John Goldworth Alger

Englishmen in the French Revolution

John Goldworth Alger

Englishmen in the French Revolution

ISBN/EAN: 9783743320178

Manufactured in Europe, USA, Canada, Australia, Japa

Cover: Foto ©ninafisch / pixelio.de

Manufactured and distributed by brebook publishing software (www.brebook.com)

John Goldworth Alger

Englishmen in the French Revolution

ENGLISHMEN

IN THE

FRENCH REVOLUTION.

ENGLISHMEN

IN THE

FRENCH REVOLUTION.

BY

JOHN G. ALGER,

AUTHOR OF "THE NEW PARIS SKETCH BOOK."

LONDON:
SAMPSON LOW, MARSTON, SEARLE & RIVINGTON,
LIMITED,
St. Dunstan's House,
FETTER LANE, FLEET STREET, E.C.
1889.

PREFACE.

THE history of the French Revolution has been written with greater fulness and from a greater variety of standpoints than any other event on the globe, yet this book takes up untrodden ground. It is well known, indeed, that the Revolution attracted to Paris men from all parts of the world, and of almost all categories—enthusiasts, adventurers, sensation-hunters; some of the best specimens of humanity and some of the worst; some of the most generous minds and some of the most selfish; some of the busiest brains and some of the idlest. Not a few of these moths perished in the flame which they had imprudently approached; others escaped with a singeing of their wings; others, again, were fortunate enough to pass unscathed. Some died in their beds just before the Terror ended, but without any assurance of its ending; others only just saw the end.

The foreigners, like the natives, who fairly survived the Revolution, had very various fortunes. Some were thoroughly disillusioned, became vehement reactionaries, or abjured politics and were transformed into sober or enterprising men of business. Others crossed or recrossed the Atlantic, and lived to a green and honoured old age, or gave way to degrading vices. Some, remaining in France, hailed the rising star of Napoleon, and lived long enough to be disenchanted, but perhaps not long enough to see the restoration of the Bourbons.

The characters of these men are an interesting chapter in psychology. The honest among them had left house and parents and brethren, if not wife and children, for the sake of what they believed to be in its way a kingdom of heaven. They appeal to our sympathies more than the cold observers, if indeed there were any such, who foresaw the lamentable collapse of all these highly-wrought expectations. No doubt some of these immigrants were restless agitators, empty demagogues, pretentious egotists; but even these are not undeserving of study. There was much base metal, but there was also genuine gold. If of some who underwent imprisonment or death we can hardly avoid thinking that they deserved their fate, there are others whom we must sincerely pity, men to whom the Revolution was a religion overriding all claims of country and kindred.

French historians have not taken, and could not be expected to take, much notice of aliens, even of those more or less actors in the Revolution. In their eyes they are but imperceptible specks in the great eddy. Their attention is absorbed by their own countrymen; they have none to spare for interlopers, none of whom appreciably influenced the course of events. If they devote a few lines to Cloots, who had to wait till 1876 for a biographer, or to l'aine, whom they often describe as an American, they consider they have done quite enough.

PREFACE. vii

French readers, moreover, while anxious for the minutest details on Mirabeau, or Madame Roland, or Danton, and while familiar at least with the names of the principal Girondins and Montagnards, do not care to hear about a foreigner who here and there sat in the Assemblies, commanded on battle-fields, or fell a victim to the guillotine. Yet for us, surely, our fellow-countrymen have an especial interest. We would fain single them out on the crowded stage of the Revolution. They are more to us, not than the actors of the first rank, but than secondary characters like Brissot or Vergniaud. Here, however, English writers will not help us. If they have not surveyed the field with French eyes, they have at least used French spectacles. French artists have painted the panorama; English connoisseurs give us their opinion of the panorama, but not of the actual scene which it represents. To vary the metaphor, or rather to state a fact, they work up the materials collected by French authors; they do not go in search of materials for themselves. Not a single English book on the Revolution tells us who represented our own country in Cloots's deputation of the human race, explains who was the hero of the Jacobin Club in December 1791, gives an accurate account of Paine's experiences, or states the number, much less the names, of the British victims to the guillotine.

If we turn from actors in the Revolution to mere spectators of it, their name is legion. There were old residents in Paris who stayed till it was too late to flee, either because they sympathised with the movement or because they took it for a mere passing storm. There were travellers, attracted by curiosity or going through France on their way to Italy. There were youths sent by their families to learn French, and suddenly immersed in the whirlpool. There were pamphleteers and insolvent debtors, fleeing English prisons only to fall into French ones. On the other hand, there were prisoners in France whom the Revolution set at liberty. There were soldiers of fortune who offered their services to the Republic. There were "bluestockings" who employed their pens or their purses in its defence; nuns who underwent captivity and privations; and ex-mistresses of royal personages. There were diplomatists astounded at the collapse of the oldest dynasty in Europe. There were two future prime ministers, one a mere child, the other a young man, destined to the longest premierships of this century. There was a future poet laureate, enraptured with the Revolution, but eventually to become an ultra-Conservative. There were versifiers who chanted the triumphs of the Revolution, philosophers who early discerned the clouds on its horizon, materialists who were stupefied at the results of their theories, inventors who counted on prompt appreciation of their merits, clubbists whose congratulations to the Convention did not avert imprisonment. There were persons of all stations, peers and grooms, baronets and tradesmen, authors and artisans, fine ladies and seamstresses, the antipodes of society being sometimes hustled together into one cell. Some had narrow escapes from detention, others spent long months of anxious suspense in the numberless improvised prisons necessitated by the improvident demolition of the spacious and nearly empty Bastille.

It may seem strange that so many British subjects, or at least those in no danger of molestation at home, should have remained in France during the Terror, but it is easy to be wise after the event. The Revolution was like a day in early spring. It commences with brilliant sunshine, light showers then pass over, black clouds next begin to collect, but there are still occasional gleams of sunshine; presently the hail pelts, the wind howls, there is a rumbling of distant thunder, yet there seems still a chance that the sky will clear, till at last the clouds lower, the horizon narrows, the thunder peals, the lightning flashes, the rain falls in sheets, and the day ends in blackness and darkness and tempest.

The capture of the Bastille was the brilliant dawn, arousing an enthusiasm in which even the English ambassador, the Duke of Dorset, shared. Before the first anniversary arrived, clouds had chequered the sky, but till the September massacres hope predominated; even after Louis XVI.'s execution it appeared still probable that the Revolution would be appeased by the blood of its foes; and there were alternations of hope and fear till the Terror commenced. We see all along what the end was to be, but these English enthusiasts were literally ignorant of the morrow, and did not easily renounce their illusions. Not till they were fairly in the toils did they recognise the gravity of their position. Flight, moreover, became increasingly difficult. Passports were refused or granted grudgingly; to depart without them was perilous in the extreme, and even with them there was constant liability to detention as French aristocrats in disguise. After the occupation of Toulon by the English, all British subjects were actual prisoners of war; and although about February 1795 there was a general liberation, Lord Malmesbury in 1797 found countrymen in Paris anxious, but still unable, to return home. It is easy to say they should never have gone to Paris during the Revolution, or should have left before the Terror commenced, but how natural was it that those whose sympathy had drawn them thither, like numbers who watched the Revolution from this side the Channel, should hope and believe that every atrocity was the last, and that these excesses were the inevitable transition to the triumph of liberty. The wonder indeed is, not that they remained till it was too late to flee, but that they suffered nothing beyond imprisonment, coupled, however, with constant apprehension of another fearful gaol delivery like that of September 1792. It must be presumed that many of them altered their opinion of their own country's stability and institutions, and learned to prefer even an unreformed Parliament to the French Convention. They cannot at any rate have failed to contrast the revolutionary tribunal with a British jury, and the guillotine with the heaviest English penalties for sedition.

The experiences of these countrymen of ours are more interesting to us than the monotonously stormy debates of the assemblies. It is true that many of them are commonplace people, justifying the remark that eye-witnesses of the greatest events, like constant beholders of the finest scenery, are the least capable of appreciation. Yet in other cases the spectators are more to us than the spectacle. Whereas, however, a multitude of French memoirs, authentic or spurious, are in existence, scarcely any English observers committed their recollections to writing. Only here and there have we an opportunity of seeing through English eyes what went on. Even the few who ventured into print mostly give us reflections in lieu of facts, and the researches of the Historical Manuscripts Commission have in this field yielded but a meagre harvest. Some who printed and even wrote nothing, yet whose character interests us, left no issue, and their collateral descendants, regarding them as the black sheep of the family, are unwilling or unable to supply any information—oftener, perhaps, unable than unwilling, for the probability is that these emigrants mostly broke off all intercourse with their kinsmen, especially as after a certain date war rendered communication very uncertain and difficult. There are, indeed, sources of information in France, contemporary newspapers and pamphlets, local and national archives, but even these are incomplete, and as regards manuscripts, rarely catalogued. The Commune of 1871, moreover, created an irreparable gap, for in the burning of the Palais de Justice and Hôtel de Ville the municipal records, the registers of deaths, and many of the prison lists were consumed. I have, however, profited by every still available source of information. I have skimmed a multitude of journals and tracts, rummaged musty documents, made inquiries of relatives which have not always proved fruitless, and collected materials which afford some idea of the enthusiasms and terrors, the festivities and privations, the honours and insults, the thrills of exultation and anguish, of the Englishmen who were voluntary or involuntary eye-witnesses of the Revolution.

This book is not written to point a moral, though it may induce moralising. It passes no judgment on the Revolution, albeit an Englishman can happily do so with as perfect impartiality as if it had taken place in a distant planet, whereas every Frenchman is more or less biassed. The Revolution is the touchstone of French politicians, not so much that their view of the Revolution governs their opinion on questions of the day, as that the latter governs their opinion of the Revolution. More deliberate falsehood, too, has been written on the Revolution than on any other historical event. Happily this ocean of falsehood but very slightly affects that side of it delineated in this book. The well of English testimony is comparatively unpolluted. We may leave Louis Blanc to credit the ridiculous story of English emissaries in the September massacres, and Michelet to regard these phantoms as eccentric Britons in search of a sensation. I have neither to justify nor impeach the conduct of the English Government towards the Revolution. International controversies have no place here. I have simply to deal with individual experiences.

CONTENTS.

I.

DELIVERANCE TO CAPTIVES.

PAGE

Lord Massareene—Capt. Whyte—Playfair—Blackwell—H. Priestley—Lord Liverpool—Dr. Rigby—Macdonagh—Rutledge 1

II.

AT THE EMBASSY.

Duke of Dorset—Lord R. Fitzgerald—Earl Gower—Huskisson—Gem—Warner—Lindsay—Monro—Somers—Elliot . 23

III.

AT THE BAR OF THE ASSEMBLY.

Pigott—Watt—Cooper—Paul Jones—Gay—Burns—Anderson —Mrs. Freeman Shepherd—Potter—Lydia Kirkham . 37

IV.

ENTHUSIASTS.

Stone—Helen Williams—Mary Wollstonecraft—Oswald—Christie 61

V.

OUTLAWS AND CONSPIRATORS.

Paine—Vaughan—Muir—Perry—British Club . . . 81

VI.

IMMIGRANTS AND EMIGRANTS.

Palmerston—Insults and Ovations—Clarkson—Wordsworth—
Fugitives—Cobbett—Edgeworth 103

VII.

PRISONERS.

Anglophobia—Ex-royal mistresses—Luttrell—Pitt's kinsmen—
Pamphleteers—Kilmaine—Nunneries and Colleges . . 139

VIII.

THE GUILLOTINED.

Dillon — Ward — O'Moran — Newton — Delany — Chambly—
Macdonald—O'Brennan—The Cemetery 169

IX.

TERRORISTS.

Grieve—Arthur—Rose—James—Duroure—Kavanagh . . 185

X.

IN THE PROVINCES.

Smith — Badger — Warburton — O'Sullivan — Bulkeley — Jane
Grey—Elizabeth Plunkett—Mrs. Thicknesse—Baron de
Bode—Colleges and Nunneries—Manufacturers . . 203

CONTENTS.

XI.

AFTER THE TERROR.

                                                               PAGE

Swinburne—Malmesbury—Prisoners of War—Anglomania—
    Sir Sidney Smith—Wright—Barclay—Mrs. Dayrell   . 225

XII.

PARIS RE-OPENED.

Fox—Rogers—Erskine—Mackintosh—Bentham—Romilly—
    Kemble—Watt—Aberdeen—High Life—Treasure-seekers 239

XIII.

NAPOLEON'S CAPTIVES.

Elgin—Yarmouth—Liberations—Refugees—Escapes—Life at
    Verdun—Release 257

CONCLUSION 285

APPENDIX.

A. Letter of Sir W. Codrington , ... 291

B. Narrative of Paris Benedictine Nuns 300

C. Narrative of Cambray Benedictine Nuns . . . 310

D. Capt. Whyte, the Bastille Prisoner 333

E. List of Prisoners in 1793 334

F. List of Prisoners in 1803 354

NOTE.

*** I am much indebted to the Proprietors of the *Edinburgh Review* for permission to incorporate in this book two articles which appeared in that journal in October 1887 and July 1888, and which form a considerable portion of chapters 1 to 9. I am also under obligations to Sir W. Codrington, Bart., and to the Rev. W. Forbes Leith, S.J., for unpublished narratives given in the Appendix; Mr. W. W. Vaughan has favoured me with information respecting his ancestor; and I have courteously been allowed to make researches at the Record Office, at the Hotel des Archives, Paris, and at the Paris Prefecture of Police.

I.

Deliverance to Captives.

"Ye horrid towers, the abode of broken hearts,
Ye dungeons, and ye cages of despair . . !
There's not an English heart that would not leap
To know that ye were fallen at last."
—Cowper's *Task*, 1784.

A

I.

DELIVERANCE TO CAPTIVES.

Lord Massareene — Capt. Whyte — Playfair — Blackwell — H. Priestley — Lord Liverpool — Rigby — Macdonagh — Rutledge.

THE Revolution, which ended by imprisoning several hundred Englishmen in Paris alone, began by liberating two, if not three, who had grown grey in captivity. The Earl of Massareene, with thoroughly British obstinacy, had remained a prisoner for at least nineteen years rather than yield to extortionate creditors. One version of his incarceration is that, arriving in Paris, a young man of twenty-three, he was deluded by a Syrian with a scheme for importing salt from Asia Minor, and signed bills to a large amount. Rutledge, however, a fellow-prisoner, who describes Massareene as the senior inmate, doing the honours of the place to newcomers, dispelling their melancholy, inviting them to supper, and encouraging them to narrate their adventures by giving his own, makes him speak thus :—

"Women, wine, gambling, rascally lawyers and doctors, lastly my own follies—behold what led to my being immured here; but the malicious people who have plunged me here will be out of their reckoning. Thanks to my philosophy, I am quite comfortable, and hope to teach them patience." *

According to the "Souvenirs" of Nicolas Berryer, father of the Legitimist orator, Massareene had been cheated at cards, and had signed bills for the amount, spent £4000 a year in prison, kept open table, and had a carriage and boxes at the theatre for his mistresses. He had attempted to escape, it is said, in woman's dress; but the turnkey, who had taken a bribe of 200 louis, betrayed him. His chief creditor was a man of considerable influence with the Parliament of Paris. Resigned thenceforth to his fate, remittances from his Irish steward enabled him to live luxuriously. Sir John Lambert, a Paris banker, himself destined to imprisonment in the Reign of Terror, writing to Lord Kerry on August 16, 1770, says:—

"My Lord Massareene's affairs are always [sic] in the same situation. You know he has miscarried in the scheme of escaping from the Fort l'Evêque, where he is still detained for want of fighting [endeavouring?] to sell his Monaghan estates, or to borrow £15,000 or £20,000, which are necessary to extract him from his present troubles." †

---

* La Quinzaine Anglaise. London: 1786.
† Lord Kerry's papers, National Archives, Paris.

On the closing of Fort l'Evêque in 1780 Massareene had been transferred to La Force, magniloquently styled by Louis Blanc the "Bastille of usury." In May 1789, Richard-Lenoir, the future reviver of the cotton industry in France, became, at the age of twenty-four, his fellow-prisoner, and his memoirs, allowing for the lapse of nearly half a century and for possible embellishments by Herbinot de Mauchamps, to whom, being himself no scribe, he apparently dictated them, may be accepted as substantially accurate. I quote the passage in full from this long-forgotten book :—

"We had for companion in misfortune an English lord, Mazaren, eighteen years a prisoner. He had married in prison the sister of another prisoner, who had since recovered his liberty. Every morning his wife and brother-in-law arrived as soon as the gates were opened, and did not leave till evening. There was something touching in the felicity of this strange household. Through them we knew of everything that was going on in Paris, and could follow, step by step, the Revolution which was beginning. Lord Mazaren especially, who had no hope except in a general overturn, was quite absorbed by it, and almost electrified us for liberty, which, indeed, for us poor prisoners, was only natural. We were not ignorant of what had happened at Réveillon's, when, on July 13, 1789, just as we were about to assemble after the opening of the doors in a kind of garden or gravelled court, Lord Mazaren suggested to us the forcing of our way out. Whether he was beforehand certain of the impassiveness of the jailors and soldiers, or whether he counted much on our daring, he assured us that nothing was easier, and that a resolute will was sufficient for success. We promptly decided. Arms had to be procured. Lord Mazaren pointed out the staircase railings, the bars of which could serve as pikes. We immediately set to work; the railings yielded to our efforts, and all of us were soon armed. The commandant, however, was speedily informed of the revolt; but fear was then gradually gaining on officials, and instead of taking strong measures, he contented himself with ordering us to carry the outbreak no further, otherwise he warned us he should be obliged to use force against us. 'So much the better,' we exclaimed on all sides. 'Kill us, and then you will have to pay our creditors.' This reply frightening him, we took advantage of his perplexity to attack the first gate, and passed through without much trouble. There were still three others to force. All the turnkeys had joined the soldiers, but several officers and privates seemed to fight with reluctance. One of them on ordering fire had tears in his eyes. However, we seized on the three gates, part of the outer wall was demolished, and we at last issued, victors, from La Force.

"Once in the street, every one thought of seeking an asylum. Lord Mazaren suggested to several of us that he should conduct us to the English Embassy. Always thoughtful and saving, I wished to re-enter the prison to fetch my things and carry them to a secure place. I was laughed at, and did not venture to insist; yet it was all that remained of my former prosperity. I therefore found myself on the streets of Paris with a more than untidy costume and twelve sous in my pocket; but I remembered my father's twelve livres, and courage did not abandon me. We were well received at the Embassy, Rue du Faubourg St. Honoré, where refreshments were offered us, and we were taken in the Embassy coaches to the precincts of the Temple, then a place of asylum for debtors. Lord Mazaren offered us a capital dinner, and while this little feast was being prepared I went to La Force to fetch my things; but alas! it was too late. The turnkeys assured me that after our departure the mob had invaded the prison. I was about to exclaim and threaten, but was answered, 'You broke open the gates, and the mob came in by the way you came out. You do not find your things? So much the worse; you should have taken them away. Good evening.' It was an impudent lie, but I had to put up with this reply."*

The Duke of Dorset in a despatch of July 16 says:—

"His Lordship, with twenty-four others in the Hôtel de la Force, forced their way out of prison last Monday morning without the loss of a single life. His Lordship, who has always expressed a great sense of gratitude for the small services I have occasionally rendered him since I first came to Paris in my present character, came directly to my hotel with six or seven of his companions, the rest having gone their different ways. I, however, soon prevailed upon Lord Massareene and the others to go to the Temple, which is a privileged place, and where he may therefore be able to treat with his creditors to some advantage. His Lordship told me that it was his intention to go thither, but that he thought it right to pay me the first visit."

---

* Mémoires de François Richard-Lenoir, p. 101. Paris: 1837. It is probable that the mob really did enter the prison, which would account for the incorrect version of the Paris papers that the prisoners were liberated by the mob.

Massareene found no obstacle to his leaving France, and on reaching Dover he jumped out of the boat, fell on his knees, and kissed the ground, exclaiming, "God bless this land of liberty!" The spectators thought him mad till they learnt who he was. He was present in August 1789, with "a French lady and her son," at Astley's representation of the capture of the Bastille. He was formally remarried to Marie Anne Barcier, on whose death in 1800 he made a second marriage, and he died in 1805, aged sixty-three, leaving no issue. His two brothers, who are said never to have written to him in captivity, succeeded him in turn, and on the decease of the second in 1826 the earldom became extinct, the viscounty passing to a daughter. Let us hope that if the steward had, as alleged, kept back half his £8000 a year, Massareene brought him to book.*

The day after this liberation another veteran prisoner recovered his liberty, but not, alas! his reason. Whyte, or Whyte de Malleville, one of the seven captives in the Bastille,† is described by

* James Swan, a Boston merchant, emulated Massareene by remaining twenty-two years in a Paris prison rather than pay what he considered an unjust claim. He was seventy-six when released in 1830 by the Revolution, and died three days afterwards. He had lived luxuriously, like Massareene, while at St. Pélagie.

† It should be borne in mind that the Bastille was not captured in order to release the prisoners, but to remove the cannon commanding that quarter of Paris, and to prevent its occupation by a foreign regiment.

some as a Scotchman, by others as an Irishman,* but there is no proof that he was ever on this side of the Channel. He may have been the son of a Captain Whyte of Clare's Irish-French Regiment, whose two daughters were on the pension list. He entered the Bastille in 1784, but had previously, probably for a quarter of a century, been at Vincennes, and at the time of this transfer was insane. In August 1788 he had refused to listen to two lawyers who called on him with papers to sign, and in the following February the governor, to whom papers in his writing had been handed, interrogated him and found him still insane. He is said when released to have styled himself "majeur de l'immensité," and to have inquired for Louis XV. The Duke of Dorset styles him Major Whyte, adding that he had been confined for more than thirty years, and that when released he was questioned by some English gentlemen who happened to be near, but the unhappy man seemed to have nearly lost the use of his intellect, and could express himself but very ill :—

"His beard was at least a yard long. What is very extraordinary, he did not know that the Bastille was the place of his confinement, but thought he had been shut up at St. Lazare; nor did he appear to be sensible of his good fortune in being released. He

---

* Charpentier's "Bastille Devoilée" gives this as a supposition, based on his speaking English well.

expressed, however, a strong desire of being taken to a lawyer."

What became of him is uncertain. One account is that a benevolent person sheltered him, but that on his beginning a few days afterwards to plunder the house, he was forced to send him to Charenton lunatic asylum. Dorset, however, could not ascertain his fate.*

The capture of the Bastille, or the procession which followed it, was witnessed by several Englishmen. Some were active participants, others simple spectators. Among the former was William Playfair, whose opinions, like his fortunes, underwent singular vicissitudes. A brother of John Playfair, the Edinburgh mathematician and geologist, he was a civil engineer, and had settled in Paris. He had patented a new rolling-machine, and in 1789 joined Joel Barlow in launching the Scioto Company, which in two months disposed of 50,000 acres in Ohio to two convoys of French emigrants. When Barlow was called back to America, Playfair acted as sole agent. He must have assisted in the capture of the Bastille, for he was one of the eleven or twelve hundred inhabitants of the St. Antoine quarter who on the previous day had formed themselves into a militia, and who, with the exception of a few detained by patrol duty, headed the attack on the

* But see new facts in Appendix D.

fortress. It is significant, but scarcely excusable, that in his "History of Jacobinism" he makes light of the capture of the Bastille, and does not hint that he was concerned in it. Indeed, the only reference to his having been in Paris at all is the remark, "I do not consider virtue to consist in the simple manners and republican phrases of a Brissot, and I have told him so to his face." A French pamphlet of 1790 on paper-money is attributed to him. It was he (not Pétion, as Carlyle represents) who courageously rescued D'Esprémenil, an old acquaintance, when half killed by a mob in the Palais Royal gardens in February 1791. Pétion simply called on and condoled with the poor man after the rescue, in which Playfair was assisted by a brave National Guardsman, a horse-dealer, who afterwards pawned his uniform to give Playfair a dinner, and was with difficulty persuaded to accept a few louis.*

Playfair speaking out too plainly on the excesses of the Revolution, Barère is said to have procured an order for his arrest, but he escaped to Holland, and thence to England.

By 1793 he was back in London, publishing pamphlets. One of these recommended that France, with the Bourbons restored, should be made permanently harmless by Savoy being given to Geneva, Dauphiny and Provence to Sardinia, a long strip drawn from Belfort to Abbeville to Austria and

* Playfair's "France as it is, not Lady Morgan's," 1819.

Prussia, and another strip from Bordeaux to Narbonne to Spain, England taking the colonies. A second pamphlet advocated a wholesale manufacture of forged assignats, as the surest and most merciful method of crushing the Revolution. He urged that this would save many lives; that American notes were forged in General Howe's camp without its being deemed dishonourable; and that there could be no fear of retaliation, seeing that Bank of England notes were payable at sight. Names, says the old song, go by contraries. Only on the *lucus à non* principle can we explain the sanguinary temper of a Rossignol, a Saint-Just, or a Lebon, and the forged assignat proposal of a Playfair. Unfortunately his suggestion did not fall on deaf ears. The British Government is alleged to have connived at the manufacture by the *émigrés* of forged assignats at Howden, near Newcastle. The local tradition is that this paper-mill on the Tyne never prospered afterwards. Some of the exiled bishops and clergy reprobated the act, but the Bourbon princes apparently reconciled themselves to it on the casuistical plea that the counterfeit notes had a secret mark by which, in the event of the restoration of the monarchy, they could be distinguished and cashed.

The Committee of Public Safety set a better example by imprisoning an English refugee named Hathway, who proposed an issue of forged Bank of England notes.

One ill deed begets another, and though the royalist issue had long ceased, Napoleon in 1803 organised a forgery of English, Austrian, and Russian notes, the plates of which were claimed by and given up to the respective ambassadors on his fall.

Playfair, who is more honourably known as an editor of Adam Smith's works, was constantly unsuccessful, despite his inventive genius. He returned to Paris after Waterloo to edit *Galignani's Messenger;* but in 1818 an article on a duel brought on him a sentence of three months' imprisonment, to escape which he fled to London, where he died five years afterwards, at the age of sixty-four. His brother, the professor, remained a staunch Whig; and a Dundee minister, James Playfair, D.D., historiographer to the Prince of Wales, who in 1790 signed an address of congratulation to the French Assembly, was probably a cousin.

Thomas Blackwell, who had been educated at the Irish College, and was studying medicine at Paris, joined in the attack on the Bastille, and was intimate with Danton. He was naturalised in France, served in the army, and in 1798 accompanied Napper Tandy to Donegal. Both escaped; but being sent on a mission to Norway, on returning to France they were given up at Hamburg to the British consul. Blackwell was imprisoned till 1801, and then went back to France.

Mrs. Schimmelpenninck, in her interesting autobiography, speaks of Harry Priestley, a lad of sixteen, bursting into her parents' drawing-room at Manchester and exclaiming, "France is free! the Bastille is taken! William was there, and helping. I have just got a letter from him. He has put up a pictorial of the Bastille and two stones from its ruins for you." Two years later William found mob-law a two-edged weapon, for he witnessed—had he been recognised he would have been in peril—the sacking of his father's house and chapel.

Dr. Priestley, who himself had the good sense to decline a seat in the Convention, offered him by two departments, bade his son William, in June 1792, "go and live among that brave and hospitable people, and learn from them to detest tyranny and love liberty." He accordingly waited on the Assembly to apply for naturalisation, and was received with plaudits. His voice being weak, his speech, which declared French citizenship a higher honour than the crown of any arbitrary state, was read for him by the President, François of Nantes. The reply of the latter compared Burke's attacks on Dr. Priestley to those of Aristophanes on Socrates, and suggested that the Birmingham rioters were the descendants of Danish pirates. The youth's gravity must have been sorely tried by this burlesque oration; but did not M. de Lesseps, in the French Academy of Sciences, once gravely hint that the English promoters of a rival Suez Canal were the descendants of Carthaginian traders? The sky soon darkened, and Dr. Priestley, his father, wrote after the September massacres to Roland, urging that unless such outrages on justice and humanity were stopped, and order and obedience to law enforced, liberty both in France and throughout Europe must be despaired of. William intended to be a merchant in France, but the war with England frustrating this purpose, he went to America, where his two brothers joined him. They contemplated buying half a million acres near the head of the Susquehanna, in Pennsylvania, to found an English colony; and their father also went over, settling at the nearest town, Northumberland, till the scheme was realised. It fell through, but Priestley remained at Northumberland, declining, however, to be naturalised. Harry died young, but William married, and had a large farm.

A young man of about the same age, the future Earl of Liverpool, then Mr. Jenkinson, also witnessed the fall of the Bastille, but merely as a looker-on.

"The whole sight has been such," he wrote, "that nothing would have tempted me to miss it;" but he either gave no description of it, or his father, in forwarding a copy of the letter to the Foreign Office, omitted a portion of it. We merely learn that "the consternation that has prevailed in Paris for the last two days is beyond all power of description. Few people have gone out of their doors, and all public amusements for the first time have been stopped." When Lord Lansdowne in 1819 argued that the Peterloo meeting was peaceable, it being attended by women and children, Liverpool replied that he saw many women busily employed in the attack on the Bastille. Young Jenkinson, even at nineteen, was able to discuss Necker's financial schemes, and he seems to have frequently attended the Assembly.

Dr. Rigby of Norwich, an old pupil of Priestley's, and his three companions witnessed the procession of the Bastille victors, were recognised as Englishmen and were embraced as freemen, for they were told, "We are now free like yourselves; henceforth no longer enemies, we are brothers, and war shall never more divide us." "We caught," says Rigby, "the general enthusiasm; we joined in the joyful shouts of liberty; we shook hands cordially with freed Frenchmen."

Ghastly trophies—two heads on pikes—soon, however, chilled their enthusiasm, and next day a mob twice prevented their leaving Paris, escorting them with hisses and insults to the Hôtel de Ville as fugitive aristocrats. To avoid further molestation they waited till July 18, and, from the Palais Royal balcony of the jeweller Sykes, saw the King pass to the Hôtel de Ville. His cold reception they considered ominous; but Rigby, though he had "seen enough to frighten him pretty handsomely and make his heart ache," was glad, having escaped all danger, to have witnessed such memorable scenes.* In 1813, when he was a grandfather and sixty-six years of age, his second wife gave birth to four infants, an event for which the Norwich Corporation voted him a piece of plate; but the whole quartette died within three months. Dr. Rigby survived them eight years.

It is a far cry from the Bastille to the Ile Ste. Marguérite; yet the 14th July echoed thither. Macdonagh, an Irish officer in the French service, had for twelve years occupied the cell of the Man with the Iron Mask. Born in Sligo in 1740, he had money left him by a great-uncle, a Jacobite refugee in France, was sent for by his guardian, and brought up in France, where he entered the army, and gained the Cross of St. Louis. In 1774, while sub-lieutenant in Dillon's regiment at Lille, he became acquainted with Rose Plunket, daughter of Lord Dunsany, and a boarder in a convent. Touched by her tale of family dissensions and her repugnance to returning to Ireland, he was secretly married to her by an Irish priest. Her brother shortly afterwards fetched her to Paris, Macdonagh going in the same coach without appearing to know her. The brother, on discovering the facts, confined her in Port Royal convent; but she appealed to the British Embassy, and there was diplomatic correspondence respecting her. "It is

---

* Dr. Rigby's "Letters from France." By Lady Eastlake.

immaterial to us," wrote Vergennes to Guines, ambassador at London, "whether the demoiselle Plunket makes a good marriage or a bad one, or even whether she allows herself indulgences without contracting marriage at all. We do not claim to be the guardians of English virginities."

To cut a long story short, Rose proved faithless, and to prevent Macdonagh's opposition to a second and more brilliant marriage, she got him arrested in 1777 under a *lettre de cachet*. On the way to prison he jumped out of the carriage by night, and villagers knocked off his fetters; but others betrayed him, and he was recaptured. He was deprived of all communication with the outer world, a turnkey who forwarded a letter for him being dismissed. Rose meanwhile married a Belgian marquis named Carondelet. Macdonagh was probably released under the decree of March 1790, cancelling all *lettres de cachet*. In the following July he met Rutledge in the Tuileries gardens, and the latter published his story to the above effect, first in Camille Desmoulins' newspaper, and afterwards in more detail as a pamphlet.* Carondelet replied to the newspaper letters by protesting that his wife had never had any acquaintance with Macdonagh beyond speaking to him once through the grating of Port Royal. According to Carondelet, her uncle, General Hussy, took her in 1771,

* "Amusements du Despotisme." Paris: 1791.

then fifteen years of age, to Belgium, as Count
O'Gara wished to make her and her brother his
heirs. She, however, desired to be a nun, whereupon O'Gara, disapproving this, placed her in the
Lille convent, and she never went outside the gate
till fetched by her brother to Paris. This version
was obviously dictated by Rose herself. Macdonagh retorted by showing Desmoulins letters in
her writing addressed to him, one of them referring
to their secret marriage. Carondelet made no re-
joinder. When Rutledge in 1791 took down the
story in full, Macdonagh, apparently not wishing,
on second thoughts, that it should be published,
asked to borrow the manuscript, but Rutledge refused. In a letter to the *Moniteur* Macdonagh
then announced that he was on his way to Hainaut
to secure the punishment of Rose and her co-con-
spirator. He was probably the Colonel Macdonagh
who, in 1804, wrote a long letter in the Paris
Argus on English misrule in Ireland.

Rutledge, as a prisoner under the old *régime* and
one of the first political prisoners after its fall, may
here be spoken of. He was the son of Walter
Rutledge, a Jacobite privateer at Dunkirk, who
joined Walsh of Nantes in lending vessels, arms,
and money to Charles Edward in 1745. The Old
Pretender repaid them the money, and conferred a
baronetcy on Rutledge, whose son consequently
styled himself the Chevalier (or Sir James) Rut-

ledge. In 1770 the latter published in London an essay comparing French and English manners, while in Paris he issued "La Quinzaine Anglaise," an account of a young lord who in a fortnight runs through £12,000 and is lodged in a debtor's prison. Wealthy young Englishmen undoubtedly at that period fell an easy prey to the tempter at Paris, and Rutledge treated this theme in other works. He also wrote farces and satires, some considered witty, others failures. He assisted Letourneur in translating Shakspere, whom he defended against Voltaire's criticism. "Frenchmen," he exclaimed, "give up your tragedies; they are cold and tedious." In 1778 he started a magazine named, after the *Tatler*, "*Le Babillard*," but it was very shortlived. Having charged his notary with fradulently obtaining his inheritance at one-third of its value, he was cast in damages, and in default imprisoned at La Force, where he made acquaintance with Lord Massareene.

This restless pamphleteer, who had been a cavalry captain, had been expelled from Poland, and now called himself a banker, was in 1789 the spokesman of the Paris bakers. Subsidised by the municipality to supply the citizens with bread under cost price, they were suspected of selling loaves to country people at a higher sum, and then of pretending that the millers had kept them without flour. Rutledge, on their behalf, covered the walls of Paris with diatribes against forestallers, and with scurrilous attacks on Necker. He is said to have declared that within four days his own head or Necker's should roll from the scaffold, and he promised the bakers a loan of two or three millions on easier terms than those offered by the municipality. A prosecution for *lèse-nation* in simulating a commission from the Assembly to treat with the bakers was instituted. Rutledge applied for protection from arrest to the Cordeliers district, which afterwards sheltered Marat, but in this case it declined to interfere. The prosecution was, however, dropped, and in February 1790 he was released. In 1792 or 1793, with the same mania of delation, he was one of the persecutors of the hapless assignat superintendent Delamarche, the nervous man whom Madame Roland showed how to die by changing places with him on the scaffold. Rutledge, like other assailants of Delamarche, had been employed in numbering the assignats, and revenged the abolition of this formality by charging him with malversation. He died in March 1794, at the supposed age of forty-four.

II.

At the Embassy.

"Why vex and torment yourself about the French? They buzz and are troublesome while they are swarming, but the master will soon hive them."—LANDOR, *Imaginary Conversations.*

II.

AT THE EMBASSY.

Duke of Dorset—Lord R. Fitzgerald—Earl Gower—Huskisson—
Gem—Warner—Lindsay—Monro—Somers—Elliot.

THE British Embassy at first fully shared in the general enthusiasm. The Duke of Dorset, though a favourite with Marie Antoinette, sent the Duke of Leeds a glowing despatch on the fall of the Bastille :—

"Nothing," he wrote on July 16, 1789, "could exceed the regularity and good order with which all this extraordinary business [the assumption of the government of Paris by a Volunteer National Guard] has been conducted. Of this I have myself been a witness upon several occasions during the last three days as I have passed through the streets, nor had I at any moment reason to be alarmed for my personal safety. . . . Thus, my Lord, the greatest revolution that we know anything of has been effected with, comparatively speaking—if the magnitude of the event is considered—the loss of very few lives. From this moment we may consider France as a free country, the King a very limited monarch, and the nobility as reduced to a level with the rest of the nation."

The Duke little foresaw that the fall of the Bastille would indirectly lead to his speedy recall. On the hasty flight of the Comte d'Artois, Dorset wrote to congratulate him on his escape. This letter, intrusted to Castelnau, the French Minister at Geneva, was intercepted on July 23. The Paris Committee, before whom Castelnau and his documents were taken, sent the latter to the Assembly, but the President sent them back to Bailly, and one of the Committee opened Dorset's letter, which was found to be merely complimentary. The Assembly was inclined to apply for its return; but being assured by Clermont Tonnerre, who had heard it read, that it contained mere trivialities, it allowed the matter to drop. Reports, however, were industriously circulated that Dorset had distributed large sums of money for the purpose of fomenting the disorders in Paris. To clear himself, therefore, he wrote to Montmorin, Minister of Foreign Affairs, protesting that England had no thought of fomenting troubles in France, and reminding him that in the previous month he had revealed a proposal made to him to seize by treachery on Brest. This letter, forwarded at his own request to the Assembly, only made things worse, for the Brest reactionaries indignantly repudiated the plot, and insisted that Dorset should give up the names of the traitors. On July 28 he reported that he had had hints from well-informed persons that it was unsafe for Englishmen to appear in public:—

"The lawless set of people," he added, "whom the late troubles have set to work, make it very unsafe travelling at present, especially by night; and I really think it necessary that some public caution be given to put those upon their guard who may propose to visit this part of the Continent."

He concluded by proposing to take leave of absence, and it is evident that his position had become untenable. He commissioned young Cox Hippisley * (afterwards Sir John Cox Hippisley), who was returning to England, to describe to the Duke of Leeds what he had witnessed. Hippisley had seen from a window the murder of the unfortunate Berthier on the 22nd July, and had endeavoured at Versailles to silence the calumnies against the English. Dorset's opinion of the Revolution had in a fortnight so completely changed—he seems to have been a purely ornamental personage, formerly "quite the fashion in the annals of gallantry," and with little diplomatic ability—that he was anxious to resign his post, and in point of fact he did not return. He continued, however, from England to supply Marie Antoinette with English gloves, and in August 1791 he transmitted to her a letter of advice from Burke, rewritten in cipher for the sake of safety, and made too concise for Burke's liking.

Lord Robert Fitzgerald acted as *chargé d'affaires*

---

* To whom the titular Henry IX., Cardinal of York, bequeathed the gauze veil worn by Mary Stuart on her way to execution.

till May 1790. His letter of instructions expressed an opinion that Englishmen should abstain from visiting France, and not out of curiosity run the risk of molestation. On the 20th June 1790, Earl Gower, afterwards Duke of Sutherland, presented Dorset's letters of recall and his own credentials. Gower's despatches speak of the expediency of embassy servants carrying guns or wearing a particular feather in their hats, so as to avoid the insult experienced by the Spanish ambassadress's attendants. English residents applied to him to obtain exemption from the capitation-tax, and information, to which he attached little weight, was offered him of plots for setting fire to English ports or fleets. A French parliamentary committee solicited data respecting transportation to Botany Bay, and he was asked to give facilities for the detection of forged assignats in London. A large importation of English buttons for the National Guard uniforms was extremely displeasing to the Paris buttonmakers, who threatened to sack shops which sold English goods. Only four days after the Feast of Pikes, the first Bastille anniversary, a number of suspicious foreigners were arrested. There were no English among them, but Gower deemed it necessary to admonish his countrymen to be very careful in word and deed, especially as an opinion had got abroad that both political parties in England had tampered with the French democrats.

The Revolution had thus already become too stormy for Gower to sing pæans over it; but Huskisson, a witness of the capture of the Bastille, who became his private secretary, was warmly interested in it. Huskisson had been brought up by his great-uncle, Dr. Richard Gem, a Worcestershire man, who went to Paris as physician to the Embassy in 1762. Almost the first time Gem spoke to Horace Walpole, who met him in Paris in 1765, he said to him, "Sir, I am serious, I am of a very serious turn," and this seems to have been his stereotyped expression. A rigid disciplinarian and parsimonious, he allowed no eating between breakfast and the five or six o'clock dinner. An avowed materialist, he was enchanted with the Revolution, and was doubtless the "Ghym, anglais," who in 1792 presented 1000 francs to the Patriotic Fund. This did not save him from being arrested, like other Englishmen, in October 1793, as a hostage for Toulon. He appears in the Prefecture of Police records as "Gesme," and as having, after nine days at the Luxembourg, been transferred to the Scotch College. The entry of his release is missing, but he was probably released under the decree of the 3rd November 1793, which, on account of the scarcity of doctors, exempted foreign practitioners from imprisonment. He seems to have gone to live outside Paris, at Meudon, and there to have been rearrested by the Versailles authorities. He was for several months in the same prison, and even in the same room, as Mrs. Grace Dalrymple Elliott. He cried the whole time, and was terrified to death, as she told Lord Malmesbury in 1796, though in her posthumous book she represents him as going to bed at dusk to save candles, getting up at four to read Helvetius or Locke, and waking her at seven to try and argue her into materialism.* Malmesbury found him living in Paris, still harping on his philosophy, anxious but unable to get away. He had Malmesbury's secretaries to witness his will: one of them was the future Earl Granville, whom he had professionally attended, refusing fees; and he died, over eighty, in 1800, leaving the bulk of his property to Huskisson.

Gem had brought over both Huskisson and his brother, the sons of his favourite niece, in 1783, on their father's second marriage. He meant them to be doctors, but the future Chancellor of the Exchequer had no turn for medicine, entered Boyd

* In the Paris *Temps*, May 22, 1888, M. Anatole France describes Mrs. Elliott as sponging Gem's tear-stained face, and asking why the prospect of death should terrify him, whereas she herself remained cheerful. He replied: "Madam, you are young, rich, healthy, and handsome, and you certainly lose much in losing life, but being incapable of reflection, you do not know what you lose. As for me, I am poor (!), old, and ill, so that to deprive me of life is not depriving me of much; but I am a philosopher and a doctor; I am conscious of being it, which you are not, and I know exactly what I lose. This accounts, madam, for my being melancholy while you are cheerful." There may be some foundation for this anecdote, but an inquiry as to the source of it elicited no reply.

and Ker's bank, studied political economy, and on
August 29, 1790, delivered a sensible address to
the Club of 1789 against an unlimited paper
currency. His notes of the proceedings of the
Jacobin and other clubs, taken for a friend at the
Embassy, were so good that Gower made him his
secretary, and he left Paris with the rest of the
Embassy on the fall of the monarchy. He told
Croker in 1826 that he and Cutlar Fergusson *
used to be waited upon at Beauvilliers' restaurant
by a smart young man whom they liked to scold
or tease, until, as the landlord told them, despera-
tion made him enlist, the waiter being none other
than Murat. The Bastide innkeeper's son, on
deserting from the army to escape punishment,
was undoubtedly reduced to a waitership at Beauvilliers', but he was not driven away by teasing, for
he had friends in the Assembly who procured
him admission to the King's Constitutional Guard,
formed in the winter of 1791.

Huskisson is said to have been recommended
to Gower by his chaplain, Dr. John Warner, himself
recommended by Lord Carlisle and George Selwyn.
Warner had long been the friend and correspondent

* Fergusson, tried with Lord Thanet in 1799 for aiding in the
attempted escape of Arthur O'Connor from Maidstone courthouse
(O'Connor had been acquitted, but was about to be arrested on
a second charge), was sentenced to twelve months imprisonment.
He went to India, had a good practice at the Calcutta bar, afterwards became M.P. for Kirkcudbright, and was Judge Advocate
from 1834 till his death at Paris in 1838, aged sixty-nine.

of the latter. The son of a rector of Barnes, Dr. Ferdinand Warner, he was more of a wit than we should consider proper in a clergyman, yet he had been a popular preacher at a chapel in Longacre, his own property, until presented in 1771, at the age of thirty-five, to a living in Bedfordshire, whence he was promoted to the Rectory of Stourton, Wiltshire. John Howard's statue in St. Paul's is attributed to Warner's exertions. "A book, a pipe, and cheerful conversation" were his delight, and if his talk was more entertaining than clerical, he should be credited with a kindly disposition and unimpeachable probity. He was so ardent an admirer of the Revolution, that he was deprived of the chaplaincy about October 1790, on account, it is said, of a sermon at the Embassy chapel. He soon afterwards went to Italy, and in 1800, shortly after his return to London, died. Like Gem, very abstemious and economical, he left a considerable fortune. He had subscribed liberally to the "Diversions of Purley," and bequeathed Horne Tooke a silver goblet.

As for Gower, he was regarded at Coblenz as a sympathiser with the Revolution. Lord Camelford spoke of him there to Burke's son, in August 1791, as outrageously democratical, and as sending dexterous despatches against assisting or countenancing the counter-revolution. This was, however, an evident exaggeration, for Gower in the previous April had congratulated himself on escaping the embraces of the fishwives, who had invaded the drawing-room of Montmorin, Minister of Foreign Affairs. When Gower called, "they were at the moment of taking leave of the Minister with the most cordial embraces, having already performed that ceremony on most of the corps diplomatique who had the misfortune of dining there." It is uncertain whether All Fools' Day, the date of the despatch, was also the date of the kissing. Anyhow, the Paris mob had so little respect for diplomatic privileges, that when they visited the aristocratic houses to slaughter the Swiss employed as porters, they made no exception in Gower's favour. Fortunately his Swiss had been sent off in disguise. Gower declined the offer of a military guard, but deemed it prudent to put in large letters over his door "Hôtel de l'Ambassadeur d'Angleterre." Gouverneur Morris tells us that he found Gower in a towering passion at the delays in delivering his passports, and that he had burnt his papers. His wife, the Countess of Sutherland, who flirted a little with Morris, was the only lady who visited Marie Antoinette the day before the attack on the Tuileries, all the Queen's timorous favourites prudently keeping away. When the royal family were at the Feuillants monastery before being consigned to the Temple, she sent some of her own dresses for the Queen, and her little boy's clothes for the unfortunate Dauphin, sixteen months his senior, but small for his age. The Queen, forbidden writing materials, commissioned Cléry to return the clothes with a letter of thanks, but the municipal commissaries refused to allow their being sent back. The little Lord Strathnavar, the future Duke of Sutherland, whose garments were thus confiscated, was then, at six years old, so accustomed to see cannon in the streets, that on arriving in London he was amazed, we are told by Walpole, at finding none.

Recalled on the abolition of royalty, Gower instructed the Embassy secretary, William Lindsay, to remain a few days, and his stay was lengthened by the difficulty in obtaining passports from the municipality. Indeed, he had to threaten to start without them, warning Lebrun, of the Foreign Office, that the result might be his being brought back or insulted, and the next morning he received them. Lindsay and other English guests were about to dine with the Duke of Orleans on the 3rd September when they heard the cries of a mob, and going to the window, saw the Princesse de Lamballe's head carried past. According to one version, Orleans looked on and said, "Je sais ce que c'est," then passed into the next room, and sat down to dinner with complete coolness; but the Bland Burges Papers, a better authority, state that he was sitting at the other end of the room, and on his guests drawing back horrified from the window, asked what was the matter. Told that a woman's head had been carried by, he said "Oh, is that all? Let us go to dinner." At table he inquired what had become of Madame de Lamballe and the other female prisoners. A guest significantly drew his hand across his throat. Orleans said, "I understand," and changed the subject. One of the Englishmen, overcome with horror, had, according to Peltier, slipped away unnoticed.

Captain George Monro, probably a son of Sir Harry Monro, Bart., also saw something of the barbarities at the Abbaye, and on December 17, describing how people were stopped in the streets, watches and rings taken, and even earrings pulled off, he wrote: "I myself never move out but with pistols in my pocket, as I find them more necessary here than in Turkey." Monro remained till the condemnation of Louis XVI., and sent despatches chiefly relating to the British Jacobins in Paris, with whom he pretended to fraternise, but his position was unofficial and indeed unsafe. "He was not only suspected, but marked here," says Somers,* who for a time took his place, and who deemed it prudent to disguise his political reports in mercantile language. One of Somers's letters announces that Morgan, the son of an Irish M.P., was in Paris, and had offered to assassinate George III. On the 1st February 1793 war was declared. In the following

---

* Somers had assisted in September 1792 in the concealment and escape of Peltier, the Royalist pamphleteer, who speaks of him as "a brave Englishman, the loyal Somers."

month the Convention prescribed that English residents should find six citizens to vouch for their "civisme," and if not in business nor landowners, should deposit their property in pledge, but until October 1793 they were not seriously molested.

Though he was not at the Embassy, and was ostensibly a mere visitor, Hugh Elliot may here be mentioned. Ex-Ambassador at Copenhagen, he had, with his brother Gilbert (Lord Minto), been at a military college with Mirabeau, and Pitt sent him over in October 1790 to ensure French neutrality in the event of an Anglo-Spanish war. Mirabeau, Barnave, and the other members of the diplomatic committee of the Assembly, gave him satisfactory assurances, and he returned to London at the end of October. Mirabeau had prepared, but not delivered, a long speech in favour of Spain, and threatening England with war if she attacked that country. His sudden change of tone reminds one of Rivarol's epigram, "Mirabeau is capable of anything for money, even of a good action."

III.

At the Bar of the Assembly.

"All hearts were open, every tongue was loud
With amity and glee; we bore a name
Honoured in France—the name of Englishman,
And hospitably did they give us hail,
As their forerunners in a glorious course."
—WORDSWORTH, *The Prelude.*

III.

AT THE BAR OF THE ASSEMBLY.

Pigott—Watt—Cooper—Paul Jones—Gay—Burns—Anderson—Mrs. Freeman Shepherd—Potter—Lydia Kirkham.

ENGLAND was represented not merely at the capture of the Bastille, but at every stage of the Revolution, in its festivities and its tragedies, in the Convention and in the Commune, in the clubs and in the armies, in the prisons and on the scaffold. She was represented on Cloots's "Deputation of the Human Race," and at the Feast of Pikes, to which that deputation solicited admission, by Robert Pigott, who had been an opulent country gentleman. The Pigotts claimed descent from a Norman named Picot, and had for eleven generations owned an estate at Chetwynd, Shropshire. They had been strongly attached to the Stuarts, and heirlooms still preserved in the family include a ring, said to have been one of four given by Charles I. on the eve of his execution, a fragment of the Royal Oak, and a portrait on ivory of the Pretender, presented by himself to Robert Pigott's father at

Rome in 1720.* This Jacobite Pigott died in 1770, and his death gave rise to a very singular lawsuit. Some hours after he had expired at Chetwynd, his son and the son of Sir William Codrington, dining at Newmarket without any idea of what had occurred, "ran their fathers' lives one against the other" for five hundred guineas. Such bets were not uncommon in those times, and were not apparently thought indecorous.† The elder Pigott was seventy years of age, the elder Codrington only fifty. When Pigott learned that his father's death had occurred prior to the wager, he maintained that the bet was off; but Codrington, or rather Lord March (afterwards Duke of Queensberry), to whom he had assigned the money, insisted on payment. The case came before Lord Mansfield, who held that the impossibility of a contingency did not preclude its being the subject of a wager, if both parties were at the time unaware of that impossibility. He consequently gave judgment against Pigott.

In 1774 Pigott was High Sheriff of Shropshire, as his grandfather had been before him. Two years later, sharing the belief of croakers that England was on the brink of ruin, he disposed of Chetwynd, as also, probably, of the manor of Chesterton, in Huntingdonshire. If, as is alleged, estates worth

* Hulbert's "History of Salop."
† In 1754 Lord Powerscourt's son made money by betting with many persons that his father, a miser, would outlive their fathers. See "Mémoires de Dufort, Comte de Cheverny."

£9000 a year realised only £70,000, he must have sold them for much less than their value. Retiring to the Continent, he lost a considerable portion of the money through the failure of the persons to whom he had intrusted it, but was still in easy circumstances. He lived for a time at Geneva, where he appears to have known Voltaire, but shortly before the French Revolution was staying in London, where Brissot made his acquaintance. A man of "fads," as we should now say, Pigott was a vegetarian—a Pythagorean was then the term— and an ardent admirer of Graham, the notorious charlatan, brother of Mrs. Macaulay's young second husband, with whose "electric beds" the future Lady Hamilton was then associated. Graham too was a vegetarian, and had perhaps made a proselyte of Pigott. The latter had, moreover, an antipathy to hats, cocked or chimney-pot, as the invention of priests and despots, and wore a cap which at the Feast of Pikes made him the observed of all observers.* When Royalist deputies, suspecting the genuineness of Cloots's deputation, sent an usher who spoke English—probably Rose, a man of Scotch extraction—to test the English representative, he was answered by Pigott in "good Miltonic English," and retired in confusion. We may imagine Pigott receiving from Cloots a certificate of his presence at the Feast of Pikes, couched, with a simple altera-

* "Anacharsis Cloots," by G. Avenel. Paris, 1876.

tion of name and nationality, in these terms, and entitling the bearer to a federal ribbon and diploma :—

"Capital of the globe, February 5, year 2.—I certify and make known to all the free men of the earth that Joseph Cajadaer Chammas, member of the oppressed sovereign [the people] of Mesopotamia, had the honour of attending the Federation of July 14, by virtue of a decree emanating from the august French Senate, June 19, year one. ANACHARSIS CLOOTS, orator of the human race in the French National Assembly." *

What a contrast between the High Sheriff of Salop paying the honours to the judges of assize and the cap-headed man at the bar of the National Assembly!

In this same year 1790, Pigott sent or presented an address to the Assembly on Sieyes's press bill. He spoke in it of his loving France as warmly as if he had been a native, and of his having hastened over with a multitude of other foreigners to enjoy the rights of man in all their fulness. He dissuaded the Assembly from taking English legislation as a model, for the shameful war with America had shown how people could be misled by a press which the Government could persecute or coerce. England, he said, was not really free, but had only a semblance of freedom. This address was read at the Lyons Club, 10th February 1791, and printed in its journal.

* "Lettre du Prussien Cloots au Prussien Hertzberg." Paris, 1791.

In the autumn of 1790, Pigott, as it appears from Madame Roland's letters to Bancal, was living alternately at Geneva and Lyons, and was desirous of buying a confiscated or private estate in the South of France. He was, however, as fickle as the wind, and Madame Roland predicted that unless he was taken by surprise and forced into a decision, he would be looking about all his life, and would build only in the air. At the beginning of 1792 he seems to have been back in Paris, and published a plea for caps, which I have been unable to find, but passages from which appeared in Brissot's paper, the *Patriote Français*. It urged that the cap allowed the face to be well seen, and could have various shapes and colours, whereas the hat was gloomy and morose. It denounced the uncovering of the head as a servile and ridiculous salutation, and appealed to Greek, Roman, and Gaulish usage, as also to Voltaire and Rousseau, in favour of caps. The effect of the appeal was electrical. For a few weeks caps were the rage, and Grangeneuve, a Girondin deputy, wore one in the Assembly, though it is not clear that they were used out of doors, any more than by Voltaire and Rousseau. When, on the 19th March 1792, Pétion wrote to the Jacobin Club so strong and sensible a remonstrance against external signs of republicanism that the president pocketed his cap, his assessors following suit, it cannot be supposed that they went home bare-headed. These caps must have been confined to indoor use; and at the club they seem to have been restricted to the president, the assessors or secretaries, and the speakers while on their legs. Pigott, however, was plainly the introducer, if not of the *bonnet rouge*, yet of the *bonnet;* for the Chateauvieux mutineers, to whom it is generally attributed, did not enter Paris till June, three months afterwards. It is true that the cap of liberty had been a symbol employed from the outset of the Revolution, but it was Pigott who made it an article of dress. He had probably quitted Paris by the summer, when it was revived, and this time undoubtedly worn outdoors, sometimes placed on the back of the head, like that of a Zouave of the present day, sometimes placed on the top of the head with the end slightly lapping over in front. Of Pigott nothing more is heard till his death at Toulouse, July 7, 1794, three weeks before Robespierre's fall. He was fifty-eight years of age, is said to have had a son who predeceased him, and left a widow, Antoinette Bontau, possibly the Mrs. Pigott who was living at Geneva in 1807–15.

There were two other Pigotts who sympathised with the Revolution, but what relation they were to Robert is not clear. Charles, the author of some plays and pamphlets, including a reply to Burke, died in London a fortnight before Robert, and was buried at Chetwynd. A John Pigott, dining at the London Coffee-house, September 30, 1793, in company with Dr. Hudson, drank " Success to the French Republic over all Europe." Other diners thereupon toasted "The King," and an altercation ensued, the result being that Pigott and Hudson were taken before a magistrate, shouting sedition from the coach windows on the way. They were committed for trial, and five days afterwards applied for release on bail, which was fixed at £250, but I find no record of any further proceedings. This Pigott may have been the " Jean Picotte " who was imprisoned in Paris from October 1793 to October 1794.

Let us pass from the *franc original*, as Madame Roland styles the Shropshire Pythagorean, to James Watt, junior, son of the great inventor, who likewise represented his country in a cosmopolitan procession. This young man of twenty-two had formed an intimacy at Manchester with an ardent politician, Thomas Cooper, a druggist, and towards the end of 1791 the Constitutional Society of that town deputed both of them to carry an address of congratulation to the Jacobin Club. Watt * was the hero of the dramatic sitting of the 18th December, so vividly depicted in Carlyle's Essays, when the British, American, and French flags were suspended from the ceiling, and when a deputation of ladies presented to the " Constitutional Whig " an ark of alliance containing the new map of France, the

* As shown by a letter from the London Constitutional Society thanking the Jacobins for their reception of Cooper and Watt.

cap of liberty, the new Constitution, a civic crown, some ears of wheat, three miniature flags, and the national cockade. After a very effusive scene "le Député Wigh" spoke of his unpreparedness for such a reception, of his having sent home an account of a previous welcome, of a letter from his society to Pétion having miscarried, and so on. The heroics thus ended in platitudes. Carlyle aptly indexes this episode as "the Jacobin Club in its early days of moral sublime," for the club had not then the sinister reputation it eventually acquired.

Watt was not only the anonymous Constitutional Whig of December 1791, but figured with Cooper in the triumphal procession of April 15, 1792, when the forty mutinous soldiers of the Chateauvieux regiment marched through Paris. The two Manchester delegates carried the British flag, together with a bust of Algernon Sidney.

Burke, in the House of Commons nearly a year afterwards, vehemently denounced them as having thus applauded mutiny and murder, and as having exchanged embraces with Marat. The Jacobin Club, on April 13, 1792, had invited the two Manchester delegates to attend all its sittings as long as they remained in Paris. Watt's biographer, Muirhead, speaks of him as horrified by the storming of the Tuileries and the September massacres; but he was so far from reprobating the former, that on August 14 he waited on the Assembly, together with Gamble and Rayment—Didot, the paper-maker, had married a Miss Gamble, and this was probably her brother—to present 1315 francs for the families of the combatants. The September massacres, however, certainly horrified Watt, and so little did he make a secret of it, that Robespierre denounced the two Manchester delegates to the Jacobins as Pitt's emissaries. Watt, whom three years' schooling at Geneva had made fluent in French, was equal to the occasion. Springing on the platform, he pushed Robespierre aside, and "in a short but vehement speech completely silenced his formidable antagonist, carrying with him the feelings of the rest of the audience, who expressed their sense of his honest British spirit in a loud burst of applause." I have found no mention in Paris newspapers of this episode, nor of a challenge between Robespierre and Danton, when Watt acted as second to the latter, and on the ground effected a reconciliation by urging the loss to the cause of liberty if either combatant fell; but Southey must have had good authority for these statements.* On going back to his lodgings, Watt had a warning that his life was not safe, and we know that the incorruptible Robespierre was also the unforgiving Robespierre. He immediately left Paris without a passport, and with some dif-

---

* "Danton" may, however, have been a slip of the tongue or pen for "Brissot," who undoubtedly had quarrels with Robespierre.

ficulty made his way to Italy. On his return to England in 1794 his father had serious apprehensions lest he should be prosecuted, and contemplated shipping him to Northern Europe or America; for though young Watt (by this time twenty-five years of age) had broken off correspondence with France, he was still a Radical, and deemed it an honour to dine with two of the "acquitted felons" of the 1794 trials. He was, however, left unmolested, went back after a time to Birmingham, succeeded to his father's business, and in 1817 was the first to cross the Channel and ascend the Rhine to Coblenz by steam. He lived till June 1848, thus hearing of the proclamation of the second Republic, after having witnessed the virtual establishment of the first.

His old colleague, Cooper, emigrated to America, was the neighbour there of Dr. Priestley, and edited a newspaper. Its attacks on the American Administration were mistakenly attributed to Priestley, who consequently incurred some danger of expulsion as an alien. Cooper, with truly American versatility, ultimately became a judge, and died in 1829, at the age of sixty-nine.

Paul Jones, as a Scotchman by birth, should not be passed over, albeit he appeared before the Assembly as an American. He was one of a deputation of Americans who, on the 10th July 1790, offered their congratulations; but the spokesman was Vernon, of Newport. Gouverneur Morris had vainly dissuaded Jones, in the previous November, from coming over from Warsaw. He was in pecuniary difficulties, and on his death from dropsy, 18th July 1792, Blackden, also one of the deputation, opened a subscription for the funeral expenses. The Assembly was invited to send delegates to the interment, and among the number was Gay Vernon, Bishop of Limoges. This was certainly the first time that a French prelate had attended a Protestant funeral, and until the Revolution, indeed, Protestants in Paris were buried at night or dawn by the police authorities. Gay Vernon, it is true, was not an ordinary bishop, for he voted for the death of Louis XVI., abjured the priesthood, and under the Empire became a consul. Jones had played many parts, and this posthumous part, the inauguration of religious toleration at funerals, was not the least singular of them. Morris had drawn up his will, which made his sister, a Mrs. Taylor, universal legatee. She went over from Scotland, is said to have been in danger during the Terror, and returned home with Jones's papers. She may be the Mrs. Taylor who figures in the list of prisoners.

One of the most striking features of the Revolutionary Assemblies was the stream of deputations, donors and suppliants, who formed interludes in the debates. It was picturesque to see children taken by their parents to offer the nation the contents of their money-boxes, a girl of twelve giving her watch, pensioners renouncing their annuities, and officers handing in their decorations; but to allow speechifying at the bar was ruinous to business, and eventually to freedom of deliberation. Frenchmen resident abroad sent or brought their contributions, and Englishmen, like other foreigners, caught the infection.

Bryan Edwards, M.P., the historian of the West Indies, forwarded a quarter of his French revenues (December 1789). Samuel Swinton, proprietor of the *Courier de l'Europe*, for which Brissot formerly wrote, offered 415 francs, the profits of the sale of the paper in France in 1789, and promised a larger sum next year; but there is no record of a second remittance. Nicholas Gay, F.R.S., waited on the Assembly (January 1792) to present 1000 francs towards the war. Amidst the plaudits which greeted his eulogy of the Constitution, a deputy objected to money being accepted from foreigners; but another deputy replied that Gay generally spent the winter in France, and might be considered naturalised, while a third remarked that all free men were brothers. Gay, too liberal even for his ample means, the author in 1799 of a pamphlet against the union with Ireland, died at Margate in 1803. Jones—probably the Hugh Jones, wine merchant, destined to imprisonment under the

AT THE BAR OF THE ASSEMBLY. 51

Terror—presented ten pieces of ordnance (October 23, 1792), on condition of their being returned at the peace, as his own country might need them. A deputy suggested the conferring of French citizenship on him, but the Convention simply voted thanks. Captain Wilson, a half-pay officer, perhaps the Scotchman who ultimately married Wolfe Tone's widow, offered a seven-barrelled gun, all the barrels of which could be discharged simultaneously. The poet Burns (February 1792) sent some guns, the equipment of a smuggling vessel which he had helped to capture, and had bought at the auction; but both letter and guns were stopped at Dover. Burns was in danger of dismissal from the Excise for this, but escaped with a reprimand.* Professor John Anderson, founder of the Institute at Glasgow, went over in 1791 to offer the Assembly "a cannon the recoil of which was stopped by the condensation of common air within the body of the carriage:"—

> "Of warlike engines he was author,
> Devised for quick dispatch to slaughter."

The Assembly accepted the model of it, and experiments with a six-pounder were made near Paris, Paul Jones being an approving spectator. Ander-

* His old schoolmaster, John Murdoch, was in France prior to or at the beginning of the Revolution, and was intimate with Colonel Fullerton, secretary of the Embassy. He returned to London, taught French, and died in 1824, aged seventy-seven.

son also suggested that, to frustrate the seizure of revolutionary journals at the German frontier, small paper balloons, varnished with boiled oil, should be sent up when the wind was favourable, freighted with manifestoes, which would fall and circulate among the Germans. This idea is said to have been acted upon. Anderson witnessed the King's return from Varennes and the second 14th July celebration.

A poor English gardener, apparently living in France, gave a six-franc piece for the war (September 1792). Another anonymous Englishman offered a pair of silver buckles (May 1792), regretting his inability to do more. Some English schoolgirls contributed 111 francs for the war (September 1792). An English officer sent a sword. William Beckett of London, in token of universal brotherhood having effaced the frontiers traced by despots, sent 200 francs (January 1791). Irishmen in Paris brought 145 francs to equip a volunteer (September 1792). Friends of Liberty at Newry sent 6850 francs. John Baptist Seymour, silk manufacturer at Rheims, gave 56 francs (July 1792). Vickery, a London tradesman, presented 160 francs for the widows and orphans of the stormers of the Tuileries (September 1792). Henry Montfort Power, born in London, but thirty-three years in the French army, had repeatedly asked for active service, but, disabled by gout, he deposited his military decorations on the altar of his adopted country, pending the time when he should be able to take the field (November 1792).

Robert Rayment, economist and statistician, offered his treatise on English finances (August 1792). Eight days later he joined with Watt, Gamble, and Anviside (Handyside?) in a gift of 1315 francs for the families of those who fell in the attack on the Tuileries. Major Cartwright sent a bundle of political tracts to the committee which was drafting the Constitution (August 1789). Cartwright was grievously disappointed at the excesses of the Revolution. Jeremy Bentham sent his book on prisons (December 1791), expressing a wish to come over and establish a prison on his own system, and to act gratuitously as keeper. The Revolution was destined to multiply prisons, but not on Bentham's system. Dr. George Edwards, an admirer of Franklin's theories of medicine, presented the Convention in 1793 with his political and economic works, and with an outline of a Constitution. Sir Joseph Banks is said to have presented as a tree of liberty the bean-tree which, till about five years ago, flourished in the quadrangle of the Paris National Library. I have not been able to verify this statement, but in 1802, when elected an Associate of the Institute, Banks scandalised his colleagues of the Royal Society by a letter of acknowledgment, in which he stated that France, during the most frightful convulsions of the Revolution, had never ceased to possess his esteem, his firm conviction being that she contained many good citizens, who would infallibly get the upper hand, and restore the reign of virtue, justice, and honour.

The voluntary offerings, both from natives and foreigners, show a marked falling off as the Revolution progressed, or rather deteriorated. Towards the end of the list comes Mrs. Freeman Shepherd, in all probability the Harriet Augusta Freeman who in 1797 translated Mercier's fanciful picture of Paris in the year 2440. She had been a boarder at the English Benedictine nunnery. Two letters addressed to her there, confiscated with other papers and preserved at the National Archives, show that she solved problems in geometry, and in a playful vein discussed metaphysical questions. She was a warm admirer of Robespierre, and in January 1792 wrote him a letter chiding him for not having cashed a cheque which she had forwarded him.

"I do not like dissimulation," she said. "I never practise it on any occasion towards anybody, and I do not tolerate its being practised towards me. You have used it, sir, with me; you have deceived me. You made me believe that you accepted for public purposes a small offering, and you have not accepted it. The debtor and creditor account just transmitted to me by my banker, according to his usual custom, proves this."

Robespierre, it appears, had called on her and told her what he intended to do with the money.

"Do not thus distrust the English; do not treat with this humiliating disparagement the stammering accents of good-will of an Englishwoman towards the common cause of all nations. The French were formerly famous for their politeness to the weaker sex, thereby the more sensitive to affront. Alas for us if the Revolution, deprives us of this precious privilege. But I claim a juster right: do not to others as you would not be done by." *

It is odd to find the golden rule enforced by a philo-Jacobin on the incorruptible Robespierre. He was apparently still obdurate, for a month later *la Citoyenne Freeman, patriote anglaise,* presented the Convention, through Beurnonville, with 200 francs towards buying shoes for the volunteers. This may, however, have been a second gift. It is the last English subscription down to the end of the Terror. Robespierre, even if he declined the gift, paid the writer the attention of preserving her letter, for it was found among his papers. It was not published in the selection issued by his enemies immediately after his fall, but was printed in 1828, the signature, however, being travestied into "Theeman Shephen," a blunder repeated by his biographer Hamel. Either the original or a duplicate figured in a sale of autographs at Paris in 1874. Mrs. Freeman seems to have escaped the incarceration which befell English residents, but I cannot ascertain when she returned to England. Her transla-

* "Papiers inédits trouvés chez Robespierre." Paris, 1828.

tion of 1797 is dated London, and is dedicated to Sir John Cox Hippisley, also, as we have seen, an eye-witness of the beginning of the Revolution.

If there is an element of vanity in some of the gifts I have enumerated, many show a touching sincerity and enthusiasm. But what are we to say of the thousand pairs of soldiers' shoes sent in November 1792 by the London Constitutional Information Society, to be followed by six weekly cargoes of the same kind? Lewis Goldsmith alleges,* on the authority of Talleyrand, that France paid for these shoes, as also for the expenses of the deputations who in 1792 congratulated the Convention on the abolition of monarchy. Neither Goldsmith nor Talleyrand bears a high character for veracity, but it is not easy to see why they should invent such a statement, which would render even more burlesque President Grégoire's reply, "The shades of Pym, Hampden, and Sidney hover over your heads, and the moment is doubtless approaching when Frenchmen will go and congratulate the National Convention of Great Britain." Anyhow, it appears that the shoes were seized in the Thames by the English Government.

Turning from donors to suppliants, we meet with Christopher Potter, who in 1791 petitioned the Assembly for a fifteen years' patent for his porcelain processes, promising a quarter of the profits to the

* "Secret History of the Cabinet of Bonaparte," ii. 152.

nation. Though not a baker, he once contracted to supply the troops at Colchester with bread. He was an unsuccessful candidate for Cambridge in 1780, and in the following year headed the poll at Colchester, but the House of Commons seated his opponent, a naval officer, afterwards made a baronet, Sir Edmund Affleck. Jokes were cut on Potter's polling batches of electors after baking batches of bread. When the Revolution stopped the porcelain works at Chantilly, established by the Condé who succeeded Orleans as Louis XV.'s Prime Minister, Potter reopened them, and turned out 9000 dozen plates a month. He informed the Assembly that he had adopted France, the country of the arts, as his own, and was employing 500 workmen.. His petition was referred to a committee, but nothing beyond compliments apparently came of it. Potter, however, prospered, and prosperity made him venturesome. He had invented new colouring processes, and he established other factories at Montereau and Forges. These did not pay, and in 1800 ruined Chantilly. The mayor reopened the works in order to give the villagers employment, but after nine years had to give them up, and it was not till the Restoration that the manufacture revived. Potter was doubtless the man who waited on Lord Malmesbury at Paris in October 1796 with an offer from Barras to conclude peace for a bribe of half a million. Malmesbury suspected a trap, and describes the scheme as *insensé;* but the venality of Barras is now so notorious that a different view may be taken. One Melville of Boston likewise offered to effect peace for £15,000,000, telling Malmesbury that he arranged peace between Portugal and France by giving the Directory ten or twelve millions. The treaty, however, was not ratified by Portugal. As for Potter, he ultimately returned to England, and died in 1817. He was very clever at mental arithmetic.

On the 22nd June 1792, François Bernet, vicar of Sainte-Marguérite, Paris, and chaplain of a section of the National Guards, waited on the Assembly with his wife, Lydia Kirkham, and three children, the youngest an infant in arms. Lydia, of English extraction but born in France, was first the wife of Thomas Lovesuch, a mercer and cap-maker at Popincourt, who fell one night into a sandpit, and died from the effects of the fall. The two elder children were his. Bernet had been twelve years a priest, but had previously been a soldier, and had written against priestly celibacy. Addressing the Assembly, he spoke of his affection for his wife, and said he had been rebuked by the Vicar-General, the Archbishop's deputy, for his marriage, but had replied that nothing would have been said if he had taken a *housekeeper*. He asked for the repayment of 330 francs which as chaplain he had expended in holding services. "I have married," he said, "this woman, who is a Protestant, but her religion does not impair mine."

He was admitted to the honours of the sitting, but does not seem to have obtained any grant, for at the end of 1792 a subscription was started for Lydia. The appeal stated that the family occupied a room in a cottage in Montmartre Quarries, and that Bernet was reduced to working on the land. Our old friend Nicholas Gay, "known for his love of liberty and as a worthy cosmopolite," had been one of the first to subscribe (40 francs), and it was proposed to buy a cottage and piece of ground, so that the children would be taught by this honest couple to study two books only, that of Nature and the French Constitution. Lafayette gave 25 francs, Cloots 20 francs, the actor Talma 10 francs, and Manneville of Boulogne 5 francs. Bernet is next heard of in December 1793 as vicar of Ecottes, near Calais. Questioned by Lebou or his satellites, he protested that he had long ago unfrocked himself by marrying a Protestant, and had no altar but Nature. He was nevertheless, in April 1794, denounced as one of the priests who had been clandestinely celebrating mass, but does not seem to have been arrested, and poor Lydia disappears from history.

Bernet was not the first priest to contract matrimony. In December 1791, a priest in the Hérault wrote a letter to the Jacobin Club, stating that in the previous August he petitioned the Assembly to abolish clerical celibacy; that nothing had been done, but that he had married, and that an expected infant would be named Mirabeau. He wished Brissot to be godfather, and the Assembly godmother.

IV.

Enthusiasts.

"They come with hot unutterabilities in their heart, as pilgrims towards a miraculous shrine."—CARLYLE.

IV.

ENTHUSIASTS.

Stone—Helen Williams—Mary Wollstonecraft—Oswald—Christie.

THE motto from Carlyle aptly describes one, and that the most to be respected, class of the motley flock of foreigners attracted to Paris by the great upheaval. Among them was John Hurford Stone, whom a family tradition represents as assisting at the capture of the Bastille, but who cannot be positively traced in Paris till three years later. He was born at Tiverton in 1763, lost his father in childhood, and was sent up to London with his brother William to assist in the business of their uncle, William Hurford, the son of a Tiverton sergemaker, who had become a coal merchant. Stone, according to information furnished me by a kinsman, was very clever and cultured, and had advanced far beyond the Unitarian doctrines of his family. He was one of Dr. Price's congregation in London. He induced his uncle to embark in speculations which ultimately proved ruinous. In October 1790 he presided at a dinner given by the Society of Friends of the Revolution (of 1688) to a deputation from Nantes. They wrote home that he was thoroughly acquainted with all the European languages and literatures, and that on dining at his house they met the leading men of letters. The poet Rogers may have been one of the number, for he knew Stone well, and twelve months later, dining with him, met Fox, Sheridan, Talleyrand, Madame de Genlis, and Pamela, "quite radiant with beauty."

In September 1792, Stone, as we learn from a letter from Bland Burges to Lord Auckland, was in Paris, whence in the following November he wrote to dissuade Sheridan from accepting French citizenship, which the Convention intended conferring on him and Fox. "Obscure and vulgar men and scoundrels"—does he include Paine?—having already received the distinction, he had persuaded Brissot to defer the proposal, especially as it would be made a handle of by the Tories. In the same month he presided at a dinner of British residents in Paris to celebrate French victories. Paine was present, as also Lord Edward Fitzgerald, whom Stone introduced to his future wife, Pamela. Stone was well acquainted with Madame de Genlis, Pamela's adoptive mother, and on having to quit Paris, she intrusted her manuscripts to him. He handed them over to Helen Maria Williams, who on the eve of a threatened domiciliary visit burnt them. The "scribbling trollop," as Walpole styles De Genlis, never forgave him for this holocaust; yet he advanced 12,000 francs with a view to procuring her husband's escape from prison.

In February 1793, Stone and about forty fellow-countrymen arrived at Dover, though without the passports then necessary under the Traitorous Correspondence Act. The captain pleaded that they had embarked at Calais during his absence on shore, and, spite of his objection to receiving them, had forced him to sail. This pretended compulsion was probably a prearranged comedy. Some of the party were "kept rolling about the vessel" for three days off Dover before they were permitted to land. Stone must have speedily returned to Paris, for he gave evidence in May 1793 in favour of General Miranda, suspected of royalism. He had heard Miranda argue in favour of a republic at Turnbull's dinner-table in London when Talleyrand was present, and he knew that his London friends included Fox, Sheridan, Priestley, and Pigott. Stone also seems to have been present at Charlotte Corday's trial, his open admiration for her rendering him in danger of arrest. As it was, he was not exempted from the wholesale arrest of British subjects in October 1793, as hostages for Toulon. After seventeen days at the Luxembourg, he was, however, released. He was again arrested, together with his wife, in April 1794, but liberated next day on condition of leaving France. He could not safely return to England, for his brother was in Newgate on a charge of treason, and he himself was described in the indictment as the principal. He went to Switzerland, probably joining Helen Williams there, but he must have been back in June, for he then obtained a divorce from his wife, Rachel Coope. This is the presumptive date of his liaison or secret marriage with Miss Williams.

William Stone was tried at the Old Bailey, after nearly two years' incarceration, on January 28 and 29, 1796, for "treacherously conspiring with his brother, John Hurford Stone, now in France, to destroy the life of the King and to raise a rebellion in his realms." The truth was, however, that he had urged his brother, "that seditious and wicked traitor," as Sir John Scott (afterwards Lord Eldon) styled him, to dissuade the French from invading England, inasmuch as they would find none of the sympathy they expected, but were doomed to failure. Scott argued, indeed, that by warning the French against a hopeless enterprise William Stone had acted as their friend and as the King's enemy; but Erskine and Adair, his counsel, urged that if promoting an invasion was treason, warding it off must be the reverse. It must, however, be acknowledged that the collecting of opinions on the chances of a French invasion, however openly done, and however adverse those opinions, was sailing very near the wind of treason. The prisoner, too, had sheltered his brother's emissary, the Irish Presbyterian minister Jackson; had corresponded with Jackson in Ireland, signing his name backwards way (Enots), and had forwarded to the Government garbled extracts from his brother's letters; but Lord Lauderdale, Sheridan, and William Smith, M.P., testified that he was merely a weak enthusiast, anxious to give himself airs, yet sincerely desirous of a peace with France. Rogers, called as a witness for the prosecution, and asked as to the prisoner's loyalty to the King and regard for his country, evasively answered that he had always thought him a well-meaning man, and he was not pressed to say more. The prisoner was acquitted, and, after a fortnight's detention for debt, retired to France, where he became steward to an Englishman named Parker, at Villeneuve St. George.

J. H. Stone would scarcely have been acquitted, for in a document read at the trial he spoke throughout of the French as "we," and of the English as "you," thus identifying himself, as Chief Justice Kenyon remarked, with France. In a published letter to Dr. Priestley, he made some caustic comments on the prosecution, incidentally extolled the Girondins, and declared his dissent from Paine's religious views and his belief in an enlightened Christianity. In November 1796 he confirmed a report that Dr. Priestley intended to settle in France. Priestley, he said, would have made France his home in 1794 but for the Terror, and Stone was keeping his books for him. While still an ardent politician, and in the confidence, if not in the pay, of the Directory, Stone had by this time started afresh in business, and became one of the chief printers in Paris.* In 1805 he brought out an edition of the Geneva Bible; he published several English reprints, and he undertook a costly edition of "Humboldt's Travels." This work, which must have made him acquainted with Humboldt, ruined him, and in 1813 he had to hand it over to Smith, likewise apparently an Englishman. He had been even reduced, in 1811, to applying to Madame de Genlis for repayment of the 12,000 francs advanced for her husband's escape. Madame de Genlis professed ignorance of the loan, and inability to repay it, but assured Stone of her esteem and gratitude; yet in her memoirs the treacherous woman represents him as having wronged her. He is described by Charles Coquerel, his quasi-nephew, as of abrupt and eccentric manners, enthusiastic, ever ready to render a service. He published, under the name of Photinus, a letter to Du Fossé in defence of Unitarianism. He was naturalised in 1817, simultaneously with Helen Williams, and died in the following year. His tombstone in Père Lachaise, "the last tribute of a long friendship," describes him as an enlightened champion of religion and liberty. A now fallen

* He printed the Government tax-papers.

stone beside it seemingly marks the spot where Helen Williams was interred nine years later.

It is now time to speak of the lady who shared his struggles and poverty, and who may have been secretly married to him by their friend Bishop Grégoire, though it is not easy to understand why they were not legally and publicly united. Helen Maria Williams, whose date and place of birth have puzzled biographers, but are cleared up by her letters of naturalisation, was born in London in 1769, and was consequently just of age when she went over with her mother and sisters to witness the Federation of 1790, "perhaps the finest spectacle the world had ever witnessed." A precocious girl, she had published a story in verse at twelve years of age, and an Ode on the Peace at thirteen, and she had been introduced to and flattered by Dr. Johnson. Enraptured with the Revolution, the Williams's settled in Paris in 1791, and Madame Roland, one of Helen's earliest acquaintances, used to take her to the Jacobin Club at the time when Brissot and Vergniaud harangued there. Madame Roland would fain have seen her married to her own admirer, Deputy Bancal, nineteen years Helen's senior; but she pleaded the recent death of her father, a retired officer, and evidently did not reciprocate his attachment. Yet Madame Roland wrote to Bancal:—

"Either I understand nothing whatever of the human

heart, or you are destined to be the husband of Mademoiselle ———,* if you manage properly, and if she remains here three months. Constancy and generosity can do anything with an honest and tender heart which is unpledged."

Bancal, destined to become a Catholic mystic, proposed on Christmas Eve 1791 the prohibition of all public religious ceremonies, as also of all reference in schools to a future state. Helen persuaded him to vote for saving the King's life; and his was no fleeting fancy, for in 1796, on his release from Austrian dungeons, he got Bishop Grégoire to repeat his offer of marriage; but by that time Helen had found her elective affinity in John Hurford Stone.

The Williams's Sunday-evening receptions were attended by the leading Giróndins. Vergniaud there rehearsed his parliamentary speeches, and Barère shed tears—probably sincere at the time—over dissensions and excesses which made him sigh for his provincial quietude. Their upper story in the Rue de Bac gave them a partial view of the attack on the Tuileries, and they with difficulty persuaded their porter to admit a wounded Swiss, who implored a glass of water, drank it, and expired. An idle story that Helen callously walked among the bodies of the victims gained currency in England, and induced Boswell to expunge in the second

* The name is left blank, or given as "M. W.," in the printed collection, "Lettres de Madame Roland à Bancal."

edition of his "Johnson" the adjective "amiable," which he had originally applied to her. Amiable, strictly speaking, she may not have been—she was too dogmatic for that; but, far from being callous, she was horrified at finding corpses in the Tuileries gardens, whither she had ventured on the assurance of everything being quiet, and hastily retreated. She wrote against the Jacobins in letters to English journals, twice visited Madame Roland in prison, and was intrusted by her with papers which the fear of domiciliary visits compelled her to destroy, together with documents of her own. In October 1793, the author of "Paul and Virginia" was drinking tea with the Williams's, and describing his projected paradise at Essonne—he had married, or was about to marry, Félicité, daughter of Didot, the great printer and typefounder, who had a papermill in that village—when a friend rushed in with tidings that all the English were to be arrested as hostages for Toulon. The next day was one of painful suspense. By evening they had heard of the apprehension of most of their English acquaintances, but still hoped their sex might exempt them. At 2 A.M., however, commissaries arrived, hurried them out of bed and to the guardhouse—a sort of lock-up—where they passed the rest of the night. Thence they were conveyed to the Luxembourg, where the porter, a Swiss Protestant, who remembered having seen them at church, was kind to them.

The prisoners, mostly English, took turns in making the fire and sweeping the rooms, and those who could not afford to send out for dinner cooked their own. The Williams's had family prayers at night, in which Lasource, the eloquent Protestant pastor, and Madame de Genlis's husband, both destined to the guillotine, joined. They had also joined in composing "a little hymn set to a sweet solemn air," which formed part of these devotions. Many, however—of the French prisoners, at least —were less serious, and were addicted to cards, music, and even love-making. Indeed, a scandal in which an outsider and a female prisoner were concerned occasioned an order for the separation of the sexes, and, while the men remained at the Luxembourg, forty Englishwomen were sent to the English Conceptionist Convent. The Blue Nuns, themselves prisoners in their own house, and compelled to convert their flowing robes into gowns and their veils into bonnets, were very kind to their distressed countrywomen, and Sister Thérèse struck Helen as the nearest approach to angelic purity she had ever seen. Exercise in the garden was allowed, and friends could speak to them through the grating, whereas at the Luxembourg they could not stir beyond the threshold, and could be seen by friends only at the common-room window.

Athanase Coquerel, a native of Rouen, settled in business at Paris, and already engaged to Helen's sister Cecilia, after two months' untiring and perilous exertions procured the release of the Williams's, which seems to have been so clandestinely effected that there is no entry of it. They risked their lives by sheltering Rabaut St. Etienne, and after a time went to Switzerland, leaving behind Cecilia, now Madame Coquerel. Helen, who had gone to France as to a land of liberty, hailed the Swiss frontier as an escape from Inferno. Perhaps after all, Barère, whom she suspected of betraying her drawing-room conversations, committed one good action in his life, and facilitated her liberation and departure. She returned after Robespierre's fall; and in July 1796, Wolfe Tone, half displeased at thus losing his incognito, met "my old friend Stone of Hackney" walking in the Tuileries gardens with Miss Williams. He dined with them "very pleasantly." Stone "was very hearty, but H. M. Williams is Miss Jane Bull completely. I was quite gentle and agreeable." This probably means that Tone had to avoid interlarding his conversation with oaths, *more suo*. After Cecilia's death in 1798 Helen was like a mother to her two boys, one of them the future pastor, Athanase Coquerel *père*. She admired the Bonaparte of Brumaire, but loathed Bonaparte the despot, and was punished by him with a domiciliary visit and a night's captivity for ignoring him in her Ode on the Peace of 1802. Fox spent an evening with her in that year. The notorious Lewis Goldsmith tells an absurd story of Bonaparte having ordered her to invite Fox, in order to worm out his opinions, and of Stone having furnished the police with a full report of the conversation. Helen and Stone, he alleges, spoke strongly against Bonaparte's tyranny for the purpose of drawing Fox out, but the latter was very reserved. All this is certainly a fabrication. Helen laid by her pen till Napoleon's fall, and she welcomed the Restoration, with the English visitors which followed in its train. Lady Morgan, in 1816, found numerous guests at her Sunday-evening reception, but Stone's increasing embarrassments affected her, and she had to write, no longer for pleasure, but to eke out her resources. Athanase Coquerel, as Pastor Marron told Lady Morgan in 1829, was for a time in ignorance of her straitened circumstances. On learning them, he fetched her to Amsterdam; but separation from friends and Dutch habits brought on confirmed melancholy. He had to take her back to Paris, and settled a small annuity on her, but she died soon after her return, in 1827. An eye-witness of the greater part of the Revolution, acquainted with the leading actors, and a ready writer, she might have given us the best contemporary account of it; but her habit of moralising spoilt her as an annalist, so that of her numerous works not one has escaped oblivion, and even the few persons who may occasionally sing her hymn—

"While Thee I seek, protecting Power,"
are probably unaware by what "Williams" it was written.

"Affected but kind-hearted" was the verdict passed on her by Mary Wollstonecraft, who, disappointed of joining Fuseli's proposed party to Paris, went thither alone in December 1792 for the purpose of learning French and of finding a situation as teacher for her sister. Walpole styles Mary a "hyæna in petticoats," because she attacked Marie Antoinette even after death; yet tears fell from her eyes when she saw Louis pass on his way to trial, displaying more dignity than she had expected. She unluckily met Imlay, heedlessly acted upon her theory of free-love, joined him at Havre in 1794, gave birth to a child there, and on business calling Imlay to London, returned with her infant to Paris. Hamilton Rowan, the Irish agitator, arriving shortly before Robespierre's fall, heard at some festival a lady talking English to a nursemaid carrying an infant,* and made acquaintance with this by courtesy Mrs. Imlay. She remained in France till the following year, having, however, previously sent off her manuscripts, for had these been found, her life would not have been worth much; but her book

---

* Poor Fanny Godwin (so called), her cradle rocked by the Revolution; her girlhood passed with a needy, tyrannical stepfather, and a stepmother styled by Lamb "a very disgusting woman, wearing green spectacles;" her end a bottle of laudanum in a Bath hotel!

on the Revolution, mostly written in a gardener's solitary cottage at Neuilly, did not advance beyond a first volume, and this contains nothing that would be otherwise unknown. She does not relate her own experiences, and, writing for contemporaries more or less familiar with the facts, she moralises rather than narrates.

John Oswald, as a fellow-vegetarian, was probably acquainted with Pigott, and, like him, did not see the end of the Revolution, but his end was more tragical. The son of an Edinburgh coffee-house keeper, he was apprenticed to a jeweller, but a legacy enabled him to buy a commission in the 43rd Foot, which he accompanied to India. He left the army, possibly on account of his political opinions, and in 1785 returned to England. He had become a vegetarian, thinking it cruel to take an innocent animal's life, and filthy to feed upon a corpse. He had a passion for travelling, had lived among the Kurds and Turcomans, and was acquainted with Arabic, French, Italian, Spanish, and Portuguese. Despising fashion, he dispensed with cravat and wig, wearing his hair à la Titus. In 1787 he published a volume of poems under the name of Sylvester Otway, a farce called the "Humours of John Bull" being inserted in it. He also started a magazine called the *British Mercury*, and issued some Radical pamphlets. The Revolution drew him to Paris, a dislike of creditors, according to some, being an additional inducement. He joined the Jacobin Club, and Brissot in September 1792 suggested the conferring of French citizenship on him, but this was not acted upon. He translated Collot d'Herbois' "Spirit of the French Constitution," which he appended to an ode of his own on the Triumph of Freedom. He was one of the founders of the *Chronique du Mois*, a political magazine. Vegetarian though he was, he considered bloodshed necessary to the success of the Revolution.

In March 1792 he placarded the faubourg St. Antoine with bills advocating the abolition of standing armies, all able-bodied citizens to be armed with pikes. He was commissioned to organise a regiment of volunteers, but found them very refractory, and being a stern disciplinarian, he had "almost as many enemies as soldiers in his corps." He had left his wife and three children in England, but he sent for his two boys, and made them drummers in his regiment. He was dispatched against the Vendée insurgents, but in almost the first engagement he and his sons perished. It is believed that they were killed by their own men. Another Englishman who fell with them may have been Dr. Maxwell, who in December 1792 joined the French army, and is not again heard of. Three months previously Maxwell started a subscription in London for the French, citing the Corsica subscription as a precedent; but his house was mobbed on the day the promoters were to meet. Maxwell slipped away unobserved, and Horne Tooke took the arrivals to his own house, where a considerable sum was raised, and an order for arms sent to Birmingham.

Another Scotchman, Thomas Christie of Montrose, paid three visits to France. He was of a Unitarian family,* and was an old pupil of Dr. Price, who in the winter of 1789 gave him introductions to Mirabeau and Necker. Enraptured with the Revolution, he counted on the regeneration of mankind. As he remained six months, he probably joined Cloots's deputation. In May 1791 he went over again, became intimate with Danton, and on his return wrote an answer to Burke. In 1792 he was once more in Paris, and when the Assembly resolved on translating the Constitution into the eight principal European languages, Christie undertook the English version, which and the Italian were the only ones executed. He knew Mackintosh and Paine. He probably left just before the September massacres, for on the 9th of that month he married in London, and became a partner in his wife's grandfather's carpet-factory. In the spring of 1793 he was again in Paris, with his wife and unmarried sister. George Forster, the German naturalist who had accompanied Cook in his voyage round the world,

---

* His uncle, William Christie, founded the first Unitarian congregation in Scotland, joined Priestley in America, became a minister there, and, like Cooper, contributed to Priestley's memoirs.

received great kindness from them, and accompanied them to the opera and in excursions to Louveciennes. Miss Christie was in love with a young Frenchman, formerly adjutant to Lafayette, who had taken refuge in England. The engagement was disapproved of by the family, and the young lady, who was in weak health, excited Forster's sympathy. She, in turn, commiserated his troubles. He was sent on a mission to Arras in August 1793, and on his return in the following November, the Christies must have quitted Paris, for he does not again mention them. Whether because the carpet-factory did not flourish, or because of a restless disposition, Christie went out to Surinam, and died there in 1796, at the age of thirty-five.

V.

Outlaws and Conspirators.

"Intriguing and discontented foreigners, who have come here because they were at war with their own Governments, and most of them with all Governments."—*Washington to Patrick Henry, on Genet's recall.*

V.

OUTLAWS AND CONSPIRATORS.

Paine—Vaughan—Muir—Perry—British Club.

THE French Revolution, like a new religion, effaced the feeling of nationality, and led men, partly from a sense of duty to the world, partly from inordinate vanity, to expatriate themselves, or even to plot their country's downfall. Prominent among these was Thomas Paine—in France he spelt his name Payne—who was the only foreigner besides Cloots who sat in the Convention, and who, more fortunate than Cloots, suffered nothing worse than imprisonment. He had twice visited Paris prior to the Revolution, but his previous career need not be related. He paid a third visit in 1790, and a fourth in 1791, when four Frenchmen joined him in constituting themselves a "Republican Society." On the king's flight to Varennes, Paine drew up a Republican manifesto, which Achille Duchatelet, though his English wife, Charlotte Comyn, was a court pensioner, translated, signed, and placarded on the doors of the Assembly.

Still clinging to royalty, that body was much scandalised, and threatened a prosecution. Paine likewise challenged Sieyes to a written controversy on republicanism. He returned to London in company with Lord Daer, son of the Earl of Selkirk, a young Scotchman enraptured with the Revolution, destined to die of consumption at Madeira in 1794, and with Étienne Dumont, Mirabeau's secretary. The latter was thoroughly disgusted by Paine's claiming the chief credit for American independence, and by his avowed desire to burn every book in existence and start society afresh with his "Rights of Man."

Almost the last act of the Constituent Assembly was to confer French citizenship on eighteen foreigners,* that they might help to "settle the destinies of France, and perhaps of mankind." Paine was elected by Girondin influence in four departments, one of them styling him "Penne." Madame Roland, repelled doubtless by his vulgarity, regretted that her friends had not nominated David Williams in his stead. To avoid being mobbed Paine had to make a detour by Sandwich and Deal to Dover, where the Custom-house is said to have rummaged all his effects, and even opened his letters; but at Calais he was greeted with military honours, cheered by the crowd, and harangued by the mayor. Paine, unable even to the

* The English "citizens" were Priestley, Paine, Bentham, Wilberforce, Clarkson, Mackintosh, and Williams.

OUTLAWS AND CONSPIRATORS.   85

last to open his mouth in French, could reply only by putting his hand to his heart. His portrait found its way even into village inns, and an English lady archly wrote home:

"At the very moment you are sentencing him to instalment in the pillory we may be awarding him a triumph. Perhaps we are both right. He deserves the pillory from you for having endeavoured to destroy a good constitution; and the French may with equal reason grant him a triumph, as their constitution is likely to be so bad that even Mr. Thomas Paine's writings may make it better." *

Captain Monro, with more seriousness and severity, exclaimed in a despatch to the English Foreign Office, "What must a nation come to that has so little discernment in the election of their representatives as to elect such a fellow?" Safely out of reach, Paine sent a defiant letter to the English Government, thanking them for extending the popularity of his book by prosecuting it, and sneering at "Mr. Guelph and his debauchee sons" as "incapable of governing a nation." When this letter was read at the trial, Erskine, reprobating its tone, could only suggest that it might be a forgery, and urge that in any case it was irrelevant.

When the king's trial came on Paine voted for his detention during the war, this to be followed by

* "Residence in France," 1792-5, edited by John Gifford (who perhaps himself wrote these pretended letters).

banishment. His reasons, a French translation of which was read by Bancal while he stood mute at the tribune, evinced humanity and sagacity. He contrasted the success of the English 1688 with the failure of 1649, excused Louis as the victim of bad training, and warned France of the impolicy of losing her sole ally, America, where universal grief would be caused by the death of a king regarded as its best friend. In a sentence, which goes far to redeem Paine's errors, he said:

"I know that the public mind in France has been heated and irritated by the dangers to which the country has been exposed; but if we look beyond, to the time when these dangers and the irritation produced by them shall have been forgotten, we shall see that what now appears to us an act of justice will then appear only an act of vengeance."

Marat twice interrupted, first alleging that Paine was a Quaker, and as an objector to capital punishment disentitled to vote, and then pretending that his speech had been mistranslated.

Danton had a friendly feeling for Paine, with whom he was able to converse in English, and dissuaded him from attending the Convention on the 2d June 1793, telling him that, being a friend of Brissot, he might share his fate. Paine said it was painful (the pun must have been unconscious) to witness such things, to which Danton replied, "Revolutions are not made with rose-water." His warning was well-timed, for in Amar's report of October 3, which ordered the prosecution of the Girondins, Paine was mentioned as having been elected by them, and as having disgraced himself by deprecating the execution of Louis XVI. He had had the effrontery, said Amar, to depict the United States, France's natural ally, as full of admiration and gratitude for the tyrant of France.

On the triumph of the Jacobins, Paine discontinued attending the Convention, quietly awaited the impending arrest, and amused himself in the garden and poultry-yard of his house with marbles, battledore, and hopscotch. On Christmas Day, 1793, he was expelled from the Convention as a foreigner; and on New Year's eve was arrested simultaneously with Cloots. An American deputation vainly pleaded for his release, and on his asking for the good offices of the Cordeliers' Club, its only reply was to send him a copy of his speech against the king's execution. Gouverneur Morris, then American ambassador, advised him as the safest course to remain quiet, and Paine appears to have acted on the advice. Morris, however, was mistaken in thinking that he would thus have nothing to fear. Not that there is any truth in Carlyle's story of Paine's cell door flying open, of the turnkey making the fatal chalk mark on the inside, of the door swinging back with the mark inside, and of another turnkey omitting Paine in the batch of victims. Even at the height of the Terror men were not executed without trial, nor without an indictment having been drawn up by Fouquier Tinville, and served upon them at least overnight, which the prisoners jestingly styled "the evening newspaper." Removal to the Conciergerie, which adjoined the tribunal, was likewise in almost all cases the first indication of an approaching trial. Not one of these preliminaries had been accomplished in Paine's case. Carlyle, contrary to his practice, cites no authority for the story, but a variation of it appeared in the newspapers in 1823, in a biography of Sampson Perry, likewise a prisoner at the Luxembourg, who may have been accustomed to tell this traveller's tale. Numbers of survivors of the Terror pretended indeed to have been ordered for execution and saved by Robespierre's fall; whereas the tribunal took a holiday on Décadi, the Jacobin Sabbath, and of the fifteen cases prepared for trial on the 11th Thermidor, there was not one of any note. Paine's death-warrant was really signed, but it consisted in this memorandum, found in Robespierre's notebook: —"Demander que Thomas Payne soit décrété d'accusation, pour les intérêts de l'Amérique autant que de la France."

This animosity can be explained. When Marat was prosecuted in April 1793, Paine gave information to the Jacobin Club that, addressing him once in English in the lobby of the Convention, Marat expressed his desire for a dictatorship, and though the letter was prudently suppressed, Robespierre was probably cognisant of it. In May 1793, moreover, Paine wrote a letter to Danton (found among Danton's papers and still preserved), advocating the removal of the Convention from Paris, in order that provincial deputies might be free from mob insults.

Paine was released in November, 1794, and Gouverneur Morris gave him hospitality for some months, though his dirty and drunken habits necessitated his exclusion from the family table. On December 8 the Convention rescinded his expulsion, and ordered payment of the arrears of parliamentary stipend; but he did not resume his seat till the next July, when he pleaded a malignant fever contracted in prison as his excuse for absence. On his journalistic and pamphleteering activity, his refusal of one of the proposed rewards to literary men, his subscription of 500 francs towards the invasion of England, which Bonaparte intended him to accompany, and his return to America in 1802, it is needless to dwell.

The prosecution of William Stone caused the flight of Benjamin Vaughan, M.P. for Calne, and uncle by marriage of Cardinal Manning. His father, Samuel Vaughan, had been a West India merchant and planter, his wife being the daughter of a Boston merchant. Samuel Vaughan, who had settled in business in London, was prosecuted by the Duke of Grafton in 1769 for having offered him £5000 to procure one of his sons the reversion to the post of Clerk of the Crown in Jamaica. The proceedings seem to have been dropped on Grafton's resignation of the premiership in January 1770, and the Letters of Junius, which had at first sharply attacked Vaughan, afterwards pronounced him "honest but mistaken." He took a warm interest in the Corsican rising, and helped to raise a subscription for Paoli's adherents.

Benjamin was born in Jamaica in 1751, and was educated at Hackney, Warrington, and Cambridge, but being a Unitarian, could not graduate. The Vaughans were related to Horne Tooke, and he may have been named Benjamin after Tooke's eldest brother, a great horticulturist at Brentford.* Lord Shelburne, also fond of horticulture, presented Benjamin Horne with some fine strawberry plants from Saratoga, the first known in England, and he frequently stayed a night with him. This may account for Benjamin Vaughan becoming private secretary to Shelburne. Both of them sided with the American colonists. In 1777 Jonathan Loring Austin, the American envoy, went with Vaughan and Dr. Priestley to the House of Lords to hear a debate on America, but admission was refused. In March 1778 Vaughan sent Franklin an outline of

* But his grandfathers were Benjamin Vaughan and Benjamin Hallowell, founder of Hallowell, Maine.

Shelburne's speech. But politics did not wholly absorb him. He fell in love with Miss Sarah Manning, but her father withheld his consent to the marriage on the ground that Vaughan had no profession. Thereupon Vaughan went and studied medicine at Edinburgh, married on his return in 1781, and became partner with Manning & Son, merchants, in Billiter Square. He acted as confidential messenger and unpaid mediator in negotiations with America, and in 1782 was four times sent to Paris by Shelburne, then Prime Minister, to confer with Franklin. His brother-in-law Manning docked him of a year's profits of the business, on the plea of his having wasted seven months in diplomatic missions.

For thirty years the friend and correspondent of Franklin, Vaughan edited a London edition of his works (1779), and assisted long afterwards from America in the new edition of 1806. He also wrote a treatise on international trade, which was translated into French in 1789. In 1790 he was in Paris, and in a letter to Shelburne (now Marquis of Lansdowne) described France as in a fever of enthusiasm. He went on to Nantes, where on the 24th November he made a speech at a meeting where Nantes delegates described the honours which had been rendered them in London. It was probably during this absence that Colonel Barré, owing to a quarrel with Lansdowne, resigned his seat for

Calne, one Morris temporarily succeeding to it; for in February 1792 Morris made way for Vaughan. Jeremy Bentham, who fancied he had been promised the seat, wrote an angry letter of sixty pages to Lansdowne, but was mollified by his reply.* Between July 1792 and June 1793, Vaughan wrote a series of unsigned letters in the *Morning Chronicle* on the partition of Poland and the threatened dismemberment of France. (These were reprinted as a pamphlet in 1795.) In February 1794 Vaughan made a speech advocating precautions against negro risings in the West Indies, on account of the emancipation of slaves in the French colonies. On the 8th May following, in common with Lord Lauderdale, Sheridan, Major Maitland, and William Smith, he was summoned to a conference with the Cabinet at the Home Office, Vaughan remaining till six in the evening. He was doubtless questioned respecting a letter from him found on Wm. Stone, seemingly addressed to or intended for J. H. Stone, and dissuading the French from an invasion of England. It dwelt on the verdicts of juries in state trials, the readiness to enlist in the army, the little opposition offered to impressment for the navy, the approval of the war by Parliament, and the temper of the nation, as proofs of the expediency of France making peace on fair terms.

* Lord E. Fitzmaurice's " Life of Shelburne."

Vaughan was so alarmed at the discovery of this letter that he took refuge in France. To avoid arrest as an Englishman, he assumed the name of Jean Martin, and lived in retirement at Passy, his identity being known to only five or six persons. One of these was Bishop Grégoire, who states that the English Government supposed him to have gone to America, or would otherwise have outlawed him. Another was Robespierre, to whom he paid secret visits. A third was Archibald Hamilton Rowan, who, lying ill at the Palais Royal, was not a little surprised by a call from Vaughan, his fellow-student at Warrington and Cambridge. Vaughan told him that Jackson, the Irish conspirator, had been introduced to him in London, and that though quite ignorant of the plot, he had thought it safest to absent himself.* In June the Committee of Public Safety detected his incognito and arrested him, but after a month's detention at the Carmelite monastery he was banished. According to Garat he was mobbed in the street as one of Pitt's spies, and narrowly escaped immediate trial and execution; but even if his apprehension really took place in this way the danger could not have been so imminent as Garat represents.

Vaughan repaired to Geneva, and had no sooner

---

* Rowan does not give his visitor's name. His editor gives it as Bingham, but Vaughan was evidently the man, and Robespierre had probably sent him.

arrived than he dispatched a long letter to Robespierre, written in a tone bespeaking intimacy and an intention of keeping up a correspondence. He advised Robespierre to contract France to her former limits, and to convert her conquests into a fringe of free and allied States. By the irony of fate this letter, written as if to an autocrat, reached Paris on the night of the 9th Thermidor, when Robespierre, arrested but released, was making his last throw for life and power at the Hôtel de Ville. It was opened by the Committee of Public Safety, perhaps at the very moment when the fallen tribune was writhing in agony, and Billaud Varennes made it the basis of an audacious or rather mendacious statement at the Jacobin Club the day after Robespierre's execution. He insinuated that Vaughan was an emissary of Pitt's, and had written a letter advocating a triumvirate—Couthon to reign in the south, Saint Just in the north, and Robespierre in the centre. Vaughan, he said, was brought to Paris after the seizure of this letter, and Robespierre wished him to be executed at once, but a hearing was claimed for him, when he told a rambling story, ended by asking for a passport for Switzerland or America, and on reaching Switzerland wrote to Robespierre, advising him to "ménager" the privileged classes, and not to put sans-culottes on a level with aristocrats.*

* "Journal de la Montagne," August 1794.

In 1796, probably before his return to Paris, Vaughan published at Strasburg a pamphlet entitled "De l'état politique et économique de la France sous sa Constitution de l'an 3." It professed to be a translation from the German, made by a foreigner who craved excuse for inaccuracies of idiom. It is an unqualified panegyric of the Directory, a system of government to be envied, according to Vaughan, even by America, much more by England, Switzerland, and Holland. There is an incidental reference to the Reign of Terror as a political inquisition whose rigour equalled that of the Spanish tribunal, and there is a very just remark attributing the atrocities of the Revolution in part to the despotism and superstition under which its leaders had been trained. Vaughan likewise observes that the mob generally respected private property, frequently yielded to the voice of reason, and were rarely intoxicated, "which"—an evident fling at the London and Birmingham rioters—"cannot be said of mobs everywhere." It is surprising, however, to find him not merely extolling the cumbrous and corrupt system of the Directory, but confidently predicting its durability and an era of peace and prosperity. He was manifestly wanting in political foresight. He was also smitten with the craze of the Revolution being a fulfilment of the Book of Daniel, and wrote a treatise on the subject, but had the good sense to suppress it, the printer saving one copy for Grégoire. A Unitarian should have escaped the prophecy interpretation mania, but the Revolution upheaval turned merchants into fanatics and rationalists into mystics.

Stone's acquittal ought to have rendered Vaughan's return to England perfectly safe, and his brother-in-law, William Manning, M.P. for Plymton and a staunch Tory, was assured by Pitt that he might resume his parliamentary duties; but Vaughan suspected a snare. This was of course absurd, but it shows the atmosphere of distrust which then prevailed. After living a year with Skipwith, the American consul in Paris, he joined his family and his brother Charles at Hallowell, where his descendants still live. He had two other brothers at Philadelphia. One of these, John, a friend of Washington and Humboldt, and secretary to the American Philosophical Society, was a bit of an oddity. Generous in other matters, he had a dislike to the non-return of borrowed umbrellas, and he printed in large letters on his own, "This umbrella was stolen from John Vaughan." A friend once took this, all unconscious of the inscription, until Vaughan's Portuguese errand-boy perceived it and claimed the article.* A fourth brother William † was a merchant in London, where Benjamin's third

---

* *Atlantic Monthly,* May 1888.

† Doubtless the Wm. Vaughan who offered a temporary home to Priestley on his being driven from Birmingham. He was a high authority on docks.

son, Petty, became his partner, and lived till 1854.
A fifth brother, Samuel, settled in Jamaica. As
for Benjamin, he was a Conservative in American
politics; he doctored his neighbours gratuitously,
was honoured and respected, and died a year after
his wife, in 1835, bequeathing parts of a fine library to Harvard University and Bowdoin College.
Of all the English exiles in Paris he seems to have
had the peacefullest old age, but not recalling his
French experiences with pleasure, was not accustomed to speak of them. "The happiest man I ever
saw," says one who knew him well.

Thomas Muir, a Scotch advocate, had the prospect of a prosecution for treason when he went to
France in 1793, for he had been one of the leaders
of the Edinburgh Convention, which, except that its
sittings were opened with prayer, imitated the forms
of the Paris Assembly. He boldly returned, however, denied that he had fled from prosecution, and
conducted his own defence. He was sentenced to
fourteen years' transportation, but escaped from
Botany Bay in an American vessel in February
1796, and made his way to Paris, where he died
three years afterwards.

Sampson Perry's departure for France was confessedly a flight from a press prosecution. He had
been fined £100 for alleging in his scurrilous *Argus*
that the ministers had published false news for
stock-jobbing purposes. In face of a conviction for

libel on the House of Commons, for denying that it represented the nation, he went, in January 1793, to Paris, which he reached in time to join the British Revolutionary Club, where he must have found congenial associates. The club originated in a dinner held on November 18th, 1792, to celebrate French victories. Stone presided, Lord Edward Fitzgerald was present, and the toasts included "The speedy abolition of hereditary titles and feudal distinctions in England," "The coming Convention of Great Britain and Ireland," "The lady defenders of the Revolution, particularly Mrs. Charlotte Smith, Miss Williams, and Mrs. Barbauld;" "Paine and the new way of making good books known by a royal proclamation and King's Bench prosecution;" "The English patriots, Priestley, Fox, Sheridan, Christie, Cooper, Tooke, and Mackintosh." On the 28th the address adopted at this dinner was presented to the Convention. It stated that notwithstanding the sudden departure of the Ambassador, the British residents had uniformly experienced the utmost cordiality and friendship from the French people. A weekly gathering commenced on the 16th December, when the president of the section delivered an address in French. The "party of conspirators here," wrote Monro on December 17th, "have formed themselves into a society," prepared for the most desperate measures against their native country. They included Sir Robert Smith, a banker at Paris,

Paine, Frost, Rayment, Sayer, Joyce, Henry Redhead Yorke, and Robert Merry, husband of the actress Miss Brunton. Dissensions soon broke out. Frost and Paine quarrelled, the latter being intolerably arrogant, and on December 31st, Monro reported:—

"Our countrymen here who have been endeavouring to ruin their country are now really beneath the notice of any one, struggling for consequence among themselves, jealous of one another, differing in opinion, and even insignificant in a body; they are, excepting a few, heartily tired of politics and addresses [to the Convention]. . . . They are now dwindling into nothing."

A second address, advocated by Paine and Merry, but opposed by Frost and Macdonald of the *Morning Post*, was near causing blows. The Convention, too, was tired of the nonsense of British addresses, perceiving the insignificance of the persons who presented them. Monro's despatches end in January 1793, for he had been denounced as a spy by Thompson, a bookseller, who recollected seeing him in London, and he deemed it prudent to quit Paris; but we learn from other sources that in February the club was dissolved, the majority, after a warm discussion, deciding to take no further part in politics. The two Sheares, "men of desperate designs, capable of setting fire to the dockyards," had previously gone back. Young Daniel O'Connell crossed over in the same packet, when their exultations over the king's fate, coupled with the excesses he had witnessed at St. Omer and Douai, rendered him a violent Tory.* The Sheares were executed at Dublin in 1798. They had gone to France because Henry Sheare's motherless children were living there with their grandfather, Swete; had been intimate with Roland and Brissot, and had denounced Irish misrule at the clubs. John Sheare is said to have been enamoured of the republican heroine Théroigne de Mericourt, who, however, had given up Venus for Mars. Frost, a solicitor, was sentenced, on his return, to six months' imprisonment and an hour in the pillory, the latter punishment being remitted because he would have been applauded. Joyce was arrested in 1794 for sedition. "He was getting up in the morning," says Lady Hester Stanhope, "and was just blowing his nose, as people do the moment before they come down to breakfast, when a single knock came to the door, and in bolted two officers with a warrant, and took him off without even my father's knowledge." Joyce, a Unitarian minister, had been acting as secretary and tutor in the Stanhope household. On the acquittal of Hardy he was discharged. Yorke, who underwent two years' imprisonment for conspiracy, changed his opinions, and in 1803 published "Letters from

* Credence cannot be given to the statement of O'Connell's son, that John Sheare exultantly displayed a handkerchief steeped in Louis XVI.'s blood.

France," which were very anti-Gallic.* Sir Robert Smith was imprisoned more than a year in Paris, went back in November 1801, in quest of his property, returned to London, and died there in 1802. Merry went with his wife to America, and died at Baltimore in 1798. He had belonged at Florence to Madame Piozzi's literary circle, satirised by Gifford. In Paris he wrote odes on the Revolution, as also in 1793 a pamphlet in which he spoke of England as rushing towards an ignominious fall, while France was rapidly rising to a pinnacle of glory and splendour, unmatched even by Athens at the meridian of its greatness. One is reminded of Goethe's distich:—

> "Seh' ich den Pilgrim, so kann ich mich nicht der Thränen enthalten;
> Wie beseliget uns Menschen ein falscher Begriff."

Of Perry's imprisonment I shall speak presently.

* He found his old acquaintance Paine equally disenchanted. "Do you call this a republic?" said Paine. "Why, they are worse off than the slaves at Constantinople."

VI.

Emmigrants and Emigrants.

"All your kings and all the kings of the earth put together have never given such an example of monstrous despotism as you have been giving for three years."—*Lavater to Hérault de Séchelles*, Nov. 21, 1793.

VI.

IMMIGRANTS AND EMIGRANTS.

Palmerston — Insults and Ovations — Clarkson — Wordsworth — Fugitives — Cobbett — Edgeworth.

UNTIL they were shocked and alarmed by the massacre of September 1792, Paris was still resorted to by people of fashion or leisure as a necessary part of a polite education. The future Duke of Devonshire was born there in 1790, and the future Lord Cholmondeley in January 1792. The Duchess of Devonshire was at Marseilles and Aix at the latter date. The Revolution, indeed, was too unprecedented to allow of forecasts. The curiosity, enthusiasm, or abhorrence with which it inspired British visitors, as also the honours or molestations experienced by some of them, typify the various phases of the Revolution.

The future Lord Palmerston, then a boy of eight, had a glimpse of the upheaval, and it would have been interesting to know what impression it made upon him, but his biographer is as silent upon it as Lord Liverpool's in similar circumstances.

Palmerston's father, indeed, was or had been a friend of Wilkes; he was walking with the demagogue in Paris, apparently about 1763, when Forbes, a Scotchman in the French army, challenged Wilkes to a duel as having insulted his country in the *North Briton;* but Forbes could not find seconds, his fellow Scots disapproving the challenge. In January 1791, moreover, Richard Burke wrote to his father from Coblenz, " Only think of Lord Palmerston being a convert " (to the Revolution), but Palmerston's diary of his visit to Paris in July 1791 is not that of a convert. It is true that he shows no sympathy for the royal family, then virtual prisoners in the Tuileries, but he was disgusted at the plaudits with which the Jacobin Club greeted Brissot's arguments for putting the king on his trial, and he predicts the dispersion of the Assembly by the mob, followed by anarchy and an eventual despotism. This forecast approximates so closely to the reality that, meagre though the diary is, it is a pity Palmerston's father kept, or preserved, no diary in 1792. We consequently know only from his mother's letter to Lady Elliot of the scene at the barrier. The gates and walls erected in 1786 by the farmers of the revenue to prevent evasion of tolls—" le mur murant Paris rend Paris murmurant "—proved a potent weapon for the Terrorists, for when the gates were shut the " aristocrats " were caught as in a trap; and those who fancy that some slight circumstance may change the whole current of events may like to speculate on what would have happened had exit from Paris been unobstructed. The influence, indeed, of the Faubourg St. Antoine on the Revolution has been exaggerated, but the principal outlet from Paris was certainly in one of the most unruly quarters of the city. Lord and Lady Palmerston's carriage was not molested, but the children's carriage which followed was stopped, probably because piled with luggage, by the mob. Carriage and occupants were taken to the " section " or district committee, but after an hour and a half's delay, the crowd having dispersed, were escorted by eight mounted National Guards out of the city. The anxiety meanwhile of the parents, who had been dissuaded from returning, may be imagined.*

The departure might, Lady Palmerston thought, have been effected in a quieter way, but travellers were at the mercy of mob caprice. Now they might be hugged, now again threatened with hanging, and sometimes the hugging had a menacing air. Even before the tiger had tasted blood its caresses were terrifying. Mrs. Damer, writing to Miss Berry in October 1791, describes a kind of blackmail then practised by Paris fishwives. They brought her a bouquet, and she gave them six

---

* "Life of Sir Gilbert Elliot, first Earl of Minto." Palmerston did not see Paris again till September 1815.

francs, but they required double the sum. When one of them proposed to kiss her she did not think it safe to decline, and was only thankful that the other half-dozen, to say nothing of the crowd waiting in the court, did not follow suit. Porters and servants were afraid of refusing admission to these intruders. Lady Rivers at Lyons found matters even worse, for she was told it was prudent to wait on the fishwives, who had just shown their power by making the Comtesse d'Artois turn back to Paris. She was graciously received, and dismissed with a "Nous nous reverrons." Mrs. Swinburne, returning to London in December 1789, was stopped by the fishwives of Boulogne, who took her for one of Orleans's mistresses about to rejoin him in England. She had to argue with them that she was neither young nor pretty, and that the Duke could not have such bad taste. Happily, the landlady of an English hotel, Mrs. Knowles, came up and pacified the viragoes. Mrs. Swinburne in the previous October had had information from her shoemaker of the intended march on Versailles. She went thither and gave warning to the wife of Marshal de Beauvau, but it was unheeded.

William Hunter, a barrister, landing at Boulogne in February 1792, was unmolested till he reached Montreuil. His landing, by the way, was somewhat singular. Women actually carried the voyagers on their backs a quarter of a mile from the packet to the shore. One of those waders, unequal to the weight of a stout traveller who had been reserved till the last, dropped him midway. This curious scene took place at night, dimly illuminated by lanterns. At Montreuil Hunter's carriage was surrounded by half-a-dozen drunken soldiers (National Guards?), who shouted "Voilà des aristocrates," but on being assured that the travellers were English and good patriots, they wished them a pleasant journey. Hunter, whom the Assembly reminded of an English pothouse, everybody talking and nobody listening, went on to Marseilles and Turkey.

Charles Wollaston, a naval lieutenant, son of the eminent scientist, and his stepbrother, James Frampton, at the last stage before reaching Paris in October 1791, had their carriage surrounded and opened by fishwives, who hailed them as friends, shook hands with them, and had to be got rid of by a five-franc note—attentions which they by no means reciprocated, for Frampton, Wollaston wrote, was in love with the queen, and vowed he would go every day to see her pass on her way to mass;* yet in August 1790 he had carried off a fragment of the Bastille.

Lingard, the future historian, driven from Douai by the revolutionary ferment, yet anxious to see something of Paris before recrossing the Channel,

* Journal of Mary Frampton.

was betrayed by his seminarist air, and was chased with cries of "Le calotin à la lanterne!"

> "The oysterwomen locked their fish up,
> And trudged away to cry, 'No bishop!'"*

or rather "No priest;" but seeing a marketwoman at the head of the troop, he dashed down a narrow alley with posts in the middle inconvenient for the passage of petticoats, and thus baffled his pursuers. This is a French version of Lingard's experiences, but his biographer Tierney gives an altogether different account, more entitled to credence. In June 1790, according to Tierney, he was walking about Douai when the mob were dragging a man whom he knew, Derbaix, to execution. Stopping to ask the reason, his seminarist dress attracted notice, and there was a cry of "Le calotin à la lanterne!" This roused him to a sense of his danger, and he hastily took to flight, but remained at Douai till February 1793. Derbaix was a printer, and commanded the National Guard. He had rescued from the mob, and was taking to prison for security, a corn merchant, Nicolon, accused of exporting wheat, when a ringleader at the prison doors snatched Nicolon from him and gave him up to the mob. Derbaix, indignant, drew his sword on the ringleader, whereupon the mob fell on him,

---

* The Royalist satirists, in the "Actes des Apôtres," drew some of their inspiration from Hudibras, and the resemblance between certain phases of the Commonwealth and Jacobinism is obvious.

hung him to a lamp-post, and then dragged his body through the streets till ten at night. His widow, prematurely confined, died from the shock. Although Tierney gives a wrong date, June instead of March 1790, he cannot have been mistaken as to Lingard's attempt to rescue Derbaix. It is just possible, however, that Lingard did go to Paris on leaving Douai, and was mobbed there. He revisited Paris in 1802 to make researches for his History.

Young Henry Swinburne, son of the Mrs. Swinburne just mentioned, had no such escape. He was a page to Louis XVI., and was at the Vaudeville Theatre in 1792, when there was a play ridiculing the Jacobins. The Royalists expelled the interrupters, but were waylaid outside the theatre by a mob who pelted them with mud and snow, forced them to shout "Vive la nation!" and made them, ladies included, wade through the mire to their carriages. Swinburne was dragged in the gutter and severely injured in the head. His aunt, Anne Swinburne, was one of thirty-five nuns who, in the following autumn, had to quit Montargis and seek refuge in England; yet the Montargis municipality, about that time, in token of international amity, burnt the flag taken from the English in 1427, and destroyed the cross commemorating the battle, such memorials being "a leaven of hatred and discord between two generous peoples." Henry was lost at sea in 1801, at twenty-nine years of age, on his way to Jamaica, where his father, a well-known traveller, had settled. Mr. Algernon Swinburne is of the same family.

There is a singular contrast between the treatment of two young men destined to be admirals. Christopher Nesham, a youth of eighteen, was living at Vernon, in Normandy, in October 1789, when a furious mob fell on Planter, a corn merchant who had been charitable to the poor, but who, having sent flour to Paris, was accused of wishing to starve Vernon. The town-hall, where he had taken refuge, was stormed, and Planter was dragged down the stairs towards the lamp-post at the corner of the building. Attempts were made to fasten the rope round his neck. Renoult, a barrister who had vainly tried to defend Planter inside the hall, pressed forward, along with the octogenarian priest Courotte and young Nesham. The latter placed himself in front of Planter, snatched a pistol from one of the mob, and with it warded off the blows aimed at himself. Knocked down, he sprang up again and vigorously resisted the mob. Planter was at last got away from the lamp-post into an adjoining street, and a door being thrown open for the priest, he was pushed in and saved. One of the first acts of the municipality, on the restoration of order, was to confer citizenship on Nesham (November 17th, 1789). The Paris municipality in the following January presented him with a civic wreath and sword. The president bade him tell his countrymen that he had found on the banks of the Seine a brave, susceptible, and generous people, formerly frivolous, but now enjoying liberty, especially as it gave them opportunities of rewarding virtue. Nesham must have reflected that if he had received the first civic wreath ever awarded in France, he would scarcely in any other country have had to defend an innocent man against a bloodthirsty mob.* He may have worn the sword at Camperdown.

The other future admiral, Henry (afterwards Sir Henry) Blackwood, whose mother became Lady Dufferin, had gone to Angoulême, when just of age, at the end of 1791, in order to learn French. In December 1792 he went to Paris, and agreed to take a bag, which he was assured contained no letters, but merely domestic articles for an *émigré* at Brussels. At Paris, however, the bag was searched, and letters were found in it. Blackwood was taken before the municipality; but as the letters did not touch on politics, he was released on bail, a Paris merchant with whom he stayed being surety for him. On January 13th, 1793, the Committee of Public Safety reported to the Convention that the letters had been

* Carlyle, following a newspaper misprint, gave the name as Needham, and spoke of the sword as "long since rusted into nothingness," but in 1854 Admiral Nesham's son corrected the mistake, adding that the sword was still preserved by him. For an accurate account of the rescue see Boivin Champeaux, "Révolution dans l'Eure." Nesham died in 1837.

H

entrusted to him by aristocratic ladies, and that he had earned 300 or 400 louis by journeys to and from *émigrés*. (Blackwood, however, insisted that most of the money was the result of a bet with a fellow-Englishman, that he would get from Brussels to Angoulême in forty-four hours.) They held that he had dealings with the enemies of the Revolution, but "to set Europe an example of the virtue of hospitality," they recommended the Convention to release him, which was accordingly done. Though authorised to remain and travel in France, we may be sure the young midshipman lost no time in returning home.

He was more fortunate than Fraser Frisell, who, taught at Glasgow University to admire the ancient republics, went over to France at sixteen, in 1792, to live under a modern one. He spent fifteen months in prison at Dijon, and there formed some lifelong friendships. He became, indeed, so attached to France, that save a short visit to Scotland in 1802, he spent the rest of his life there. At the rupture of the peace of Amiens he was again arrested, but in consideration of his literary pursuits and his previous imprisonment, was released, with permission to remain in Paris or to travel about France, for travelling, coupled with shooting and Greek, was his passion. Chateaubriand styled him the "Greco-Anglais," and while in prison in 1832 for supposed complicity with the Duchesse de Berri, wrote an elegy on his daughter Louisa, who died at the age of seventeen. Joubert was another of Frisell's friends. Frisell published an essay on the English constitution, to correct French misconceptions. He married a Frenchwoman, a daughter by whom is still living, and expired in 1846, at the age of seventy.

Lord Sheffield, on his way to Lausanne in the summer of 1791, was horrified at the Revolution, and he found his friend Gibbon so reactionary as actually to deprecate the abolition of the Spanish Inquisition. Clarkson, on the other hand, thought, or rather Wilberforce thought for him, that the revolutionary zeal for the suppression of abuses might be directed against the slave trade. Clarkson accordingly went over in August 1789, and remained six months. Lafayette, as we might have expected, was ardent, and Clarkson was agreeably surprised to meet at his dinner-table two Dominican mulattoes in the uniform of National Guards. Necker was friendly, and Mirabeau not only showed him the outline of a speech he intended to deliver, but asked for further data. Clarkson accordingly, for more than a month, sent him every other day a letter of sixteen or twenty pages, but the speech was never delivered. The Abbé Sieyes and Brissot warmly supported him, and the leading members of the Assembly listened to him with respect; but the Creoles in Paris denounced him as a spy, and addressed him threatening letters. Recalled to England to prepare evidence for a parliamentary committee, he enjoined moderation and prudence on the coloured deputation which had arrived from St. Domingo. He was disappointed with his want of success, due partly to the political turmoil, partly to the counter efforts of the colonists, who saw no inconsistency in excluding negroes from the rights of man. Neither, indeed, did some English sympathisers with the Revolution, as for example Colonel (afterwards Sir) Banastre Tarleton, M.P. for Liverpool, who was in Paris in 1791. He was a zealous defender of the slave trade, though he regretted having fought against American independence.

A closer view of the Revolution sobered or saddened some who from this side of the Channel had been enchanted with it. Mr. (afterwards Sir) John Stanley of Alderley, after a month at Paris in 1790, when he accompanied Huskisson, Windham, and Pelham (afterwards Lord Chichester) to the Jacobins, informed Lord Auckland that his enthusiasm had been dispelled; but he had not turned round the other way, for the violence, unfairness, and ignorance of both sides equally disgusted him. David Williams, the Unitarian minister, whose creed was ironically said to be, "I believe in God: amen," had been invited over to assist in framing the constitution. This was done at the suggestion of Brissot, who had translated his "Letters on Political Liberty," and he spent the winter of 1792 in Paris, but was glad to get back to England. He is said to have warned the Girondins that unless they put down the Jacobins, whose club had denounced him as a Royalist because he excused Louis XVI., they would be destroyed by them. Aghast at the confusion in the Convention and the uproar in the galleries, he told Madame Roland he expected little good from deputies unable to listen. "You French no longer study that external propriety which stands for so much in Assemblies; heedlessness and coarseness are no recommendations for a Legislature." The clamour in the Assembly shocked, indeed, all English observers, who by 1791 were getting disillusionised; yet even then there were deceptive lulls. George Hammond, afterwards Under Secretary at the Foreign Office, writing to Bland Burges in March 1791, expresses surprise at the tranquillity which prevailed. "Except a greater number of men in military uniforms parading the streets, all the common occupations of life proceed as smoothly and regularly as if no event of consequence had occurred, and the public amusements are followed with as much avidity as in the most quiet and flourishing periods of the monarchy." Lafayette, however, about this time bowed, but said nothing when congratulated on the calm by Samuel Rogers, who had fancied on landing at Calais that France might soon prove even to Englishmen a welcome asylum, but who found the best judges in Paris full of misgivings.* Rogers conversed, indeed, with the Duc de la Rochefoucauld, Condorcet, and other leading men, but obtained no knowledge of the real state of the country.

How, indeed, could young men just of age be expected to foresee the total eclipse of law and order? Wordsworth, who made the acquaintance of Watt in Paris in November 1791, accompanied him to the Assembly and the Jacobin Club—

> "In both her clamorous halls,
> The National Synod and the Jacobins,
> I saw the revolutionary power
> Tossed like a ship at anchor rocked by storms,"

and took away with him a fragment of the Bastille as a relic.

> "The senselessness of joy was then sublime."

When, however, he returned to Paris from Orleans and Blois, just after the September massacres, he was horrified on visiting the scenes of carnage, and for years, it is said, would dream that he was pleading for his own life or that of friends before

---

* Lafayette had an English aide-de-camp, John Hely (afterwards Lord) Hutchinson, younger son of the Irish Secretary of State, whose rapacity made Lord North remark, "If he had England and Ireland given him, he would ask for the Isle of Man as a potato garden." Young Hutchinson was with Lafayette from 1789 till his flight in August 1792, succeeded Abercromby in Egypt, became Earl of Donoughmore in 1825, and died, aged seventy-five, in 1832.

the infamous Maillard. Yet he returned home reluctantly, was still for a time a Republican, and expected Robespierre's fall to usher in a second dawn of liberty.

The Englishmen who left before the Terror set in must have been numerous, but there are few traces of them. As early as the winter of 1789 a London newspaper, remembering the adage of the ill wind, commented with real insular egotism on the benefit to England of the Revolution. Not only had many rich Frenchmen sought refuge here, but many British residents had returned home. Reckoning, too, the English visitors to Paris as 5000 a year, and their expenditure as £100 a head, England, it said, would save half a million per annum. Now, as for visitors, possibly as many were for a time drawn over by the Revolution as kept away by it, but residents were certainly frightened off. Lord and Lady Kerry—she was Anastasia, only child of Peter Daly, of the county Galway, and had been divorced by her first husband, a cousin Daly—had lived mostly on the Continent since their marriage in 1768, and had paid several visits to Paris. In 1792 they occupied the mansion of M. de Caze in the Rue des Champs Elysées, when the storming of the Tuileries and the recall of Lord Gower showed them the necessity of leaving Paris. This, however, was not so easy. On the 1st September, Kerry, in a letter to Lindsay at the Embassy, stated that he had vainly applied for a passport for himself, his wife, and such servants as were not French, but had been told, "I must prove that we and our servants are foreigners." He had given up the idea of taking French servants, and thought of applying for a passport for the provinces, of going to Calais with it, and of there waiting a chance of departure; but he feared his property would be seized and confiscated. He must have gone away very hurriedly, for he left not only considerable property —his heirs were in 1820 awarded £145,000 from the indemnity fund—but a large bundle of papers, likewise confiscated, revolutionary logic declaring an Irish peer an *émigré*. These documents, comprising some hundreds of bills and letters, extend from 1768 to 1790, and the correspondence with the Irish steward shows that the collection of rents was almost as difficult then as now. A patriotic gift of 117 francs to the Assembly in November 1789, from "eleven servants of an English lord," must have been approved, if not inspired, by Kerry, yet Nicolas, probably one of the eleven, was guillotined in May 1794 for dealings with the enemy; and Louise Blaizeau, wife to the man-cook Riquet whom Lord Gower had taken back with him to England, suffered the same fate, partly for endeavouring to get the seals removed from Kerry's property. Kerry was in

Belgium about the end of 1792, for Fersen, the Swedish count associated with the King's escape to Varennes, met him there. Lady Kerry died in 1799, and her husband in 1818, both being buried in Westminster Abbey, and the title and estates passing to his cousin, Lord Lansdowne.

One of Fersen's confederates also quitted France in time—Quintin Craufurd, the nabob from Manilla, whose maxim was, "Make your fortune where you like, but enjoy it at Paris." A confidant of Marie Antoinette, he provided, or at least housed, the famous carriage which the royal family overtook and entered at Bondy, it having already started when Fersen drove them to Craufurd's. Craufurd himself had gone to London and Brussels, perhaps to avoid suspicion, leaving his valet, Tom Sayer, to make all the arrangements. When the fugitives were brought back, one of his coachmen in the crowd incautiously exclaimed that he knew the carriage, but a fellow-servant curtly told him he was mistaken; the mob would otherwise have stormed Craufurd's house. Not discouraged by the failure, he busied himself in trying to get foreign Powers to interfere. On leaving in November 1792, he, too, was classed as an *émigré*, and his furniture, pictures, and statues were sold. Stormy times these for an inveterate cardplayer, who in 1787 was fetched home at nine in the morning from the British Embassy by his Italian mistress and eventual wife Mrs. Sullivan, alleged ex-wife of the future King of Wurtemburg,* and grandmother that was to be of Comte d'Orsay! When the Terror had passed over, Craufurd returned. Under the Empire he had whist parties with Talleyrand, and formed a collection of historical portraits which was one of the sights of Paris till his death in 1819. The Duke of Wellington was returning from a call on Craufurd when shot at by Cantillon in 1818, and he was at Mrs. Craufurd's when the intelligence of Napoleon's death arrived. Talleyrand was also there, and when some exclaimed "What an event," he replied, "*Non, ce n'est qu'une nouvelle.*" Benjamin Constant secreted himself for a few days in Craufurd's house on Napoleon's return from Elba, Madame de Stael having probably made them acquainted with each other. Though so devoted to Marie Antoinette, Craufurd, in a memorandum to the English Government, spoke of Fersen as "generally supposed to be the father of the present Dauphin." †

Henry Seymour, nephew of the first Duke of Somerset, left in June 1792, and like Kerry and Craufurd, was declared an *émigré*, which implied confiscation of property. A widower, he was the neighbour and penultimate lover of Madame Dubarry, and eight of her letters to him were sold at Paris

---

* Who married George III.'s eldest daughter.
† Papers of Bland Burges.

in 1837 and afterwards published by Goncourt. "And what a romantic passion!" says a contemporary gossip in December 1778,* "what sensibility, what warmth, what transports! It was a real love drama, with elegies, pastorals, and eclogues enough to satisfy the least sentimental man in the world." The passion soon cooled down, but Seymour was not supplanted by Brissac, perhaps not unwillingly, till about 1782, when he went to London to see a daughter married. In June 1792, three months before poor Brissac perished in the Versailles massacre, Seymour returned to his seat at Northbrook, Devon. His granddaughter Harriette Felicité married Sir James Tichborne. She was mother of the young Sir Roger personated by "the Claimant," and her identification of the latter, as also her death in 1868 before the trial came on, will be remembered. Danby and Alfred Seymour, M.P.s for Poole and Totnes, were Henry's grandsons.

Charles Jerningham, of Cossey, Norfolk, brother of Edward, the poet, was another fugitive. He was a colonel in the French army, and had invested his patrimony in France. In 1796, when Swinburne found his property all sold and irrecoverable, he was "dying to return to Paris," but he had to wait till 1802. Returning to Cossey, he died there in 1814.

* "Nouvelles à la Main sur la Comtesse du Barry." Published by Cantrel in 1861.

Disney Ffytche, elder brother of Dr. John Disney, (a Lincolnshire vicar who became the Unitarian minister at Essex Street chapel), apparently beat a hurried retreat, for in February 1794 his furniture was sold as that of an *émigré*. Sir Robert Gerard, a young Lancashire baronet, with his schoolfellow, hereafter to be known as the informer Reynolds, "ran up" from Liège to see the men who were revolutionising France, but after seeing the King's return from Varennes they were advised by Lord Gower to hurry off. They were stopped eight or ten times on the way, and their papers scrutinised, lest they should be *émigrés*.

Cobbett may be numbered among the fugitives, for tidings of the King's dethronement and the massacre of the Swiss made him turn back at Abbeville on his way to Paris and embark at Havre for America. He had spent his honeymoon in France in the previous year. Back in London, he charged officers of his old regiment with peculation, but when a court-martial met, he failed to put in an appearance, either because he had taken hush-money or because he knew he could not substantiate his charges. He fell into further odium by allegations in support of an agitation for increasing soldiers' pay, and England being too hot for him he went in March 1792 to St. Omer, where he spent, he says, the six happiest months of his life. He found the French very hospitable, and intended

IMMIGRANTS AND EMIGRANTS.

passing the winter in Paris to perfect his knowledge of the language. It would have been interesting to know what he saw and did, but unfortunately he tells us nothing. We only know that in America he sharply attacked the sympathisers with the Revolution.

Two Englishwomen who left before the Terror figured long afterwards as partisans of the sham dauphins, Bruneau and Naundorff. Mrs. Atkyns—probably Charlotte Walpole, wife of Edward Atkyns of Ketteringham, or possibly the wife of his brother John, M.P. for Oxford, for she is described as the widow of an M.P.—had been presented to Marie Antoinette before the Revolution, and on the Queen becoming a prisoner resolved to save her. A municipal commissary promised her admission to the Temple in the disguise of a National Guard, on condition of nothing secret being said or given to the Queen. Mrs. Atkyns offered the latter a bouquet, and her emotion made her drop the note accompanying it. The commissary was about to seize the document when Mrs. Atykns snatched it up and swallowed it, whereupon the man angrily drove her out. She procured a second and this time a private interview, when she expounded a plan of escape, but the Queen refused to abandon her children, professed resignation to her fate, and begged Mrs. Atkyns to devote all her efforts to the deliverance of the Dauphin. This deliverance she arranged for with Madame de Beauharnais and the Comte de Frotté, and then left for England. The Dauphin's escape is said to have been effected, but he was not brought to her by Frotté, and she did not see him till 1818, when he (the alleged Bruneau) was in prison as an impostor, she herself then living in Paris on a small pension allowed her by Louis XVIII. She is said to have died in Paris shortly before 1830. All this has the air of a romance, more especially as Mrs. Atkyns is dubbed Duchess of Ketteringham—Ketteringham, Norfolk, had been in the Atkyns family since its purchase by the son of Chief Baron Sir Robert Atkyns—but absurd as the Bruneau legend is, it seems clear that a Mrs. Atkyns really endeavoured to effect Marie Antoinette's escape.

Catherine Hyde's story is still less credible. In her "Memoirs respecting the French Royal Family during the Revolution"—professedly a translation from the English, but I can find no English original—she represents herself as the illicit offspring of the Duke of Norfolk and a Lady Mary Duncan. She says she was brought up in an Irish convent in Paris—no such convent existed—was long kept in ignorance of her parentage, learned to speak German and Italian, in addition to her English and French, was taught music by Sacchini, and was so accomplished a musician that the childless Princesse de Lamballe virtually adopted her.

Marie Antoinette, by whom she was called "la petite Anglaise," entrusted her with secret missions abroad, and she accompanied the Princesse de Lamballe, in 1791 or 1792, to England. Just prior to the capture of the Tuileries the Princesse, to place her out of danger, sent her on a mission to Italy, and they never met again. Catherine married in Italy the Marquis Broglio-Solari, who was Venetian ambassador at Brussels in 1803. She there dined with Barras, and heard him say— *in vino veritas*—" He " (Bonaparte) "will not succeed in his ambitious projects, for Louis XVI.'s son is still living." In 1840 she made an affidavit in London that Naundorff, whom she had just seen, had given her proofs of his being the Dauphin. Now it is not easy to see how Venice, part of the Cisalpine Republic in 1803, could have had an ambassador at Brussels, then French territory. I can find no trace of a Lady Mary Duncan, and though this Catherine Hyde may have really served the unfortunate Princesse de Lamballe, her book, with its professed quotations from the Princess's diary, is a romance, possibly founded on fact.

The Countess of Albany, though no Englishwoman, may as titular Queen of England receive mention. The Young Pretender's widow, in company with Alfieri, was living in Paris from 1787 to 1792, after a visit to London, where she had been presented to the rival Queen, thus virtually acknowledging the Hanoverian dynasty. She and Alfieri left just after the attack on the Tuileries, but had almost to fight their way out at the gates. Their two carriages full of luggage and five servants attracted a mob, whom Alfieri harangued with his stentorian voice, while his wife (for she was by this time his wife) lay back frightened in the carriage. A presentiment is said to have made them start two days earlier than they originally intended. Two days afterwards the very section which had granted them passports ordered their arrest, and seized all their horses, furniture, and books. Alfieri, who had written a poem on the fall of the Bastille, never forgave the French this injustice, nor the loss of his own and the Countess's pension. For him they were "monkey-tigers," and he vented his wrath in verses entitled "Misogallo."

The Countess of Albany's—predecessor shall I say?—also witnessed the beginning of the Revolution. Clementine Walkingshaw bore a daughter to the Young Pretender at Liège in 1753. According to Dr. King, a non-juring clergyman, Gordon, gave the infant Protestant baptism. The parents then openly cohabited, but in 1760 Clementine secretly left the Prince, whose courtiers had vainly endeavoured to separate them.* She went to Paris, and placed the child in a convent. Mother and

* Her sister being housekeeper to Frederick, Prince of Wales, they suspected her fidelity.

child were afterwards in a convent at Meaux, and were ignored by Charles Edward until 1784, when, wifeless and lonely, he sent for the so-called Lady Charlotte Stuart to join him at Florence, acknowledged her as his daughter, and created her Duchess of Albany. She remained with him till his death in 1788, and died at Bologna the following year. Clementine—Countess of Albestroff she styled herself, having perhaps lived in the Lorraine village of that name—did not accompany her daughter to Italy. Walpole in 1784 believed her to be dead, but Lord Braye possesses two letters addressed by her from Paris in 1790 and 1791 to "His Majesty the King of England at Rome"—that is to say, to the Cardinal of York. When and where she died I cannot ascertain.

Walter Boyd, the banker, of whom we shall hear again, and to whom Egalité entrusted his diamonds, left in October 1792; his partner Ker soon followed him, and Kerly, a Scotchman, agent for the banker Herries, a regular frequenter of the Jacobin Club, but ultimately denounced as a spy, also fled. The Republic had evidently no more need of bankers than of *savants*. As for visitors, the great stampede was caused by the capture of the Tuileries. Richard Twiss (uncle of Horace) tells us that whereas there had been only thirty in Paris, above two thousand arrived in less than a week from all parts of France, all eager for passports to get away. Twiss waited on the Assembly with a petition, and, as nothing came of this, was getting up a collective remonstrance when the recalcitrant municipality gave way.* This was, perhaps, due to a strong protest by Deputy Kersaint, who urged that England was the only really neutral country, and was very sensitive to violation of the laws of hospitality, yet that everything had been done by the Commune to irritate Englishmen by domiciliary visits or refusal of passports. These visits were sometimes disguised burglaries, for on the 18th September 1792 an Englishman complained to the Convention that about £20 had been thus taken from his house at Chaillot, and that the tribunals dared not arrest the malefactor. Yet in the previous month Courtenay, the joker of the House of Commons, who related his French and Italian tour in rhyme, shed tears of joy at the republican spirit of the Parisians and their determination to resist the invaders.

No Englishman perished in the storming of the Tuileries or the September massacres, though two Irish priests, Flood and Corby, narrowly escaped the latter.† The English had, however, to be on their guard, particularly on August 10th, for a foreigner might easily have been mistaken for a

* "Trip to Paris in July and August 1792." (Anonymous, but by Twiss.)

† Flood was presented to the Assembly by two municipal officers who had saved him, and was declared to be under the safeguard of the nation.

Swiss or an aristocrat. Dr. Moore, father of Sir John, was denounced as an aristocrat by the head of a troop of pikemen, but fortunately had a French valet with him, whose assurance that Moore was English was accepted. Next day, in the Assembly, he heard the fate of the royal family discussed in their presence. "The Queen," he noted, "has lost all her beauty, and no wonder." * Nevertheless he felt no uneasiness when the arrests were going on. Shopkeepers told him the sanguinary feeling was confined to the people in the galleries and at the Jacobin Club. His landlord, boasting of a night of domiciliary visits and of the arrest of four priests, "could not have had a prouder air if he had quartered the Duke of Brunswick." Moore approached the Abbaye during the massacres, but turned back with horror. He found the noisiest sitting at Westminster a calm compared with the Assembly, where fifty deputies were shouting at a time, yet so sudden were the alternations of violence and quietude that on the 19th August the Champs Elysées had their usual shows and concerts. He left Paris without difficulty, but returned in October and remained till December. He was travelling as medical attendant with the Earl of Lauderdale, whose carriage was once stopped by a sentry because the hammercloth had coloured fringes. Such a distinction was contrary, said the sentry,

* "Journal during a Residence in France," 1793-94.

to equality. The coachman, proud of the fringe, had disobeyed his master's orders to use only plain cloth. The new rulers, indeed, were as punctilious on costume as the old monarchy had been. Arthur Young, more interested in agriculture, even during the Revolution, than in politics, was stopped in the provinces in 1790 because he wore no cockade.

General John Money, who went to France in July 1792 to raise a foreign legion, was aroused near midnight by his aide-de-camp, and told that the Tuileries were about to be attacked. He put on his uniform, went to the palace, and asked for a musket. "Voilà un véritable Anglais!" was the welcome cry of a hundred officers mustered there. When informed that the King was going to the Assembly he vainly tried to get thither, then doffed his uniform and went back to his hotel. When again aroused a few hours later and told that the Marseillais were pointing cannon at the palace, he tied a white handkerchief to his gun, and would have gone to the Carrousel to try and stop the fighting, but his fellow-countrymen at the hotel would not allow him thus to rush to certain death. Going out to look a little later, he was insulted by a man among the mob, deemed it prudent to return, and passed an anxious week before he could obtain a passport for Valenciennes. He then served under Dillon and Dumouriez, and though ignored in their despatches, claims a considerable share in the success of the campaign. This plucky Norfolker, who had served in Germany and Belgium, had offered his services to the Brabant insurgents in 1790, and had gone to France owing to no prospect of employment at home rather than to sympathy with the Revolution, for while a Whig, he was no Jacobin. In January 1793 he made an offer to the English Government to go over to Paris and arrange with Dumouriez to save the King's life. He believed that £100,000 would have turned the majority in the Convention the other way; but his proposal was not accepted, and on the King's death he sorrowfully returned to England. He was a witness for the defence of Hardy in 1794, and his name appears in a list of guests at the George III. Jubilee dinner at Norwich in 1809. He died at Trowse Hall, near that city, in 1817, aged seventy-seven.

In 1785 he had a perilous balloon adventure. He went up alone in Zambeccari's balloon from Norwich, in the presence of 40,000 people, was carried out of sight in an hour, and was driven out to sea, the valve being too small to allow of his descending. After being buffeted about for two hours the car dropped into the sea, and the balloon being torn, and hanging merely like an umbrella over his head, he had great difficulty in keeping afloat. A Dutch crew, inhuman or frightened, passed in sight, but took no notice of him. A boat chased him for two hours till dusk, but then bore away. The car sank inch by inch, and Money, resigned to the fate of Pilate de Rozier, was up to his breast in the water, when, shortly before midnight, a revenue cutter rescued him, so weak that he had to be lifted on board. "Any man with less strength than myself," says Money,* "must have perished."

Richard Twiss, who had visited Voltaire at Ferney, and had employed Rousseau in copying music, had also repaired to Paris in July 1792. He was a clever violinist and chess-player, and had lost much money in a scheme of making paper from straw. So little did he foresee the impending horrors that he intended spending several years in France. He expected indeed a counter-revolution. On the capture of the Tuileries he went out at three in the afternoon and found all quiet, but the gardens were strewn with corpses of Swiss, which were being stripped and mutilated by ruffians *of both sexes*.

I have left to the last the Abbé Edgeworth, and this for two reasons. His flight was latest in date, and he had virtually become a Frenchman, yet he cannot be omitted from a book on Englishmen in the French Revolution. It is, moreover, well to clear up misconceptions as to his relations with the

---

* Copy of newspaper cutting (at back of an old picture of the balloon at sea, belonging to Mr. J. J. Colman, M.P.) furnished me by Mr. E. A. Tillett, of Norwich.

French court. His father, Robert Edgeworth, great-grandson of Francis, who went over from England about 1582, and gave his name to Edgeworthstown, county Longford, resigned the rectory of that parish in 1749, on his conversion to Catholicism. The son, Henry Essex Edgeworth—Edgeworth de Firmont, as the family now styled itself, from an estate called Firmount, near Edgeworthstown—never saw Ireland again after thus leaving it at four years of age. Educated at Toulouse and Paris for the priesthood, he joined the seminary of foreign missions, but was dissuaded from his plan of becoming a missionary, and devoted himself to the poor, especially the poor Irish in Paris. He declined, when the Revolution assumed a threatening air, a pressing invitation to return to Ireland, his reasons being the long cessation of correspondence with his family (his elder brother Ussher had gone back to Ireland), his imperfect knowledge of English, and the spiritual needs of his flock. Princess Elizabeth, on her confessor accompanying the King's aunts to Italy in February 1791, appointed Edgeworth as his successor, and he frequently visited her at the Tuileries till August 1792, but was not introduced to the rest of the royal family.

When the King's trial was impending, Elizabeth recommended Edgeworth to her brother for the last spiritual ministrations, in the hope that his obscurity would save such a confessor from molestation.* Edgeworth accepted the mission, and in a letter to a friend in England, dated 21st December 1792, explained that this was his reason for remaining in France. "I prepare myself," he added, "for death, for I am convinced that popular rage will not allow me to survive one hour after that tragic end." He fully expected, indeed, to be torn to pieces by the mob, and he made his will before leaving his mother and sister (the former ignorant of his danger) for the Temple. Rigidly searched at the gate, lest he should carry poison for the King, Edgeworth, bursting into tears, fell at Louis's feet. Louis read him his will, and Edgeworth, through a glass door, heard the piercing sobs at the King's parting with his family. He remained with the royal prisoner till ten at night, took some hours' rest in an ante-room, administered the sacrament at five next morning, dissuaded the King from another interview with his family, and rode with him to the scaffold. As two gendarmes seated opposite in the hackney coach made private conversation impossible, Edgeworth offered his breviary to the King, and recited with him alternate verses of suitable psalms. He had no recollection of exclaiming, as the axe fell, "Fils de St. Louis, montez au ciel," and Lacretelle half confesses to having invented this for a report in a Paris newspaper. Edgeworth did, however, say, when the King, averse to being

* Hébert, king's confessor at the Tuileries, was guillotined in 1794.

pinioned, looked appealingly to him, "Sire, in this last insult I see only a last resemblance between your Majesty and the God who is about to be your recompense." When all was over, Edgeworth, rising from his knees, and bespattered by the King's blood as the executioner held up the head to the mob, looked to see where the crowd was least dense, and being in the lay dress then obligatory on the clergy, walked away unmolested.

He had promised Princess Elizabeth not to leave France till her death, and letters concealed in balls of silk occasionally passed between them. He had various disguises and several narrow escapes, his mother and sister being meanwhile prisoners, and the former dying in captivity. In 1796 he effected his escape to England, and conveyed to the Comte d'Artois (afterwards Charles X.) his sister's farewell message, the tenor of which is unknown. He was about to repair to Ireland when a mission to Louis XVIII. in Brunswick led to his becoming that prince's chaplain,* and he died in that post at Mittau in 1807. On the loss, through the dishonesty of the borrower, of the £4000 produced by the sale of Firmount, he accepted in 1806 the

* When Louis was expelled from Russia in 1801, the Duchesse d'Angoulême supported him on one side and Edgeworth on the other at a spot where he had to alight from his carriage and force his way through the snow. At a village inn at Ilmagen where he stayed a night, only two bedrooms being available, Edgeworth and Comte d'Avaray shared Louis's apartment, while the Duchesse d'Angoulême and her attendants occupied the other.

pension from the English Government which he had previously declined. By a singular coincidence, while Edgeworth attended Louis XVI. to the scaffold, his kinsman, Admiral Sir Thomas Ussher—both were descendants of Archbishop Ussher—escorted Napoleon to exile. Napoleon at Elba, in December 1814, inquired of Lord Ebrington for "my good friend Ussher."

VII.

Prisoners.

"Rousseau is to this Revolution what the germ is to the tree. He who thoroughly probed Rousseau's life would see the Revolution, in good and evil, enveloped in it; he bequeaths it not merely his ideas, but his temperament. He professes that all is good in man: he ends by finding mankind 'suspect.' A philanthropist, he daily advances towards an implacable misanthropy. Not a friend whom he does not immolate to his idol, suspicion. . . He lost himself in a vision of mysterious spots in which his reason totters."

—QUINET.

VII.

PRISONERS.

Anglophobia — Ex-royal mistresses — Luttrell — Pitt's kinsmen —
Pamphleteers — Kilmaine — Nunneries and Colleges.

AT the beginning of the Revolution the English were regarded as freemen to be imitated, at the end as slaves to be liberated or as enemies to be subjugated. The stage eagerly adopted the latter view. In October 1793 a play by Sylvain Maréchal, *Le Dernier Jugement des Rois*, represented all the monarchs of Europe on a volcanic island, George III. being dragged in chains by an English sans-culotte. Charged with ruining his people and fomenting civil war in France, he pleads madness in excuse. This piece was ordered to be performed at all the Paris theatres on the anniversary of Louis XVI.'s execution. A little later, Lebrun Tossa brought out his *Folie de George*. In this play the recapture of Toulon has brought on a relapse of insanity, and the King, in dressing gown, bestrides the stage, whip in hand, imagining that he is hunting. Pitt is anxious to prevent his opening Parliament in this condition, but the Prince of Wales threatens to reveal everything to the public. The fit passes over, and George in royal robes goes to open Parliament, but the Prince, by his side, endeavours, by whispering to him of a plot, to cause a relapse. He succeeds but too well, and in his delirium George apostrophises the Whig leaders, flings his robes on the table, and in boxing attitude challenges Sheridan. Pitt with great difficulty leads him away. The debate then begins, and the Opposition are demanding a regency when a French landing is announced. Grey proposes to go and welcome the French; a republic is proclaimed, the heads of the Prince of Wales and Pitt are cut off and paraded through the streets. George, shut up in a carriage, is drawn to Bedlam by Burke, Grenville, and Chesterfield. Fox and Sheridan in red caps insult him, and the curtain falls on Fox's exclamation that if the King recovered his reason he would be the first to demand his death.

Desnoireterres * finds something Shakesperean in this sorry burlesque, the author of which afterwards fawned on Napoleon. The proceedings of the Convention were almost as grotesque. On the 1st February 1793 it issued an address to the English people, Paine being one of the framers, though a small minority objected to it as useless, as all England was for war. In the following

* *La Comédie Satirique au XVIII. Siècle.*

August, Simon complained of the multitude of Englishmen in Paris. They insulted the French, he said, by their anti-revolutionary *redingotes*, paraded their luxury at the very moment when spying on and betraying their hosts, and ridiculed Frenchmen who did not adopt their manners or dress. Every day, too, they were at the Bourse, "bearing" the market. On the 7th September a deputation pressed for the extension to the English of the confiscation already applied to Spaniards. Gaston, in supporting this, denounced the English as perfidious monsters who were employing the most atrocious means to destroy French liberty. "As to the objection that the English might retaliate by repudiating debts to Frenchmen, there was not a single honest Frenchman in London, all were traitors, and the worse the English served them the better." The Convention annulled debts to Englishmen, but the finance committee overruled this, whereupon a second deputation urged the prohibition of all British goods. "The Romans," exclaimed Germain, "were not a commercial people, yet they conquered Carthage; and London is our Carthage." The Convention, moreover, subsidised David and other artists to caricature George III.

The delivery of Toulon to the English exasperated the Convention, especially as it was led to believe that they had hung Deputy Beauvais. On the 18th October 1793 it decreed that all English,

Scotch, Irish, and Hanoverians of both sexes and all ages should be arrested, their papers seized, and their effects confiscated. Factory operatives and children under twelve in French schools were alone excepted.* On a motion to rescind this decree, or else to extend it to all foreigners, Saint Just said, "Make your children swear eternal hatred to that Carthage, the Court of London,† not to the English people." He proposed the arrest of all subjects of powers at war with France. Robespierre in seconding it said, a few philosophers and friends of humanity might suffer, but they would be generous enough not to resent it. Barère carried a proviso exempting Englishwomen with French husbands, such as Madame Calas, married to the eldest son of the Toulouse victim. All British merchandise in stock was to be given up, an indemnity being promised, and ultimately even English placards and shop-signs were forbidden. A teacher of languages had even to announce lessons in *American*.‡

* Ferrières in February 1794 was expelled from the Jacobin Club for having liberated English children under twelve years of age, though he urged that not only did he thus rescue them from prison vices, but secured employment for sans-culotte teachers.

† This perhaps suggested Barère's impudent legend of Pitt having in boyhood been made by his father to swear eternal hatred to France.

‡ Yet Danton took Young's "Night Thoughts" to prison with him, and the poetaster Roncher translated Thomson's "Seasons" while awaiting the guillotine. He discussed a puzzling passage with three fellow-prisoners.

There was a sort of precedent for this wholesale arrest of peaceable English residents or travellers. In 1746 it was ordered that they should be apprehended as hostages for the Young Pretender, and after his escape the arrests were continued or maintained against persons not acknowledged by him as Jacobites. The object then, however, was to get rid of spies and cavillers, and most of the English were released on condition of quitting France. Lord Morton with his family was incarcerated in the Bastille because, being related to a man in high office in London, he would not apply to the Pretender for protection. There is no complete list of the English so-called hostages for the Toulon patriots. A number of the prison lists were consumed in 1871, when the Communists burnt down the Palace of Justice. The late M. Labat, archivist to the Prefecture of Police, compiled from the remaining lists, and from such warrants of arrest as have been preserved, a catalogue of the prisoners during the Revolution. These two bulky folios in manuscript I have carefully examined, and am indebted to them for most of the names of British prisoners given in the Appendix, but there are probably many omissions. The prison statistics tend to show that about 250 British subjects were arrested between the 10th and 14th October 1793, and the list in the Appendix contains over 200 names, several of which are, however, of doubtful nationality.

K

Very few of these prisoners have left any account of their experiences. There appeared, indeed, in 1859 a small book entitled, "Journal of my Life during the French Revolution," by Grace Dalrymple Elliott, daughter of Hew Dalrymple, a barrister engaged in the Douglas case, divorced wife of Dr. (afterwards Sir) John Elliott, successively the mistress of Lord Valentia, the Prince of Wales, and the Duke of Orleans. Had the work been trustworthy it would have been the best narrative of a British eye-witness of the Revolution. Unfortunately, though accepted by Sainte Beuve, who wrote a preface to the French translation, it has been shown by Vatel, Madame Dubarry's biographer, and other critics, to be a mixture in unknown quantities of reality and fiction. Mrs. Elliott professes to have been in four Paris prisons, but her name is not in the list of any. She describes a heartrending parting at the Carmelite monastery between Custine and his wife, whereas Custine was never at the Carmelites', and his wife was not arrested till two months after his execution. She describes the embarrassing meeting of Josephine and her husband as fellow-prisoners after years of separation, whereas the reconciliation had taken place long previously, and Josephine for weeks visited him in prison till herself arrested. She speaks of Harrop, eventually guillotined, as eighteen years of age and as a student at the Irish College, whereas he was twenty-two and in business.

She describes Santerre as released before Robespierre's fall, whereas he was released immediately after it. After this it is needless to discuss the cutting off of Mrs. Elliott's hair preparatory to execution, her offer of marriage from Bonaparte, and other marvels. All that is certain is, that she was in France from about 1786 to 1801, that she was Gem's fellow-prisoner at Versailles, and that she knew a Mrs. Myler or Miglia, widow of an Italian, who was really a prisoner in Paris, and whose experiences she has apparently appropriated and embellished. She was watched, as a suspected political intriguer, after the Terror was over; she returned to England in 1801, went back to France about 1816, and died there in 1823. Had Mrs. Elliott really been imprisoned at St. Pélagie, she might have made acquaintance with an Irishwoman, Maria Louisa Murphy, who, if not like herself the mistress of two princes, had been openly lodged at Versailles, and had borne a son to Louis XV. The daughter of an ex-soldier turned shoemaker, whose widow dealt in old clothes, she had, by Madame de Pompadour's contrivance, posed for a picture of the Virgin in the Queen's oratory, so that the King might send for her. She was divorced by her third husband, Dupont, a member of the Convention, in 1798.*

* The first inmate of the Parc aux Cerfs, she was succeeded by her sister, Mary Bridget. She was born at Rouen, had a pension of 12,000 francs till the Revolution, and died at Paris, 11th December 1814, aged seventy-seven.

Failing Mrs. Elliott, Sir William Codrington gives us a vivid picture of prison life. Codrington is the man who made the strange bet with Pigott in 1770. A boon companion of the Prince of Wales, he was disinherited by his father (M.P. for Tewkesbury in 1769), who twice paid heavy debts for him, the second time on condition of his renouncing all claim to the estates.* These went to a cousin, who fancied he inherited the baronetcy also. Codrington retired to Brittany, and his father's death in 1792 made him Sir William. I give in the Appendix the interesting letter received from him by friends in London in February 1795, and privately printed by his grandson, to whom I am indebted for a copy. Written just after his release, it is entitled to entire confidence. All that need be added is that he continued to reside in France, married Eleanor Kirke, and died in 1816. His son received £23,000 compensation after the peace, and his grandson still inhabits Brittany.

The Temple Luttrell, an ex-M.P., mentioned by Codrington as a fellow-captive, was a son of the Earl of Carhampton, whose daughter married the Duke of Cumberland. Luttrell's arrest was triumphantly announced as that of the King of England's brother, because his sister was the King's sister-in-law. The Colonel Luttrell seated for Middlesex in opposi-

---

* Codrington's wife, Mary, daughter of the Hon. William Ward, whom he married in 1776, had probably died, and without issue.

tion to Wilkes was his brother, and Henry Luttrell, a noted wit and man of society, was an illegitimate brother. Temple Luttrell, arrested at Boulogne 18th September 1793, was liberated on the 14th February 1795. Liberty was his valentine.* Three days previously Colonel Richard Grenville had been discharged. He was a son of James Grenville, brother of Lord Glastonbury, and nephew of the George Grenville who was Chancellor of the Exchequer in 1763. He was the "dear little captain" of seventeen spoken of in the Grenville correspondence. While quietly living in a mansion at Cominet, near Dinan, in September 1793, he was pounced upon by Carrier, who exultantly announced the arrest of a "nephew of Pitt." He was really a cousin of the younger Pitt, and this unlucky relationship involved his detention at the Luxembourg till February 1795. He rose to be a general, was M.P. for Buckingham, and died in 1823.

If supposed kinship with Pitt had disagreeable consequences, imagine the result of bearing the same name! On the 4th October 1793, Deputy Dumont wrote to the Convention from Abbeville to announce the arrest of a relative of the infamous Pitt. "This shrew, named Elizabeth Joanna Pitt, had prudently conceived the idea of absconding, but she was in a town whose inhabitants are no longer ruled by moderantism and aristocracy.

* He died at Paris, January 14th, 1803.

She met on the road Republicans who patriotically *pressed* her to remain. All her effects are seized. . . . As she is an additional hostage, I am going to send her to Paris." At Paris accordingly the poor woman arrived, and I presume she is "la nièce Pitt" who was liberated in June 1795. According to the letters published by Gifford, she had been a nun at Abbeville, and was of impaired intellect. Benjamin Pitt, an elderly tradesman, and his wife Elizabeth Atlay, were also sent to Paris, and detained till February 1795. The announcement of their arrest by Barère, "the licensed liar of the Convention," as Michelet styles him, created unbounded delight.

Sampson Perry, militia surgeon, quack medicine vendor, and journalist, has given in his "History of the Revolution" some particulars of his own captivity. On his first visit to Paris, Paine took him to dine at the Hôtel de Ville with Pétion, the guests including Dumouriez, Santerre, Condorcet, Danton, and Brissot. Prosecuted for asserting in his *Argus* that the King and Pitt had kept back information for stockjobbing purposes, he fled to France in January 1793. He was a witness at the mock trial of Marat, but merely gave evidence as to a young man named Johnson, who, his mind unhinged by fears for Paine's safety, had attempted suicide, after making a will in Paine's favour. He states that, for want of room elsewhere, the English were kept in a guardhouse, men and women having to sleep as well as eat in one room. A baronet and a groom, a fashionable young lady and a cook, were thus companions for many weeks before they were drafted off into prisons. A secret police report, indeed, describes the English of the Section du Roule as lying, men and women, on straw, straw itself being scarce, and as lacking even water to drink. The Comtesse de Bohm, too, saw forty Englishwomen brought to Plessis, cooped at night in a room so small that their beds touched, and spending the day on the stairs, utterly impassive and torpid. Perry was at first sent to Madelonnettes, where the keeper was a humane man, and on a relaxation of rigour was transferred to the Luxembourg. Many English without means might, he says, have obtained release, but preferred remaining prisoners. Teachers, grooms, and domestic servants must obviously have been deprived of their livelihood by the exodus of the rich. Perry believed himself to be in imminent peril when, on the trial of the Dantonists, Hérault de Séchelles proposed calling him as a witness to the innocency of his negotiations with English Whigs; but the defence, as we know, was suppressed, and Perry after fifteen months' detention was released. He bore no grudge against his gaolers,—he wrote in his "Appeal," dated "the felons' side of Newgate, March 25th, 1795,"—

for many innocent natives and foreigners had inevitably to suffer, and Frenchmen, lamenting that Englishmen had had to sustain so long a captivity, did everything in their power to make them forget their past sufferings. Released from Newgate on a change of ministry, he subsequently edited the *Statesman*, had cross suits for libel with Lewis Goldsmith, the jury giving him a farthing damages, and died in 1823, on the eve of discharge by the Insolvent Debtors' Court. A contemporary sketch of him,[*] apparently copied from a newspaper, is the sole authority I have been able to find for the fable of Paine (and Perry also) having escaped the guillotine by the cell door swinging open and being chalked on the inner side.

Henry Stevens, described like Perry as a man of letters, was imprisoned at the Abbaye, the Carmelites, and the Luxembourg from October 1793 to the end of January 1795. He also was a friend of Paine, and had written a book, which I have been unable to find, entitled "Les Crimes des Rois d'Angleterre." He called on Lord Malmesbury at Paris in 1796.

General Kilmaine should not be passed over, though he had in thirty years become to all intents and purposes a Frenchman. His real name was Charles Jennings, and he was born at Dublin in 1751, but was apparently related to the Jennings

---

[*] Annual Biography, 1824.

family of Kilmaine, Mayo. When eleven years old he accompanied his father to France, was brought up a soldier, and made a good cavalry officer. He served under Lafayette in America, and afterwards in Senegal. He was enraptured with the Revolution, and distinguished himself at Jemappes. In June 1793 he was at the head of the vanguard in Flanders, and was anxious for a command in chief, but the Convention commissaries, while acknowledging that he was brave and dashing, deemed it imprudent to give him a higher post. "He is a foreigner; he is Irish; republicanism does not easily penetrate such skulls." Dubois-Dubay, however, recommended him for the command in Vendée, as the only general on whose ability and energy he could rely. But instead of promotion came eighteen months' imprisonment for falling back before the enemy, his wife Susan being also incarcerated till July 1795. Kilmaine afterwards served in Italy, commanded the "armée de l'Angleterre," which should have invaded us in 1798, and died in 1800, having not long previously been divorced. His rapacity was notorious.

Denis de Vitré, an Englishman by birth, Canadian on the paternal and English on the maternal side, was a prisoner for at least some hours, though I have not found the conclusion of his history. His father was the Denis de Vitré who was believed to have piloted the English fleet up the St. Lawrence in 1759. He had just been captured at sea, and was coerced by threats of hanging into thus betraying his native Quebec, but coercion is a poor excuse for treason. He petitioned Pitt, moreover, for compensation or reward, and it is said with success. The son went to France about 1777, managed a manufactory for Philippe Egalité apparently at Montargis, joined the revolutionary clubs there, next went to Rouen, and then to Paris, where he stayed at the Hotel de Philadelphie, the resort of English and Americans, and sedulously attended the Jacobin Club. On the 16th December 1793 he was denounced at the Club as an agent of Pitt, and if his father's career was known this is not surprising. He was sharply interrogated, and sent to the Committee of Public Safety. As the Club usually sat till ten, Vitré doubtless passed that night in confinement, but the Committee probably discharged him. Anyhow, he is not on the guillotine list.

The British Catholic communities in France, twenty-eight in number, with about 1000 inmates and £15,000 revenue, were nearly all despoiled and broken up by the Revolution. The Embassy for a time, indeed, obtained their exemption from the law-suppressing monasteries, on the ground that their property was derived from British benefactions, and that to confiscate it, after the invitations and assurances given by French sovereigns to the founders, would be like the hanging out of false lights by wreckers. There should at least be permission to sell out and withdraw to England. But the respite was very short, and there came a series of tribulations. The nuns in Paris might have given us interesting accounts of their own experiences; but domiciliary visits rendered it unsafe to keep diaries, and only one convent out of three subsequently drew up a record of its sufferings. We know from the minutes of Jacobin commissaries that, unlike some of their French sisters, the English nuns unanimously declined to re-enter the world, and they felt the full force of the revolutionary hurricane. Their lives, indeed, were never in danger, except from a possible repetition of the September massacres, but they suffered great privations.

The Austin nuns, since 1634, had carried on a school, to which leading Catholic families, Pastons, Towneleys, Fermors, and Blounts, sent their daughters. Dr. Johnson and the Thrales called on them in 1775, when the sub-prior Frances Fermor, niece of Arabella, the heroine of the "Rape of the Lock," described Pope as a disagreeable man, the poem as rather an insult than an honour to the family, and her aunt as rendered troublesome and conceited by it. Mrs. Thrale (then Madame Piozzi) paid the nunnery a second visit in 1784, when she made in her diary some sarcastic comments on the easy, care-free lives of the inmates. The flippant lady little foresaw the ordeal in store for them, yet they were comparatively fortunate in remaining at their convent. They would have been buffeted about like others but for the overcrowding of the prisons and the spaciousness of their heterogeneous buildings, so graphically described by George Sand, afterwards a boarder there. Their journal, which the present chaplain, the Abbé Cédoz, has allowed me to inspect, has a gap of several years, followed by a brief statement of the cause.

A motley throng of prisoners, good and bad, rich and poor, occupied the convent. They included several actresses; Malesherbes's daughter, Madame de Rosanbo, guillotined with eleven other inmates; George Sand's grandmother, Madame Dupin; and the birdseller's daughter, Victoire Delaborde. Curiously enough, these two did not then make each other's acquaintance, and Maurice Dupin, then a boy living at Auteuil, who agreed with his mother that at a certain hour in the day both should fix their eyes on the dome of the Pantheon, had no presentiment that his destined wife, Victoire, might also be gazing at it. Disparity of station kept the two women apart.

A number of British subjects were detained there, among them the Abbé Edgeworth's sister, Betty, who was "dragged from prison to prison." His mother, too, was probably there also, for she was arrested while he was still in concealment in Paris, and soon succumbed to grief. Another inmate, arrested not as an Englishwoman but as the widow of an aristocrat, was the Marquise de Châtellux. Mary Bridget Josephine Charlotte Plunket was lady-in-waiting to the Duchess of Orleans, the wife of Egalité. Her father, Thomas Plunket, a kinsman of Lord Dunsany, was an Austrian field-marshal, had distinguished himself in the Seven Years' War, and had died governor of Antwerp in 1770. Mary, born at Louvain in 1759, was educated at the Austin convent, her future prison. A husband was found for her by a singular stratagem. The Marquis de Châtellux, a member of the Academy, and the first adult Frenchman who underwent inoculation, had published an account of his travels in America. It was contrived that he should be sent to Spa, and should steal unawares on Miss Plunket while absorbed in his book. He fell in love with her on the spot, and marriage speedily followed; the bridegroom was fifty-three, the bride twenty-three. Washington sent him a bantering letter of congratulation—"Married, my dear Marquis? You, too, caught! I have a great mind to laugh." Captain Swinburne, who saw the happy pair in 1787—by a slip of the pen he says Carondelet instead of Châtellux—writes: "He is the most passionate lover ever seen, and cannot bear to be absent from her for a moment, and even sits by her at table." Madame de Genlis was jealous of the Marchioness, whom she accuses of supplanting her in the favour of the Duchess of Orleans. Possibly she opened the Duchess's eyes to the relations between Egalité and his children's governess. The bride was in twelve months a widow, but gave birth to a son, Alfred, who was petted by the Duchess, his godmother. Gouverneur Morris, the American ambassador, was very friendly with Madame de Châtellux, who introduced him to the Duchess, and whom he describes as "an amiable woman, not the less lovely for the tears she sheds to her husband's memory." Morris was so fond of discussing financial and political programmes that Madame de Châtellux used to tell him that her patriotic gift—patriotic gifts were then in vogue—would be to present him to Louis XVI. as one of his ministers.* Her English coachman Archley was among the captors of the Bastille, yet she was regarded as one of the instigators of the departure of the King's aunts, who, poor ladies, thus escaped revolutionary horrors. Perhaps on this account she was a prisoner from November 1793 to November 1794 at the Austin nunnery, where she had been at school just twenty years before.

Mirabeau's mother was also at the Austin convent. The Marquis de Mirabeau, the self-styled "friend of man," but not the friend of his own household, describes his life with her as "twenty years of

* *Scribner's Magazine,* January 1887.

nephretic colic," but the fault was certainly not all on her side. On her going to visit her sick mother in 1763, her husband forbade her return home, and procured a *lettre de cachet* for her detention in a Limoges convent. The Marquis died the day before the capture of the Bastille. The widow lived in poverty in Paris; her son refused to see her, and when he was dying she vainly waited six hours outside for permission to see him, for her daughter, doubtless by Mirabeau's orders, refused her admission. She threatened to dispute his will, which left her nothing, but as he died in debt his legacies were nugatory. The poor woman, poor in two senses, was a captive about a year, and died shortly after her release, 18th November 1794, at the age of sixty-nine.

No prisoner at the convent has left any narrative. The nuns were required to assume secular dress, and were not allowed religious services, but they were permitted to remain in their cells and to walk in the vineyard. The tombs were profaned for the sake of the lead, and church plate and ornaments were plundered. The velvet draperies, bearing the royal arms embroidered in gold, from the royal pew in Whitehall chapel, presented to the convent on James II.'s death, had disappeared. In March 1795 the gaoler and guards were withdrawn, and the school was reopened, but in 1799 the sale of all the British establishments was ordered. The nuns were on the point of quitting France, and had sent off their luggage to Calais, when Consul Lebrun's sympathy, and his good offices with Bonaparte, enabled them to remain. Removing in 1860 to Neuilly, just outside Paris, they celebrated in 1884 their fifth jubilee.

The Benedictine convent was likewise converted into a prison, with a brutal gaoler who delighted to threaten his captives with death—no empty threat, for the Princess of Monaco, Madame Sainte Amaranthe, and others, left the nunnery for the Conciergerie, and the latter for the guillotine. The nuns not only witnessed distressing partings, but anticipated a like fate. Stonyhurst College possesses a manuscript, which, evidently written after their return to England, depicts in an artless way the alarms, insults, and privations undergone by them.* After several domiciliary visits they were declared prisoners in October 1793. Their street was called the Rue de l'Alouette, from the ground having been formerly frequented by larks. They were now themselves caged birds, if indeed they had the heart to sing. Commissaries next came to fit up the convent as a prison, but to tranquillise the nuns promised that the captives should be only Englishwomen, a promise which was not long kept.

The prison became so full—Foignet found eighty inmates, two-thirds of them men—that in the work-

* See Appendix B.

room were placed as many beds as could stand, which were removed during the day. Refectory, cloisters, and outhouses were also crowded with beds. The cemetery was turned into a promenade for the prisoners, the tombstones being laid flat or carried away. All their rents being stopped, the nuns for the last three months of 1793 had to live on the small sum in hand, barely sufficient to keep them alive. Their papers were catalogued in a sarcastic style by a revolutionary commissary. One of the nuns had been in the habit of complaining to the chaplain, Naylor, of real or imaginary unkindness from the abbess or sisters, and these letters were inventoried as "squabbles of conventual life," "mystical extravagances," &c. The poor nuns must have shivered at the thought that all their documents, from religious correspondence down to recipes for making snuff, were overhauled by scoffing *sans-culottes*. Their library of a thousand volumes was dispersed. The Girondin deputies, indeed, after being huddled with criminals at the Madelonnettes, found the nunnery clean, spacious, and airy, with an agreeable prospect and a delicious promenade, the only drawback being that the female prisoners had had to be crowded to make room for them, yet according to Foignet, study was impossible and even conversation dangerous, it being construed as conspiracy.

In July 1794, the nuns were removed by night

L

to the castle of Vincennes, where they were cooped up in narrow cells, with windows too high to see out of. Four months later they were carted back to Paris, to the Austin nunnery. On their liberation they managed, by the sale of their linen and furniture, to leave for England, where they found a new home, first in Dorsetshire and ultimately in Staffordshire.

The Conceptionists in the Rue Charenton, very near the Bastille, were removed to the Austin convent in November 1794, and shared its alarms and privations. On their release they petitioned the Convention, giving a lamentable picture of their condition. "While prisoners we were at least sure of food, but we are now reduced to starvation, subsisting only on the scanty alms of charitable persons acquainted with our situation. Our property is not restored; we are despoiled of everything. We have no family, and shall have no country if the Republic abandons us. You will not suffer despair to reduce us to regret having escaped the axe of assassins. Grant us temporary shelter and succour until you have decided whether our property shall be restored. We shall not cease to bless your justice, and to cry 'Vive la République Française, vive la Convention Nationale.'" This appeal seems to have secured them a temporary allowance of two francs per head daily, and in 1797 Captain Swinburne found them tolerably comfortable, their convent having been restored to them, though in a dilapidated state. They were living upon what they could earn, and he dissuaded them from returning to England. A fresh confiscation, however, befell them in 1799, and they sought refuge with the Jerninghams at Cossey, Norfolk, where the community died out.

The Benedictine monastery and the three British seminaries were closed or turned into prisons, but the priests and monks mostly escaped. The Irish college, which then had lay as well as clerical students, had stormy times. In December 1790, one of a party of its students, walking in the Champ de Mars and mounting the Federation altar, leaned against and accidentally knocked down a wooden pedestal. The sentry tried to arrest the delinquent, his comrades defended him, a mob collected, and had not Lafayette with 100 horsemen hurried up, six of the Irish youths would have been hanged on the spot for the supposed insult to the altar. As it was, they spent a fortnight in prison, and were then acquitted. Later on a mob attempted to break into the college; but Mac Canna, a student, pistol in hand, planted himself at the gate, threatened to shoot the first man who advanced, and improvised a speech on the position of Irish exiles confiding in French hospitality, whereupon the mob applauded and dispersed. In September 1791, the congregation at the college chapel, including French worshippers, were mobbed on leaving, a lady being shamefully flogged, but the authorities took measures against the recurrence of such outrages. After the Terror the ten remaining Irish students were allowed to return to their own country. James Coigley or Quigley, a priest destined to the gallows at Maidstone for treason in 1798, had left in 1789, having proved an unruly spirit, but he had witnessed the beginning of the Revolution, and mistaken for a royalist priest, had had a narrow escape from the *lanterne*. He was in Paris again in 1797, conspiring against England.

The Scotch college, adjoining the Austin convent, was made a prison, and St. Just was taken thither on the 9th Thermidor, but the gaoler refused to receive him. The gilt-bronze urn, containing in a leaden case the brain of James II., was wrenched off the monument to his memory, and the case was not discovered till four years ago, in laying a pipe under the chapel floor. James's manuscripts, sent for safety into the provinces, were ultimately destroyed. His coffin at the Benedictine monastery was opened, and the body made away with.

Of this "resurrection" we have two accounts. An anonymous correspondent of the *Gentleman's Magazine* in 1798, a prisoner at the Scotch college, was told by a Miss White, an eye-witness, that James's nose was very prominent, the end of it being long and "abundant," whereas the lower part of his long oval face was anything but prominent, for his cheeks were lantern-jawed. She gave the correspondent a piece of the black silk velvet which enveloped the body. In *Notes and Queries* for 1850 appeared a rather fuller account, taken down ten years previously at Toulouse from the lips of an octogenarian Irishman, Fitzsimons, doubtless the Gerard Luther Fitzsimons, born at Quilca, County Cavan, in 1765, who retired from the French army in 1821 on a pension of 2400 francs. He states that there was a wooden coffin, enclosed in lead, and this again in a wooden case. The lead was wanted for bullets, and the body lay exposed nearly a whole day. It was swaddled like a mummy, and tied with garters. When the Jacobins took it out of the coffin, there was a strong smell of vinegar and camphor. The corpse was quite perfect, and the hands and nails very fine. Fitzsimons moved and bent every finger. The teeth were the finest set he had ever seen. A young lady prisoner wishing for a tooth, he tried to pull one out for her, but they were too firmly fixed. The feet were very beautiful, and the face and cheeks as though alive. He rolled the eyes, and the eyeballs were quite firm under his finger. The French and English prisoners gave money to the Jacobins for permission to see the body. The Jacobins said James was a good *sans-culotte*, and they were going to put him into a hole in the churchyard, like other *sans-culottes*. The body was carried away, but where it was thrown he never heard.

A decision of the Privy Council in 1825, for reasons more technical than equitable, excluded the monastic communities from any share in the indemnity fund. Sir John Leach, Master of the Rolls, delivered judgment to the effect that these communities being illegal by English law, they must be regarded as French establishments, and as such not entitled to share in the lump sum given by France to indemnify British subjects. Even as recently as 1874 the House of Commons was petitioned to reconsider the question.

A word as to the history of the Irish college, the only British institution besides the Austin nunnery which still exists in Paris. Macdermott and several of the remaining students took refuge at St. Germain, where Jerome Bonaparte was Macdermott's pupil. The school was afterwards reinstated in the college, and altogether lost its religious character. The students were young men of fashion, more conversant with Voltaire and Rousseau than with the Bible. In 1801 the English and Scotch colleges in Paris, as also the provincial ones, were amalgamated with the Irish college; that is to say, the wreck of their property left by the Revolution was lumped together, and the scholars all congregrated in one building, an arrangement still in the main continued. In 1813

Walsh, the superior, was removed. According to
Richard Ferris, who supplanted him, he had refused to render any accounts, and had sold to the
butterman for 500 francs the 2700 volumes of the
English Benedictines, including a unique edition
of the Fathers. Ferris, displaced by Paul Long,
whom Archbishop Murray sent over on the fall of
the Empire to restore the College into a seminary,
was reinstated during the Hundred Days, was then
again superseded by Long, but in 1820 recovered
his post. He had been quartermaster under
Condé in 1792, now kept his carriage, and had
so completely unfrocked himself that he had a
wife (?) and children. He resigned after a time, and
bought a mansion near Soissons, where he died in
1828. His collaterals in Ireland claimed his
property, on the ground that his son was illegitimate, and that the grandchildren were consequently
not heirs-at-law; but the distance and expense
deterred them from proceeding with the suit, or a
compromise may have been effected. Papers on
this unedifying episode are still preserved at the
College, which I believe has since been as harmoni-
ously managed as for many years, both before and
after the Revolution, it was the reverse. Ferris was
unmistakably "a character," for though a priest,
and with a right hand paralysed, he challenged
Hély d'Oissel, his co-trustee, who had rebuked him
for his quarrelsomeness. Reminded by Captain

Myles Byrne, whom he asked to act as second, that his right hand was helpless, he replied—" No matter, I shall hold my pistol in my left hand, and my opponent will do the same." This left-handed duel did not, however, come off.

VIII.

The Guillotined.

"France had shown a light to all men, preached a gospel, all men's
   good;
Celtic Demos rose a Demon, shrieked, and slaked the light with
   blood."

—TENNYSON.

VIII.

THE GUILLOTINED.

Dillon—Ward—O'Moran—Newton—Delany—Chambly—
Macdonald—O'Brennan—The Cemetery.

ALTHOUGH about a dozen men of British birth and as many more of British extraction fell victims to the guillotine, it must not be supposed that they were executed as English subjects. Little respect as the Revolution showed for international rights, it did not wantonly massacre foreigners. A fear of reprisals would alone have sufficed to deter it from this. Even Paine, had Robespierre lived long enough to behead him, would have been beheaded as a naturalised Frenchman and ex-deputy. The British victims were mostly men—alas, that we should have to add, *and women*—who by birth or long residence, or by service in the army, were really French citizens, and with one exception were not of high position.

The exception was General Arthur Dillon, son of the eleventh and brother of the twelfth Viscount Dillon. The Dillons had for nearly a century and a half been an amphibious family, so to speak, and their career in France would of itself fill a chapter, but I have already given a summary of this in the "Dictionary of National Biography." It is enough here to say that General Dillon's uncle, Archbishop of Narbonne and virtual viceroy of Languedoc, a man of much ability and of liberal views, who in June 1789 became bankrupt for two million francs,* was an *émigré*, and died in London in 1806. Arthur Dillon was born in Berkshire in 1750, entered the Franco-Irish regiment which bore the name of his family, and in 1767 became its colonel. After service in the West Indies, and acting as Governor of St. Kitt's, he was nominated brigadier-general in 1784, with a pension of 1000 francs. He was for three years Governor of Tobago. Martinique elected him as its deputy to the National Assembly, and he made numerous speeches on colonial subjects. When the Assembly, in May 1791, conferred the franchise on freeborn negroes, Dillon with the other colonial deputies ceased to attend, and the colonies were not represented in the Convention. He was appointed in June 1792 to the command of the army of the Ardennes. On hearing of the storming of the Tuileries, he issued a general order pledging himself and his troops to uphold the monarchy. He ordered Dumouriez, his subordinate, to issue a

---

* "Every one acquainted with his mode of living, and his general character for irregularity in his payments, is only surprised that this event did not take place long ago."—Duke of Dorset's despatch, June 25, 1789.

similar order, but Dumouriez refused. On the arrival of commissioners from Paris a few days afterwards, Dillon made profuse apologies for his manifesto, as being due to misinformation, and accepted the Republic. The command-in-chief was, however, transferred to Dumouriez, Dillon serving under him. He claimed a large share of the credit for the successes in the Argonnes passes, but according to General Money, who was with him, he was careless and indolent, lying in bed till noon. A letter written by him to the Landgrave of Hesse, offering him an unmolested retreat, was disapproved by the Convention, which declared that he had lost its confidence, and he was imprisoned for six weeks at St. Pélagie. The Convention, however, rescinded its declaration, and he was released. He attended the British dinner mentioned in a previous chapter, and gave a toast—" The people of Ireland, and may Government profit by the example of France, and Reform prevent Revolution."

Camille Desmoulins about this time formed a friendship with Dillon, who seems to have been a fascinating talker, and to have given luxurious dinners. Desmoulins fancied him to be a great strategist, and the only man who could repel the invader. Attacked in the Convention by Bréard, who taunted him with his intimacy with an aristocrat like Dillon, Desmoulins replied that six months previously Dillon had predicted to him the military reverses which had just happened, and which had his advice been taken would have been prevented. "Dillon," he added, "is neither royalist, nor aristocrat, nor republican," and he had drawn out a plan of campaign which filled generals with admiration. The very next day (July 11th, 1793), Dillon was rearrested, charged with a plot for liberating the Dauphin and proclaiming him king. Desmoulins in the Convention denounced this as a ridiculous fable, but was refused a hearing. Dillon was kept in solitary confinement at the Madelonnettes, and repeatedly interrogated. He vainly asked to see his friends or to be confronted with his accusers. In a letter to Desmoulins he protested his innocence, and complained of incarceration in a heated cell without air. Desmoulins replied in a letter, which he published as a pamphlet of thirty-eight pages, sharply attacking the Committee of Public Safety. It was pretended that the note-book of an English spy had been picked up at Lille, and Dillon was mentioned in it as in Pitt's pay. Dillon denounced it as a forgery, which it evidently was. Desmoulins, on admission into the Jacobin Club in November 1793, had, however, to repudiate Dillon, and to confess he had been mistaken in him, as in Mirabeau. Robespierre warned him to be more cautious thenceforth in his friendships.

Dillon, meanwhile, had been transferred to the Luxembourg, where he had comparative liberty.

Indeed, he had too much society, for Amans, a *mouton*, as prison spies were called, reported his real or alleged conversations to Robespierre. He is said to have drunk too freely, and to have amused himself with backgammon. When Danton, Desmoulins, and others, were arrested, a prison plot was invented as a pretext for cutting short their sham trial. The sole foundation for this was that prisoners, Dillon among them, had resolved, in the event of another September massacre, to sell their lives dearly. Dillon had also written to Desmoulins' wife, enclosing 3000 francs, as was alleged, to be used in exertions for her husband's release, but the turnkey, on second thoughts, detained the letter. (He was guillotined for not having divulged the fact.) After eight months' confinement, Dillon, with Lucile Desmoulins, and nineteen other persons, was tried for this prison plot, his name heading the list. They were all guillotined on the 14th April, 1794.

Dillon was twice married, and had two daughters. One of them, Fanny, married General Bertrand,[*] and was with Napoleon at Elba and St. Helena. He was not, as is sometimes stated, the brother of General Theobald Dillon, who was murdered by his soldiers at Lille in 1792. Theobald was born at Dublin in 1745, entered Dillon's regiment in 1761, was at the attack on Grenada and the siege of

---

[*] "Altogether English, and adores her husband," says Stendhal's diary of her in 1809.

Savannah in 1779, won the cross of St. Louis, and was a member of the Order of Cincinnatus. Brigadier-General under Dumouriez in Flanders, he was ordered to make a feigned attack on Tournay, to prevent it from assisting Mons, which was to be simultaneously attacked by Biron. According to Lord Gower's information, Dillon ventured too near the enemy, and was attacked while his horses were grazing. He ordered a retreat as prearranged, but the retreat became a headlong flight, and the soldiers, thinking Dillon had betrayed them, cut him to pieces in a barn where he had taken refuge, threw the body on a fire in Lille market-place, and danced savagely round it. The Convention conferred a pension on Josephine Viefville, with whom Dillon had cohabited for nine years, but, as he said in a will made the previous day, had not had time to marry, as also on their three children.

Brigadier-General Thomas Ward, born at Dublin in 1748, had a similar fate to Arthur Dillon. He lodged at the same hotel as Paine, and related to Paine a conversation he had had with Marat. The latter said, Frenchmen were mad to allow foreigners to live among them. They should cut off their ears, let them bleed a few days, and then cut off their heads. "But you yourself are a foreigner," remarked Ward. Paine, in May 1793, informed the Convention committee of this episode, and suggested that they should question Ward upon it. Though a general in the French army, Ward was arrested in October 1793, with all the British subjects, as a hostage for Toulon. Robert Plumer Ward, the author of " Tremaine," relates a singular story of his being arrested by mistake for General Ward. Plumer Ward had gone to Barèges for rheumatism, and had been visiting at various country houses. He was arrested, he says, " for having the same name and the same coloured waistcoat as another Ward, guilty of treason, was ordered without trial to Paris to be guillotined, and only escaped by their catching the real traitor. I was, however, banished the Republic merely for my name's sake." It is not easy to reconcile this story with the fact that Thomas was at least twenty years older than Robert, and that Englishmen were not banished but detained. Ward was condemned for the pretended prison plot at the Carmelites, and was executed on the 23rd July 1794. His servant, John Malone, born at Limerick in 1765, shared his fate. Five days more, and Robespierre's fall would have saved them.

General James Ferdinand O'Moran had been guillotined four months previously. He was a native of Elphin, Ireland, and was fifty-six years of age. He was arrested in his camp at Cassel in Flanders, on a charge of designing to betray the army to the enemy. It was alleged that he had refused to advance on Furnes, pleading that the Austrians were in superior force, whereas he knew

M

the contrary, and that when forced into marching he laid a mine on the road, intending to blow up his own men. His real offence seems to have been a refusal to drink to Marat's health. Custine superseded him. O'Moran was at first screened by Carnot, who, however, said, "He has a prudence which makes me desperate, and which I should call pusillanimity if I did not respect his talents." Released from St. Lazare, he was rearrested, tried for "manœuvres tending to favour the enemy," and executed on the 6th March 1794. His aide-de-camp, Etienne de Jouy, charged with complicity, fled from Cassel and took refuge in the house of Robert Hamilton, a Jamaica planter claiming kinship with the Dukes of Hamilton. Hamilton had married a daughter of Lord Leven and Melville, widow of a Dr. James Walker. They had two daughters, one of whom fell in love with the refugee, a modern d'Artagnan, who had lost two fingers in battle, and who had probably many tales to tell of his adventures in America and the East. Jouy fled for greater security first to Paris, where he saw O'Moran pass on his way to execution, and then to Switzerland. Returning after the Terror, he married Miss Hamilton, but this alliance, soon followed by a separation, exposed him to imputations of intrigues with England. He threw up his commission in the army out of disgust with these repeated vexations, and became a prolific dramatist.

Of his mother-in-law, Lady Mary Hamilton, we shall hear again.

William Newton, born in England in 1762, had been a captain in the dragoons, and had also been in the Russian army. In 1792 he twice pressed his services on the Convention. He was made a cavalry colonel, and was the contractor for a new kind of military waggon. He was arrested along with the other English in Paris. He appears to have been denounced by a prison spy for having remarked, after reading Barère's indictment against England, "Has Barère ever been in England? What crimes can the English Government have committed?" He was also in the habit of comparing Robespierre to an Eastern despot. He was executed June 6th, 1794. On the scaffold he exclaimed to the mob, "I am happier than your tyrants, for they tremble, whereas I am quite composed."

One of his fellow-victims was Thomas Delany, a youth of seventeen. His history is told by Yorke, apparently on the authority of Paine, whom he visited at Paris in 1802. Yorke states that a youth, whose name he withholds, was sent by his mother to acquire French polish. He was incautious and vehement, and openly denounced the Revolution. Thrown into prison, he retained his high spirits, and made the walls ring with "Rule Britannia" and "God save the King." Put on trial along with Newton, he did not utter a syllable, and had not the slightest notion that he was being tried. Only when placed in the cart did he awake to a consciousness of his fate, and lament that he should see his mother no more. He was heir to a considerable fortune. This evidently relates to Delany, but it is, to say the least, highly embellished. Delany—sometimes called Lainy or Laing, perhaps because he had renounced the first syllable of his name, lest it should be mistaken for the aristocratic particle—was accused of being a spy. So far from not understanding that he was on his trial, he energetically denied the charge, and in confirmation of his denial asserted that he had taken the first opportunity of offering to join the French army. As, moreover, three fellow-countrymen were tried with him, Newton, Roden, and Murdoch, they would manifestly have enlightened him as to his danger, had he been unconscious of it. Other parts of the story may, however, be authentic, and in any case the execution of a lad of seventeen was a barbarity which, except in the sanguinary annals of the Revolution, would bear a special mark of infamy.

Charles Francis Chambly, a native of Louisburg, Canada, was guillotined in the same batch as Ward. Patrick Roden, a deserter from the English army, was executed in the same batch as Newton. Charles Edward Frederick Henry Macdonald (he is styled Count in the pension list, where he figures for 1800 francs), born at Dublin in 1750, had served in Ogilvie's Franco-Scotch regiment, had retired on account of ill health, and had travelled in Italy and England. He returned to France in 1791, and was perhaps the Macdonald who in December 1792 wrote for the *Morning Post*, was a speaker at the British Revolutionary Club, and left with the two Sheares. "All three men," the English Government was warned, "are men of desperate designs, capable of setting fire to the dockyards." There may, however, have been two Macdonalds, which is the more likely, inasmuch as Charles was condemned on account of a letter addressed "Donald Macdonald." It contained only some trivial news, but the poor man was executed as a spy of Pitt's. Charles Harrop, a Londoner of twenty-two, was sent in January 1793 to buy military stores in the German ports. With or without reason he was afterwards arrested, and perished as one of the Carmelite conspirators. He is said to have talked against the Revolution in a Café, and as M. Wallon remarks of Newton, "had not stipulated for retaining his native country's liberty of speech." James Murdoch, an Edinburgh wigmaker of twenty-nine, had deserted from an English regiment at Gibraltar, came to France in 1782, and was a servant to Prince Poniatowski and to a Polish count. Apparently pressed to join the army, he offered to serve against the Austrians, but objected to fight the English, because if captured they would hang him. He would have done better to run the risk, for he was guillotined on the 6th June 1794.

Pierre O'Brennan, a priest manifestly of Irish extraction, was executed on the 23rd July 1794, for having spoken against the authorities and concealed some old title-deeds; and the last batch of Terrorist victims included two Moncriefs, father and son, of remote Scotch extraction. There is no foundation for the story of the St. Antoine mob stopping the tumbrels on the way to the scaffold, and of Henriot forcing the drivers to proceed. The batch of the 9th Thermidor had been sacrificed before tidings of Robespierre's overthrow could have reached the Faubourg St. Antoine.

Most of these English victims were interred in a garden adjoining Parc Monceau, which for the last six weeks of the Terror was the political cemetery. Robespierre himself found a resting-place there, if indeed it could be called a resting-place, for the bodies were stripped, thrown into a trench, and covered with quicklime. The garden belonged to a house called the "Maison du Christ," and it was styled the "Enclos du Christ," because a Calvary had formerly stood close by. After Waterloo the garden was offered for sale to the Crown, for Princess Elizabeth had been buried in it; but Louis XVIII., who was sceptical even as to the remains of Louis XVI. and Marie Antoinette, found in the Madeleine Cemetery, declined the offer, and the ground was partly built upon. Michelet, in an unpublished chapter of his "History of the Revolution,"* describes it in 1852 as the site of a cheap dancing saloon. He found a Sunday ball going on. People were literally dancing over the bodies of Princess Elizabeth, Danton, and Robespierre— of Dillon and Arthur. So quickly does Paris forget its horrors! In 1863, when the Rue de Miromesnil was extended, some of the bones were found, and others were discovered a little later in laying down a sewer or gas pipe, but nobody reflected how they came to be there.

* Given in the *Revue Bleue*, June 2nd, 1888.

IX.

Terrorists.

"The character of this tyranny was . . . in the name of liberty to erect into civic virtues anarchy, debauch, delation, ferocity."
—CARNOT, *July 28th*, 1797.

IX.

TERRORISTS.

Grieve—Arthur—Rose—James—Duroure—Kavanagh.

It is sad to find Englishmen among the Terrorists, even though foreign birth or long absence had made them English only in name. George Grieve, who hunted Madame Dubarry to death, was an hereditary agitator. His grandfather Ralph, a scrivener, at a contested election of a clergyman in 1694 headed the unsuccessful party, and was expelled from the Common Council of Alnwick. Ralph's son Richard, also an attorney, was agent for Lord Ossulston, the Whig candidate at the election of 1748, and he headed a mob which stormed the town hall, thus frustrating the attempt of the Council to procure an unfair return. Ossulston was, however, unseated, while Grieve—his conduct denounced as "partial and villainous, and in defiance of all ties, both human and divine"—was expelled from the Council. This happened only a few weeks before George's birth. With such a lineage George Grieve could scarcely fail to be an ardent politician; yet his elder brother, Davidson Richard, was a quiet country gentleman, high sheriff of Northumberland in 1788. He must have taken after his mother, Elizabeth Davidson. George, on coming of age, had to sue the Common Council for the right to take up his freedom, the Council arguing that he was not a freeman's son, inasmuch as at the time of his birth his father had been disfranchised, though subsequently readmitted. George won his case, and in 1774 he headed the opposition to the Duke of Northumberland's attempt to fill up both seats for the county, in lieu of being content with one. The opposition secured a narrow majority of sixteen, Alnwick itself pronouncing for the Duke, who, as he told Dutens, spent £7000 on the election. Four years later Grieve led a mob which levelled the fences of part of the moor wrongfully presented by the corporation to the Duke's agent. He was of course a fervent admirer of Wilkes, and a zealous advocate of parliamentary reform. His affairs, however, became involved, and like Pigott he fancied England to be on the brink of ruin. Accordingly, about 1780 he sold his patrimony, crossed the Atlantic, made acquaintance with Washington and Paine, and is said to have partly supported himself by his pen. He appears to have been sent on a mission to Holland, and then, about 1783, settled in Paris.

That such a man would throw himself into the revolutionary movement is evident; but although he knew Mirabeau, there is no trace of Grieve's activity till 1792, when he took up his quarters at an inn at Louveciennes, the hamlet inhabited by Madame Dubarry. Here he formed a club, which, the lady being in England in quest of her stolen jewels, audaciously met in her drawing-room. Her Hindoo servant Zamore, whom she had brought up, had stood sponsor to, and had named after one of Voltaire's tragedies, proved unfaithful. She had loaded him with kindness, and as a boy he used, dressed like Cupid, to hold a parasol over her as she went to meet Louis XV. in the garden; but Grieve wormed all her secrets out of him, got an order for seals to be placed on her property, and inserted her name at the head of a list of persons to be arrested. The power of the municipality to make arrests was, however, questioned, and for four months Madame Dubarry remained free, though in perpetual anxiety.

On July 1st, 1793, Grieve escorted the municipality to the bar of the Convention, vehemently denounced her, and obtained authority to apprehend her, but a petition from the villagers, who had profited by her bounty, procured her release. Thereupon Grieve issued a pamphlet describing her luxurious life, and holding her up to odium as a conspirator. He signed himself "Man of Letters, *officieux* defender of the brave *sans-culottes* of Louveciennes, friend of Franklin and Marat,* factious (*factieux*)

* Marat perhaps made his acquaintance at Newcastle, or while teaching French at Edinburgh in 1772.

and anarchist of the first water, and disorganiser of despotism for twenty years in both hemispheres." Madame Dubarry, who had already dismissed one treacherous servant, now dismissed Zamore also. In September, Grieve secured a fresh warrant against her, and singularly enough rode part of the way to Paris in the hackney carriage with her. What passed between them is a mystery. Was he enamoured of her, and repelled with horror, or did he offer life and liberty if she disgorged? In any case it is strange that Madame Dubarry, whose last lover but one had been an Englishman—Henry Seymour, nephew of the Duke of Somerset, the Sunday evening dancing in whose park at Prunay was remembered by old women still living in 1870—should have been hunted to death by another Englishman. The inhabitants again obtained her release, but in November she was a third time arrested. Grieve superintended the search for her jewels concealed in dungheaps, and got up the case against her. Not merely did he collect evidence, but he was himself a witness, and had it not been for his relentless persecution it seems likely that she would have been left unmolested.

Grieve was to have dined with Marat the very day the latter was assassinated. To dine with Marat sounds anything but tempting. Marat's squalor was, however, all external, an affair of parade, for he liked comfort and good fare. Grieve unwarrantably denounced the Jacobin ex-priest, Jacques Roux, as Charlotte Corday's accomplice, on the ground of having met him at Marat's house and seen him "look furious." * Evidently

> "His mind
> Had grown suspicion's sanctuary."

This denunciation had no effect; but Roux, who had pretended to continue Marat's newspaper, was forced by his relict's protestations to renounce the enterprise. Grieve is said to have boasted that he had brought seventeen persons to the guillotine. If the vaunt was true, it can only be hoped that his reason was temporarily impaired. Five months after Robespierre's fall he was arrested at Amiens and taken to Versailles, where twenty-two depositions were taken against him, but on unknown grounds the prosecution was stopped. In 1796 he was back in America, where he published a translation of the Marquis de Châtellux's Travels, unaware perhaps that John Kent, likewise an eye-witness of and pamphleteer on the Revolution, had brought out a translation in London nine years earlier. He eventually settled in Brussels, and died there February 22, 1809. He was apparently unmarried, and had broken off all relations with

---

* Roux had been expelled from the Cordeliers' Club on the motion of Marat. He stabbed himself in December 1793, to avoid being guillotined.

Northumberland. The entry of death described him as a native of "Newcastel, Amérique," instead of Alnwick, England. His manuscripts, still preserved at the National Archives, Paris, are in irreproachable French, and his pamphlet, the copy of which in the Paris Library contains autograph corrections in a bold hand, is sprinkled with classical quotations. His tool and confederate Zamore, also arrested after Robespierre's fall, but said to have been released on Grieve's representations, lived, morose, miserable, and a vilifier of his benefactress, till 1820.

John James Arthur,* a member of the Paris Commune, was a much more prominent personage than Grieve, but though he was often spoken of as "l'Anglais," he was born in Paris, and had probably never quitted France. He does not therefore call for any lengthy notice. He may have been descended from a Jacobite banker named Arthur, or from an Irish refugee who served in the French army. He was a manufacturer of paper-hangings, at that time used only by the rich, and mostly imported from England. He also made cameo fans and other ornamental articles, and was employed by the Court, for in 1791 the Assembly paid him 13,000 francs, a debt due by the Crown prior to 1789. No man had therefore less to gain from a

---

* Jean Jacques was probably an assumed name, out of admiration of Rousseau.

Revolution which drove away wealthy residents from Paris, but of course nobody at the outset foresaw this result. Arthur, moreover, had suffered under the injustice of the old system of government. About 1786 he bought a house on the boulevard, at the corner of the Rue Louis-le-Grand. At the opposite corner stood the wing added to his mansion by the notorious *roué*, the Maréchal de Richelieu, great-nephew of the famous Cardinal. The municipality had allowed the Marshal to encroach on the street for this corner building, which commanded a view of the boulevard, and which the Parisian wits or populace had nicknamed the " Pavillon de Hanovre." The nickname implied that the money expended on it was a bribe received by the Marshal at the capitulation of Closterseven in Hanover. The old man seems to have cynically accepted the title, which remains to this day, for though the rest of the mansion, converted into an hotel after the Revolution—Fox stayed there in 1802—has long disappeared, the Pavillon de Hanovre is unaltered, still projects into the Rue Louis-le-Grand, is occupied by the jeweller Christofle, and was renovated two years ago. Arthur began adding another story to his house, but Richelieu, whether because it would really have spoilt his view, or whether displeased at his consent not having been asked, objected. Litigation commenced, and Richelieu even claimed Arthur's house, alleging that the Duc d'Antin, of whom Arthur bought it, had had no title to it. Exercising, moreover, a privilege of the nobility, he had the case transferred from the ordinary tribunals to the Intendant, where he was sure of indefinite delay, if not of a favourable decision. Arthur, after vainly trying to conciliate the old man, induced friends to threaten him with odium or lampoons. Richelieu at length withdrew his opposition, and had he not done so his death in 1788, at the age of ninety-two, would have settled the matter.

It is not surprising, then, that Arthur welcomed the Revolution. In September 1789 he presented 600 francs to the patriotic fund, his partner Robert gave another 600 francs, and his clerks, painters, engravers, &c., contributed 556 francs, which shows that the concern was a large one.* In July 1790 Arthur and his men assisted in preparing the Champ de Mars. He became president of his section (Section des Piques, the Rue Louis-le-Grand being rechristened Rue des Piques), and must have known Lavoisier, who was in the same division of the National Guard. He was a member of the Jacobin Club, was a not infrequent speaker there, and was one of the committee which, in December 1793, "purged" away the less extreme members. In 1792 he was elected—it was a sham election by an

* In May 1792 Arthur's workmen made a second gift of 600 francs.

insignificant minority—on the Paris Commune or municipality, and was placed on the chief or central committee, a kind of Cabinet. There were plenty of foreigners to keep him company, for Pache and Marat were Swiss, Dubuisson and Pereire Belgians, Proly and the two brothers Frey Austrians, Guzman was a Spaniard, and Dufourny an Italian. Foreigners, indeed, formed the majority. It was at Arthur's suggestion that the name of all inmates had to be inscribed on the door of every Paris house. As a "municipal" Arthur took his turn in guarding the royal family in the Temple, and in March 1793 he denounced two of his colleagues for secretly conversing with Marie Antoinette and making her laugh. They were consequently struck off the roll, and one of them confessed long afterwards that he secretly carried newspapers to the Queen, and was plotting her escape.*

Delation became habitual with Arthur. He denounced speculators who melted down the copper coinage. He charged Pitt's agents with a plot for slaughtering cows and sheep, so as to starve France, and suggested that every citizen should be required to keep a cow. He accused Delamarche of dishonesty in the manufacture of paper money, alleging that he had in private conversation at his dinner-table advocated national bankruptcy. Arthur's father was cited to confirm this, but Delamarche

* "Souvenirs de J. F. Lepitre," 1817.

replied that the old man, whom he much respected, had often groaned over his son's fanaticism. He added that he himself had obtained a grant of 1800 francs a week to enable Arthur to continue employing his 400 men. Delamarche was deprived of his post, and was eventually executed, though on a different charge. Arthur suggested that the Convention should issue an address to the English people, pointing out how they were dishonoured by their Government in conniving at the issue of forged *assignats*. He was on the list of witnesses against Danton, and though not called at the trial, he at Robespierre's suggestion made his deposition before the Jacobin Club. He charged Danton with complicity with Dumouriez, with having reprobated the execution of Marie Antoinette as destroying all hope of peace, and with having condemned the execution of Custine, because such treatment of the best generals made victories impossible. He would also have given evidence against Clavière but for his suicide before trial.

In Robespierre's notebook Arthur is on the list of "patriots having more or less ability." In the summer of 1794 the Committee of Public Safety sent him to the Haute Marne, ostensibly to stimulate the manufacture of gunpowder, but really, according to Lombard de Langres, to inquire into the *civisme* of certain ironmasters whose fortunes they coveted. An urgent summons from Robespierre brought him back to Paris on the eve of the 10th Thermidor. He was on the committee of eight appointed by the Commune on the 9th to support Robespierre against the Convention. Six of the eight were foreigners. Robespierre, after much hesitation, was signing an insurrectionary address to the Section des Piques, when he was fired at and disabled. On the triumph of the Convention the "municipals," already outlawed, were executed without trial. Arthur apparently was in hiding till the 11th or 12th Thermidor, for he was guillotined, not with the eleven who accompanied Robespierre on the 10th, nor with the large batch of sixty-eight on the 11th, but with a third batch of ten on the 12th. He was thirty-three years of age, and seems to have been unmarried. One of his partners, Grenard, shared his fate, but Robert continued the business. The house was afterwards demolished in order to widen the street. Fanatic as he was, Arthur may be absolved from the horrible charge of devouring the heart of a Swiss killed in the defence of the Tuileries. This is one of the many legends of the Revolution which will not bear examination.

Arthur must have been confronted at the very climax of the struggle by a man like himself of British extraction, Auguste Rose, one of the ten ushers to the Convention. Stone had his letters from England sent under cover to Rose, perhaps to prevent their being opened at the London post-office. When Robespierre and his confederates were declared under arrest by the Convention, Rose, on account of his firmness and courage, was deputed to conduct them to the Committee of General Safety, who gave him a receipt testifying their safe delivery. In the evening the Convention sent him to the rebellious Commune with a summons to appear at the bar and hear its orders. The Commune, on learning his arrival and errand, had him arrested and brought before them. He showed such boldness that Fleuriot, the president, bade him go back and tell the Convention they would appear arms in hand and enforce their rights. Taking this insolent message as a release, Rose left the room, fought his way on the stairs past two men who tried to stop him, and ran at full speed. He had scarcely left the Hotel de Ville than the Commune on second thoughts decreed his arrest, but it was too late. When the Commune was outlawed, Rose also accompanied several deputies who went and harangued the troops brought by Henriot to the Carrousel to crush the Convention. Let us hope that Merlin de Thionville, to whom Rose sent a statement of his services, secured him the reward due to his intrepidity.

Arthur had two colleagues in the Commune of British birth or extraction. James, doubtless the William Benjamin James who took part in the capture of the Bastille, was a teacher of English.

He took his turn in watching poor Louis XVI. at the Temple, and Cléry tells us that once when the King withdrew after dinner to his study to read, James went in, sat down by him, and refused to leave, though the King urged that he could be sufficiently watched from the anteroom through an open door. The unhappy monarch gave up reading for that day. James was one of the secretaries of the Jacobin Club in 1794. He may have been related to the Captain Charles James, "one of the many hundreds who helped to demolish the Bastille," who published in London in 1792 " An Extenuation of the Conduct of the French Revolutionists." He gravely alleged that Marie Antoinette had said she should never be satisfied till she had bathed in the blood of Frenchmen. He insisted, too, that from the 14th July 1789 to the 4th September 1792 there had not, with the single exception of Theobald Dillon's murder, been any case of " unprovoked severity, misnamed barbarity."

Louis Henri Scipio Beauvoir, Comte Duroure, was the grandson of Bolingbroke's sister, Lady Catherlough. The name Scipio, which fitted in so conveniently with Jacobin usages, and in favour of which he dropped his other names, had for several generations been a family one. A Scipio Duroure, probably his grandfather, entered the English army in 1705, and became a colonel. He himself was born at Marseilles in 1763, but was educated in

England. He knew Josephine, returning with her in the same vessel from Martinique in 1791. As a "municipal," he proposed and carried a resolution, that the 6th January, the anniversary of Louis XVI.'s death, should be styled the *fête des sans-culottes*. He did not, however, side with Robespierre, and was imprisoned at St. Lazare during the latter part of the Terror, nor did he again figure in politics. Under the Empire he studied jurisprudence and grammar, and translated Cobbett's English Grammar. He died in 1822 in London, whither he is said to have gone to claim an inheritance.

Joseph Kavanagh, a shoemaker, though a native of Lille, was evidently of Irish extraction. He seems to have been a coward when there was danger, an assassin when there was none. On the 13th July 1789, according to a detective named Blutel, who was guillotined at Arras in 1794, Kavanagh headed a band of roughs who ransacked the Tuileries, seizing twenty-five muskets and a chest of money. Next day he intercepted five carts bearing arms from Metz for the Vincennes garrison. He erected a barricade, on a rumour that the carts would be demanded. Going to the Hotel de Ville, he found the mob, in the belief of a massacre by the soldiers in the Faubourg St. Antoine, talking of going to the Invalides for arms. "Let us march thither," shouted Kavanagh, but after going a short distance he slackened his pace and slunk home. In September 1792 he was one of the butchers of unarmed prisoners. What became of him we do not hear.

Among the revolutionary judges in the provinces were two men apparently of British extraction. Duplessis-Smith, in Finistère, endeavoured in May 1794 to save from the scaffold twenty members of the former Girondin local administration, but his efforts were unavailing. O'Brien, at St. Malo, was more successful in securing the acquittal of six children—two of them only five years old, the others between eight and ten. To such lengths had the Terror gone that even children were not safe. Well might a caricature, seized by the St. Denis municipality and forwarded to Robespierre, represent him as seated on a sarcophagus inscribed, "Noblesse, clergé, Girondins, Hébertistes, peuple," Robespierre and the executioner the only survivors, and Robespierre preparing to guillotine the executioner.

X.

In the Provinces.

"Alas, poor country ;
Almost afraid to know itself. It cannot
Be called our mother, but our grave ; where nothing
But who knows nothing, is once seen to smile."
—*Macbeth.*

X.

IN THE PROVINCES.

Smith—Badger—Warburton—O'Sullivan—Bulkeley—Jane Grey—Elizabeth Plunkett—Mrs. Thicknesse—Baron de Bode—Colleges and Nunneries—Manufacturers.

THE list of persons executed in Paris is complete, so that English names can be easily extracted, but of many who perished in the provinces there is no known record. Documents have been lost, destroyed, or abstracted by men ashamed of their revolutionary antecedents or by their descendants. Louis Blanc imagined that only eleven or twelve provincial tribunals existed, whereas Berryat St. Prix has shown that there were no less than 149. If the list of victims is very defective, still more so is the list of prisoners. Departmental and municipal archives are believed, indeed, to contain many documents on this subject, but the process of cataloguing has scarcely been begun. The last official report mentions only nineteen departments in which there is as yet any possibility of knowing what documents exist subsequent to 1790. Histories of the Revolution in particular departments or regions are now, it is true, being written, and two monthly magazines, taking opposite sides, are throwing much light on what happened in the provinces, ignored by Louis Blanc and Michelet; but scarcely more than a beginning has been made. It may, however, be conjectured that as many Englishmen suffered imprisonment or death outside Paris as within it.

When Lyons was recaptured by the Jacobins in October 1793, four persons of British nationality or descent perished in the wholesale fusillades perpetrated by the victors. The most prominent of these was Joseph Smith, a civil engineer born in Paris, who happened to be at Lyons, and rendered great service by casting cannon. He bore the rank of lieutenant-colonel of artillery. According to Balleydier, he solved an important engineering problem the very day he was shot, and carried the secret to the grave. Précy, one of the few leaders who escaped, gives a minute account of the last desperate sortie. On entering the village of Bagnols he heard that two fugitives had been arrested there. He demanded their release. The municipality hesitated, but he threatened, and at last the two men were brought. One of them was Smith, who urged Précy to leave his troop and try to escape alone. Smith gave him his cloak and his provision of chocolate. Précy with great difficulty got to Switzerland. Smith with the rest of the troop was captured, and two days afterwards (October 14th) was shot. He was at least saved the long suspense which befell his fellow-countrymen.

Two of these were silk-weavers, Louis Badger, aged thirty-five, and Pierre Badger, twenty-seven, natives of Lyons, and apparently sons of John Badger, who in 1789 was receiving a pension of 2300 francs for having introduced spinning-machines and for selling English tin-ware. He was seventy-seven, and had lived nearly forty years at Lyons. According to Beaulieu, Pierre Badger, when the town surrendered, was laid up with a wound received in the rising of the previous May, was arrested by mistake for his brother, might have saved himself by a word, but went cheerfully to execution. If this statement is correct, the sacrifice was unavailing. Pierre was shot on the 28th November, and Louis on the 5th December. The latter was one of 208 prisoners who were pinioned by the wrist to a long rope, the two ends of which were fastened to willow trees. Soldiers were stationed four paces behind, and fired on the signal being given, but not nearly all were killed. The survivors uttered fearful cries; the cavalry charged them with their sabres; it was a long and horrible butchery.

On the following Christmas Eve, Samuel Warburton, a retired English officer, fifty-eight years of age, and described as a Londoner, was shot with another batch of victims. One of them was a woman who in male dress had acted as a gunner during the siege. When asked how she could fight against her country, she replied that she was defending the country. Strange destiny for an English officer to pass unscathed while fighting under his own flag, and to perish in a stand for Moderate Liberalism, as we should now call it, in France!

If at Lyons one brother sacrificed his life to save the other, at Angers there were two brothers of Irish extraction, one of whom betrayed the other. One was executed by the Jacobins, while the other was put on trial, after Robespierre's fall, as a Terrorist. How long the O'Sullivans had been in France I cannot ascertain. A Daniel O'Sullivan, who taught fencing, and in 1766 published a treatise on it, may have been the grandfather of the two men of whom I am about to speak. He, too, may have been the O'Sullivan who was quartermaster with the Young Pretender in 1745, and, according to "Ascanius, or the Young Adventurer" (London, 1812), was very chicken-hearted in embarking on a French cutter and leaving the Prince to his fate. O'Hanlon, however, speaks highly of O'Sullivan's bravery and ability, and says Charles Edward passed at one time for his son.

Charles O'Sullivan, collector of stamp duties at St. Georges sur Loire, took part in the Vendée rising, and terrible to say, was given up by his brother, John Baptist, for the latter, when himself on trial at Paris, said: "As for my brother, he was with the rebels. He murdered patriots, and wanted to murder me. When he found there was no other hope for him, he came and threw himself into my arms; but he was my country's enemy, I performed a republican's duty and denounced him, and justice pronounced his fate."* Charles was guillotined at Angers, December 31st, 1793. He was twenty-eighty ears of age.

Jean Baptist O'Sullivan was a fencing master like his presumptive grandfather. In 1791 he was sub-lieutenant in a company of volunteers at Nantes. At the end of 1793 the infamous Carrier made him adjutant of Nantes, and he took part in Carrier's atrocities. According to Madame de la Rochejaquelein, John owed his life to his brother, four years his junior, being saved by him when captured by the Vendeans. She adds that after Charles's death he was a prey to remorse, fancied himself pursued by his brother's ghost, and stupefied himself by committing fresh crimes. His wife, a handsome and virtuous woman, reproached him with his baseness. Summoned to Paris as a witness against Carrier, he was himself placed in the dock. It was alleged that, dining with a party of men in a garden, he had boasted that when superintending the "noyades" he would distract a prisoner's attention by bidding him look at something on the

* What a subject for a thrilling drama!

shore, and when the man turned his head stuck a knife into his throat. This he denied, but he admitted that he might have said in a moment of indignation that if the "brigands" (royalists) were in his hands he would knife them. In a conversation on muscular strength he was alleged to have said that his brother was stronger than himself, so that the guillotine had to strike twice before his head fell. It was also said that he had boasted of having slaughtered men like sheep with his pocket-knife. Yet he is described as a handsome man, adored by women, and wonderfully dexterous with his sword. One of the forty survivors of a gallant band of 400 men who in June 1792 frustrated a night attack on Nantes, he was acquitted at Paris, like twenty-seven others, as not having acted with counter-revolutionary designs. They were not, however, released, were threatened with a second trial, and were transferred to Angers prison, but were ultimately liberated. O'Sullivan settled as schoolmaster at Buchesne, was highly esteemed there, was a republican to the last, and survived till 1841. A letter from him, but without his signature, appears in Guépin's "Histoire de Nantes." He left two daughters, one of whom, a widow, kept a china shop at Nantes, retired on a competency, and died in 1875, at the age of ninety-one. Her father spent his latter years with her.*

* Information from M. Dugast Matifex.

Before quitting Vendée I should mention William Bulkeley, lieutenant in Walsh's regiment, who married a widow possessing an estate near La Roche sur Yon, and in 1793 placed himself at the head of his peasants. He was one of the tallest and handsomest of the Vendean officers, and his wife, still young and handsome, fought with him under Charette. His descent from an old Irish family is spoken of. He was guillotined at Angers in January 1794. He is the last victim mentioned by Argens in a letter to the Paris Commune— "Our holy Mother Guillotine is busy. In the last three days she has shaved (*sic*) eleven priests, one ci-devant (noble), one ci-devant nun, one general, and a splendid (*superbe*) Englishman of six feet, whose head was *de trop;* it is now in the sack." M. Dugast Matifex, the Vendean historian, possesses several of Bulkeley's letters, which show him to have been well educated, though devoid of military ability.

The butchery in French Flanders, under the auspices of an ex-priest named with cruel irony Lebon, included two Englishwomen. Jane Grey, widow of one Griffiths—"Milord Griphèse," says a letter by the Jacobin Leroulx—"was thirty-five years of age, and so far from being in the peerage, was a working woman at Hallines. She was a native of London, and was charged with making voyages to England to carry money from Madame

Fournier of St. Omer to her son." She was executed at Arras, and Leroulx, who speaks of her as a fine tall woman of thirty-six, says—" She did not show the slightest concern at the sentence, but on her way in the cart was laughing like a *diablesse.*" Elizabeth Plunkett, one of twenty-nine victims furnished by the small town of Aire, was executed at Cambray, June 13th, 1794. She was born at Montreuil in 1758, but her name bespeaks Irish extraction. Imprisoned for nearly two years as a royalist, she was acquitted, but the very next day, when she had scarcely rejoined her mother, was rearrested, for it had been discovered that in 1791 she had carried round for signature an address thanking Louis XVI. for vetoing the bill against recusant priests, and asking that one of the churches might be assigned them. She had prepared a written defence, still preserved, in which she argued that the act was not at the time criminal, and could not be retrospectively so, but she was not allowed a hearing. When Lebon was brought to justice, one of the documents against him was a letter addressed to him by a juror, who, speaking of five executions, said—" The first of the five is a *scélérate* whose anti-revolutionary sentiments it would be impossible to describe. Suffice it to say, that since I have been on the revolutionary tribunal I have never known effrontery approaching hers. Her anti-revolutionary principles were shown not merely in her answers but in her line of defence. The wretch's name was Elizabeth Plunkett, of Aire."

I can only mention, for I have no particulars of them, André François Buckle, guillotined at Rochefort, March 14th, 1793; John Baptist Carr, executed, with sixteen other recusant priests, at Poitiers, March 18th, 1793; Charles Eliot, at Rennes, October 28th, 1793; Martin Glynn, Irish recusant priest, at Bordeaux, July 19th, 1794; John Joseph Goff, a deserter from the army, at Auxonne, June 15th, 1794; and Margaret Rose Gordon, born in France 1733, executed with six other nuns at Orange, July 15th, 1794.

Several persons bearing English names were acquitted by the tribunals or subjected to non-capital sentences. Joseph Joachim and Joseph Martin, sailors and prisoners of war, were condemned at St. Brieux to fifteen years' imprisonment for forging assignats. Captain John Bayer, John Fleet, Richard Westerman of Southampton, and eight other sailors from Jersey, wrecked in the cutter *Felix*, off Blainville, had a quantity of forged assignats in their possession, but were acquitted of intending to pass them. They were, however, ordered to be detained till exchanged. Marie Lesueur, of Jersey, who on business visits to France received money for refugee priests, was arrested at Flamainville (Manche) with 1700 francs of such money. She was convicted at Cherbourg May 11th,

1795, of exporting coin, and sentenced to six months' imprisonment, then to be detained as English. Charlotte Thomson, wife of François Laisin, who was interrogated and had her property sequestrated, April 6th, 1794, was apparently of British extraction, though born at Vienne.

As for the hostages in the provinces, they were most numerous in the north of France, for Boulogne even before the Revolution had a considerable English colony, retrenchment or fear of creditors attracting some of them.* Richard Warburton Lytton, Bulwer's grandfather, was one of those who fled in time, leaving his house to be confiscated. Englishwomen married to American Quakers at Dunkirk—the Quakers had been invited over to introduce whale-fishing—were, on the appeal of one of the husbands to the Convention, October 26th, 1793, declared exempt from arrest, unless "suspects" or married to suspects. Others were less fortunate. Mrs. Thicknesse, second wife of Governor Thicknesse —her stepson became Lord Audley—had started with her husband for Italy in 1792, when on the very day of leaving Boulogne he expired in the carriage. She returned to Boulogne for the funeral, and was erecting a costly monument over his remains when she was arrested, and, with other Englishwomen, confined in the Ursuline convent. The

* Byron's father, Captain Byron, died at Valenciennes, out of reach of his creditors, in August 1791.

prisoners were at first treated indulgently, but when Lebon became proconsul rigour set in. Mrs. Thicknesse fancied that but for her obtaining a few hours' delay in the execution of an order for their transfer to the Annunciata convent—news of Robespierre's fall arrived in the interim,—they would have been stripped of their money and jewels and then massacred; but these hairbreadth escapes at Robespierre's overthrow must be distrusted. Shortly afterwards came an order that all who could earn their livelihood should be liberated, whereupon Mrs. Thicknesse sent the local authorities specimens of drawing and music-copying. There was some demur to allowing a lord's stepmother to profit by a decree in favour of working women, but Dumont effected her release, and she returned to England. A lively old lady, with well-preserved teeth and unbleached hair, she was seventy-nine at her death in 1826.

Sophia Kingdom, the future Lady Brunel, was among the captives at Rouen. The youngest of the sixteen children (nine surviving) of a deceased naval contractor at Plymouth, she had in 1792 accompanied West India friends, the Longuemars, to Rouen, as a good opportunity of learning French. Illness prevented her returning home when the Longuemars, uneasy at the political prospect, went back, and she was left in charge of the American Consul, Charpentier, whose wife was an Englishwoman. There young Brunel, a kinsman of Charpentier, made her acquaintance. Common sympathy with the royalists and common danger helped to make them attached to each other. Brunel started for America in July 1793, thus escaping imprisonment. Sophia was afterwards arrested, and in a convent found scanty accommodation and fare, but the kind nuns taught her artificial flower-making, a conventual accomplishment. She was released in 1794, and rejecting more brilliant offers on her return to England, waited till 1799 for Brunel's arrival from America. "To you, my dearest Sophia," he wrote after forty-six years of wedlock, "I am indebted for all my success."

Near the eastern frontier of France, at Soult-sous-Forêt in Alsace, the Baron de Bode with his wife and son had to flee for their lives, and his large estate was confiscated. A Franconian nobleman in the French army, he made the acquaintance at Dunkirk in 1775 of Miss Kynnersley, who was yachting with her friend Lady Ferrars, and followed her to Loxley Hall, Staffordshire, where the marriage and the birth of a son took place. His son and grandson—the latter died near Moscow in 1887, aged eighty-one—devoted much time and money to a fruitless attempt to obtain compensation out of the lump sum paid over by Louis XVIII. to England to indemnify the losses of her subjects.

The British convents in the provinces experienced greater brutality than those in Paris, doubtless because provincial manners were rougher, and because there was at Paris, even at the height of the Terror, a public opinion which prevented wanton ill-treatment of prisoners.

The English college at St. Omer had enjoyed a pension of 2000 crowns, originally given by the Spanish, and continued by the French kings. In May 1790 it made a patriotic gift of 600 francs to the Assembly. In 1793 its sixty-four inmates were sent as prisoners to Arras. Gregory Stapleton, who in 1773 had succeeded Allan Butler as superior, obtained a considerable remittance from friends, which he forwarded to his old fellow-collegians of Douai, who were suffering great privations in the citadel of Doullens. In May 1794 Stapleton and his comrades were also sent to Doullens, but in the following October they were permitted to return to St. Omer, though as prisoners in the French college. At the beginning of 1795 Stapleton was allowed to go to Paris to plead for the release of the British communities of St. Omer and Douai. By dint of persuasion and money he eventually succeeded, and they landed at Dover in March 1795—viz., thirty-two from Douai, and sixty-two from St. Omer. One of the St. Omer professors, Richard Brettergh, had succumbed under the hardships of imprisonment. Stapleton himself died at St. Omer in May 1802, having gone thither to try and recover the property.

An account of the sufferings of the Douai, and

incidentally of the St. Omer prisoners, was given in the *Catholic Magazine* for 1831 by Joseph Hodgson, vice-president, and William Poynter, a professor, ultimately Vicar Apostolic of the London district. (He laid the first stone of St. Mary's, Moorfields, and was buried there.) The serious troubles of the Douai college began in February 1793, when commissioners installed themselves in the building, sealed up much of the furniture, and forced the inmates to retire to their country house at Equerchim. In October they were brought back to Douai, and lodged in the Scotch college, but a week later were transferred to Doullens. Their pupils had, of course, mostly taken flight—Charles Kemble in 1792, Daniel O'Connell in January 1793, and Lingard a little later. Some, indeed, both of the professors and students, had not returned after the Christmas holidays of 1792. The forty-seven captives were hooted as they passed through Arras. At Doullens they were at first shut up in a casemate under the rampart, with no bed but straw, and even for this they had to pay. They were afterwards lodged in an attic, above the room of a sergeant whom, on account of his dictatorial airs, they nicknamed Cromwell.* They managed three times clandestinely to say mass, a baker's basket serving as the altar, at an early hour in the morning, but had to be very quiet in their move-

---

* A recent French writer, Deramecourt, seriously gives this as the man's real name.

ments for fear of being overheard by "Cromwell." They were eventually transferred to the ground floor, and from their windows they witnessed the demolition of a Calvary. The cross on the summit of the citadel had given place to a red cap, and on this being carried away by a storm, Good Friday was chosen for placing a second cap. On the 24th November 1794, reduced to twenty-six by some escapes, they were taken back to Douai, were lodged in the Irish seminary, and after a while were allowed to walk about the town.

In 1802, John Philip Kemble passed through Douai. When sent there as a youth, his father intended him for the priesthood, but he returned to England before he was twenty, and took to the stage. He found his old college in indescribable desolation, and had not the heart to go up to the room occupied by him nearly thirty years before. In 1863 a search was made for church plate, vestments, and relics buried by the monks just before quitting it in 1793. Father Penswick, the only surviving witness (he died the following year, at the age of eighty-six), had given directions where to search, and the plate and vestments were found, but the relics, including Thomas à Becket's shirt and St. Charles Borromeo's barretta, could not be discovered. The portrait of Mary Stuart, given by Elizabeth Curle to the Scotch college at Douai, was more fortunate. Rolled up and concealed in a chimney recess, it was found intact in 1815, and is now at Blairs College, Aberdeen.

At Dieulouard, near Pont-à-Mousson, was an English Benedictine monastery founded in 1609. The monks introduced hop-growing into the district, and themselves made beer on a considerable scale, supplying the Lorraine court, as long as there was a court, and exporting some to Germany. In 1790 the Assembly allowed the monks to remain as secular priests, and to retain all the property proved to have been bought with English benefactions; but in October 1793, after passports had been granted to the younger inmates, a mob broke into the monastery, and plundered and destroyed everything. Two monks and two lay brothers were arrested. The other inmates, warned in time, had escaped. The prior, Richard Marsh, has given a full account of his adventures—how he waded across rivers, avoided towns, was sheltered by friendly tenants, parried embarrassing questions, and at length got through a strictly guarded frontier to Treves. After three days' rest he walked on to Liège, where he was received with open arms by the English college, which supplied him with the means of getting to Ostend and thence to England. In May 1802 Marsh went to see what had become of the monastery. He heard how the prisoners had been kept eighteen months on bread and water, and found one of the survivors, tutor and chaplain to a French viscount. The abbey was in ruins, and Marsh went back to England heart-broken. He became president-general of his order, and died in 1842 at the age of 80. In 1882 two monks from Ampleforth, where Marsh had established a priory, went over to Dieulouard to see whether the community could return to their old site, but the visit does not seem to have led to any result, beyond the publication of a French translation of Marsh's manuscript.

Of the sufferings of the Benedictine nuns of Cambray I give their own interesting account in the Appendix. Other provincial convents underwent equal hardships. The twenty-six Poor Clares of Rouen were arrested in October 1793. All religious monuments and symbols were removed or destroyed, and the house was converted into a prison for 320 inmates, while the poor nuns were cooped up in granaries and other outbuildings. In the spring they were sent to another prison, suffering much from crowding and scanty food. In January 1795 they were liberated, and eventually went to England. The twelve Poor Clares of Aire were also declared prisoners in their own house, and one night in June 1794 were turned out without money or passports. Kind townspeople sheltered them, and in September they left for England. The Benedictine nuns of Dunkirk had their chapel appropriated by a Jacobin Club, and in October 1793, at a few hours' notice, they were hurried off amid a line of soldiers to the Convent of the Poor Clares. Four days later both communities were crowded into a small boat, guarded by fifty soldiers, and were taken to the Poor Clares at Gravelines. But for charitable people they would have been starved. Two of the nuns died. The winter was severe, and the insufficiency of fuel obliged them to burn cupboards and wainscoting, and to cut down the trees in the garden. They all left for England in April 1795.

English manufacturers, encouraged by the monarchy to settle in France, appear to have been in general unmolested. Potter at Chantilly, as we have seen, was no sooner arrested than liberated. Foxlowe, who had a cotton mill with 2000 hands at Orleans, the Duke of Orleans as sleeping partner finding six-sevenths of the capital, was allowed, after the Duke's death, to buy up his share from the State, under the right of pre-emption given by the deed of partnership. A cannon foundry managed by two Englishmen near Nantes, and a copper-sheathing factory for ships, near Louviers, also in English hands—both were visited by Arthur Young in 1789—were apparently undisturbed. Morgan and Massey, at Amiens, who in 1789 had a grant of 12,000 francs from the Government for inventing a jenny with 280 spindles; Lawrence Bennett, of Stockport, who had introduced spinning jennies at

Les Andelys, in Normandy;* and Milne, a machine
maker pensioned by the monarchy, who died at
Paris in 1804, do not figure in the list of prisoners.
O'Reilly, described as a Scotchman, probably the
ex-Benedictine who, in January 1792, proposed
grinding corn by compressed air, achieved a reputation in Paris for his engraving on glass. Ffrench
and Johnston, wine-merchants at Bordeaux, seem
likewise to have continued their business operations. But Didot's paper-mills at Essonnes, Corbeil,
where assignats were made, was visited by Camille
Desmoulins and district commissaries, in October
1793, for the purpose of arresting several English
employed there. Jules Didot explained that his
wife, Maria Gamble, was English; she had been
governess to his children in his first wife's lifetime.
She was perhaps the "citoyenne Didot mère," to
whom Bernardin de St. Pierre wrote in January
1800, saying that his son Paul was much grown,
was anxious to embrace his dear Virginie (Didot) and
would accompany his father to Essonnes next décadi.
Sykes, optician and agent for Wedgwood's pottery,
gave up the Palais Royal shop which commanded so
good a view of revolutionary jubilations and horrors,
and in 1792 erected a cotton mill at St. Rémy,
not far from Dreux, his only child marrying

* Gay, a Scotchman, secretary to the Jacobin Club in that town,
a jovial but rapacious fellow, was probably his foreman. See
Contemporary Review, 1867.

William Waddington, a London merchant. One of their sons, William Pendrell Waddington—the Waddingtons were descendants of the sister of the Richard Pendrell who concealed Charles II.—died at Rome in 1821; another was the father of the present French diplomatist. Sykes, English, but born and bred in Holland, seems to have escaped the imprisonment which befell Thomas Collow, a Scotchman, who after living in Tobago, settled in 1785 as a merchant at Havre. In a time of scarcity he bought foreign corn for the municipality, charging no commission, and he gave the first tidings (received from Bryan Edwards) of the St. Domingo rising, instead of speculating on his priority of information; yet he was arrested as a hostage in 1793. He twice petitioned the Convention, urging that merchandise for America was spoiling in his warehouses during his detention, and the municipality endorsed his request for release; but he apparently had to await the fall of Jacobinism. He remained at Havre, and died there in 1803. Another Tobago man, Daniel King, who had been naturalised and had settled as a shipowner at Dunkirk, was also arrested as an Englishman, with his partner Peter Watson.

XI.

After the Terror.

"Down came the storm! In ruins fell
The worn-out world we knew.
It pass'd, that elemental swell—
Again appear'd the blue;
The sun shone in the new-wash'd sky,
And what from heaven saw he?
Blocks of the past, like icebergs high,
Float on a rolling sea!"
—MATTHEW ARNOLD, *Obermann once more.*

XI.

AFTER THE TERROR.

Swinburne—Malmesbury—Prisoners of war—Anglomania—Sir Sidney Smith—Wright—Barclay—Mrs. Dayrell.

As the wholesale arrest of British subjects, from which only artisans and schoolchildren were exempt, was grounded on the loss of Toulon, its recovery four months later should seemingly have been followed by their release; but the Revolution did not condescend to logic. There was no general gaol delivery for the English captives till the end of February 1795, and even then the war prevented their return to England unless by special favour, though an American brig, *The Two Friends*, Captain Gilbert, was allowed to make frequent passages to Dover and back. In August 1795 there was a cartel of exchange, but this applied only to soldiers and sailors. One of these was Captain O'Hara, captured at Toulon, "the most perfect specimen of a soldier and courtier of the last age," says Miss Berry, who but for a misunderstanding would have married him. He died a bachelor, Governor at Gibraltar, in 1802.* Captain Henry Swinburne, sent over to Paris in 1796 to try and effect the exchange of Sir Sidney Smith, tells us that he was accompanied by Major Gall, ostensibly as secretary, Gall's real object being to fetch his two daughters, released but still unable to leave. Gall obtained passports for himself, his sister, and daughters, but the vessel in which they sailed was captured off Calais by a French privateer and taken to Dunkirk. They were, however, promised release. Gall was a friend of Warren Hastings, and when in Paris in 1791 attended the Jacobin Club, but was suspected of being a spy. Swinburne found in Paris Mitford, brother-in-law of Lord C. Annesley, Chenevix, son of the Bishop of Waterford, and Walter Smythe, brother of the famous Mrs. Fitzherbert. Relegated to Fontainebleau during the elections, he there met Lady Rodney * and her daughters. There were nine English prisoners of war in the Palace, and he sent them clothes. Recalled because Sir Sidney Smith mistakenly thought him wanting in zeal, Swinburne was joined at Calais by a Captain Davies of Hull, who had escaped from Arras, and who crossed over with him in the guise of his servant.

Lord Malmesbury, also at Paris in 1796 trying to negotiate peace, met the sons of the Rev. Charles Este, a well-known Whitehall preacher. One of them, a journalist, was but too friendly with the

---

* The Admiral married a Lisbon lady; she died in 1829, aged ninety.

wife of Sir Robert Smith, the banker already mentioned.* Malmesbury dined with George Hamilton, of Jamaica, and his wife Lady Mary, daughter of Lord Leven. Their two daughters had married French officers. Malmesbury, on account of his fine eyes and profusion of white hair, was compared by a Paris newspaper to a white lion, which made his friends playfully style him "the lion." He had so frequently to send to London for instructions that the caricaturists represented Lacroix as asking him how he was, and Malmesbury as writing to London to know what answer he should give. His bust figured in the waxwork exhibition of Curtius, uncle and predecessor of Madame Tussaud, but was withdrawn immediately on his departure.

International animosity had much cooled down since May 1794, when the Convention ordered that no quarter should be given to the English, a decree which the army refused to execute.† There were, however, recriminations respecting the treatment of prisoners which we must hope were, to say the least, exaggerated. While in France it was alleged

---

* Paine beguiled his captivity by a correspondence with Lady Smith.

† Robespierre only a fortnight before his fall complained that the English captured at Nieuport had been spared, and General Dugommier was gently rebuked by the Committee of General Safety for not shooting General O'Hara. O'Hara, speaking to a French fellow prisoner at the Luxembourg of the freedom of the press in England, might well say—" We can exclaim, ' King George is mad,' but you dare not say, ' Robespierre is a tiger.' "

that French prisoners were fed on dead cats and dogs, Captain Swinburne was informed that at Dunkirk the English captives had very few blankets, at Amiens none, and that at Brest sixty captains or passengers of merchant vessels were debarred exercise and in want of necessaries. Sir William Eden (afterwards Lord Auckland) went to Dieppe in May 1795 to propose an exchange of sailors, but the Convention would only agree to an exchange of naval officers. When the expedition to Ireland was being prepared, Nicholas Madgett,* a priest born at Kinsale, County Kerry, and a friend of Tone's, was sent to Orleans to pick out Irish prisoners to be enrolled in it. The result was a quarrel between English and Irish, and the removal of the former to Valenciennes. Three or four hundred seamen were induced to join the expedition, by being plied with drink and assured that England had left them to their fate for the sake of one man, Sir Sidney Smith. In February 1798 France agreed to England's proposal that each should feed and clothe its own subjects, and in the following September it was arranged that officers should be free on parole and civilians liberated without exchange; but in October the

---

* Himself a prisoner from May to November 1795, having landed with a passport under the name of Hurst. The open, not to say ostentatious way in which the expedition was organised is explained by the fact that it was a mere sham, designed to frighten England into peace, and became serious only on Lord Malmesbury's departure.

Directory, on the plea that French officers had not been allowed reciprocity, ordered all English prisoners without exception to be imprisoned in certain departments at a distance from the coast. Many, accordingly, had to march on foot from Brest nearly 500 miles.

Anglomania revived under the Directory, as was indeed inevitable in the general reaction against the Terror. Dandies riding in the Bois de Boulogne greeted each other with "weri wol" (very well), and French dressmakers having migrated to London, the latter city had become the seat of fashion, so that English bonnets and dresses were the rage. Despite the nominal prohibition, the Palais Royal shops were full of English goods. In September 1797 Braham and Signora Storace arrived in Paris to give concerts, which, though admission was a louis, whereas the usual price was six francs, were so popular that the visit was extended from three weeks to eight months. Yet Arndt in 1799 saw "Guerre aux Anglais" placarded in the streets, in cafés, and even in churches, including the temple of the Theophilanthropists. The spy mania also existed. An Englishwoman married to a foreigner, in her "Sketch of Modern France" (1796-7) met at Abbeville a cart containing an Englishman, his wife, and three children. They had been some months in prison, all their effects had been confiscated, and they were being escorted to Calais for embarkation.

Sir Sidney Smith cannot be passed over, for although prisoners of war, as concomitants of all wars, receive little notice here, his was an exceptional case. Indeed, his long detention was due to the demand of France that 4000 Frenchmen should be exchanged for him, a great though unwitting compliment. He and his brother Spencer had been educated at a military college at Caen. While trying to cut out a privateer from Havre in April 1796 he was captured, with twenty or thirty officers and men. The Directory refused to treat "this monster" as a prisoner of war, on account of his burning of the French ships at Toulon, and consigned him, with his secretary, John Wesley Wright, to the Temple, though not, as is sometimes said, to the rooms in which the royal family were confined in 1792. He was interrogated, with a view to a prosecution for arson. Lord Malmesbury notified in 1797 that unless Smith was liberated on parole no French officer in England would be allowed a similar privilege. When Babœuf's followers attempted to break out of the Temple, Smith helped to overpower them. Swinburne, when recalled, thought himself on the point of arranging the affair, but his successor, Captain James Cotes, accomplished nothing. Bribery and stratagem were, however, more effective than diplomacy. Count Tromelin, a Vendean *émigré* captured with Smith, passed himself off as his English servant, John

Bromley by name, pretended to speak broken French, and was exchanged without difficulty, whereupon he returned from England in disguise, and in concert with Philippeaux arranged Smith's escape. On the 5th May 1798 Tromelin and a confederate, dressed as French officers, presented themselves at the Temple with an order from the Minister of Marine to give up Smith and Wright that they might rejoin the other prisoners of war at Fontainebleau. Printed form, signature, and seal were genuine, but had been stolen by a Dalmatian, Wiskowich. Smith's affected reluctance to leave helped to throw the keeper off his guard, and the two prisoners, given up without demur, made their way to England, where Smith was enthusiastically received.*

What bribes were paid, and to whom, is unknown, but as Bonneville puts it, "the age of murderers has been succeeded by the age of thieves." The keeper, Boniface, was sentenced as a scapegoat to six months' imprisonment for remissness, albeit he had immediately notified the surrender of Smith to three of the ministers. These notices were apparently kept

* One of the confidants of the plot was Hyde de Neuville, a lineal descendant of Lord Chancellor Hyde, but whose Jacobite grandfather had settled in France. Out of regard for Tromelin's wife, Hyde hired a house adjoining the Temple, and made an underground passage from the cellar to the prison wall. A piece of the latter unexpectedly fell in, in broad daylight, under a sentry's eyes, and the conspirators had to flee from the house. Hyde was not personally concerned in the second and more successful attempt. He was a deputy and diplomatist after the Restoration.

back, for the escape was not ostensibly discovered till a week afterwards, when Smith had reached London. Arndt in 1799 found Smith's rooms as much visited by the curious as those of Louis XVI. and Marie Antoinette. They still contained pictures which he had hung on the walls, and Arndt was told that Smith not only had the run of the building, but used to receive numerous callers of both sexes.

Tromelin afterwards served under Smith in Syria, was captured in 1804 at Stuttgart together with Spencer Smith, abjured royalism, entered the French army, fought at Waterloo, and was deputed by the provisional Government to apply to the Duke of Wellington for a passport for Napoleon. He was certainly a man who played many parts. Smith, too, had a singular influence on Napoleon's career. "That man," Napoleon when at the height of his power used to say, "spoilt my fortune. If St. Jean d'Acre had fallen I should have been Emperor of all the East." Supremacy in Europe did not apparently console him for the evaporation of his Oriental dreams. Yet newspapers sent to him by Smith while negotiating an exchange of prisoners are said to have induced him to return to France, by convincing him that the Directory was so unpopular that it could easily be overturned. Indeed, Nakoula, a Syrian in the service of the Emir of the Druses, who was in Egypt at the time, states in an Arabic book translated by Desgranges in 1839 that on returning to

Alexandria from Acre, Bonaparte gave a grand dinner to Smith, loaded him with attentions and presents, and obtained permission to send three small boats to France. Not till two days afterwards did Smith learn that Bonaparte had himself left in one of these boats, and he vainly pursued him. Michelet argues that the English Government winked at Bonaparte's escape in the hope of his restoring the Bourbons, but this theory, like Nakoula's story, has a dubious air. If Bonaparte and Smith really dined together it was a curious sequel to their exchange of incivilities at Acre, where Smith endorsed and distributed a Turkish proclamation inviting the French to desert, as the Directory had sent them there merely to get rid of them; Napoleon responded by vilifying Smith, who sent him a challenge, which Bonaparte declined.

After Waterloo Smith, to avoid his creditors, settled in Paris, died there, and was buried in Père Lachaise. His brother Spencer, a diplomatist, went to reside at Caen, where he died in 1845. The Duke of Wellington, who met Smith at Paris in 1815, could not believe that a man so silly in all other affairs could be a good naval officer, and he told Croker an anecdote of Smith waiting on Louis XVIII. at the time of the English expedition against Algiers to represent that Lord Exmouth was incompetent, and that failure was inevitable unless he himself were appointed. The king heard him out, and then archly told him that news had arrived that very morning of the success of the expedition. Smith's vanity, indeed, was inordinate.

His secretary, Captain Wright, also died at Paris, but under strangely different circumstances. In March 1803 he was sent over as attaché to the Embassy, and Lord Whitworth feared that this would be an additional obstacle to peace, as his escape from the Temple might be recollected. However intelligent he might be, a less known man would have been equally useful. Cruising off Morbihan in 1804, Wright was captured and again imprisoned in the Temple. He was identified by two of the prisoners implicated in Georges' conspiracy as having landed them, and he was produced as a witness at the trial, but refused to answer, maintaining that he owed no account of his naval operations except to his own Government. There is reason to believe that he was tortured to extract a confession, and that this having failed, the authorities, afraid to release him lest he should expose their infamy, strangled him in prison and then pretended he had committed suicide.

Sidney Smith's nephew, George Sidney Smith, was captured with Wright, was several years a prisoner at Verdun, and owing to his knowledge of French, commanded the boat which conveyed Napoleon to Elba.

Two other inmates of the Temple in the closing

years of the century may here be mentioned. Sir Robert Barclay was captured in a merchant vessel early in 1799, with despatches from Lord Grenville in his possession. He had been officially employed on the Continent. He was closely confined in the Temple, and was interrogated by a military commission respecting a supposed mission to the Hague. He is said to have been acquitted, though of what charge is not clear, but was nevertheless detained till November, when, after an interview with Bonaparte, he was released. He appears to have claimed kinship with Sheridan, which may have conduced to his liberation, and his wife was Elizabeth Tickell, granddaughter of Addison's friend and Queen Anne's Under-Secretary of State. Barclay was elected M.P. for Newton, Hants, in 1802, and died in 1839, at the age of eighty-three.

Mrs. Dayrell, the widow of an English officer, probably one of the Oxfordshire Dayrells, a handsome woman of twenty-eight, settled with her little girl at the beginning of the Revolution at La Chaussée, near Blois. She there married Courtin de Clenard, who in February 1792 sold the Clenard estate, which he had just inherited, to Edmund Dayrell, his wife's brother-in-law. Courtin having emigrated, the sale was declared collusive, and in 1793 the property was confiscated. Madame Dayrell-Courtin subsequently went to Paris and obtained an order that the estate should be restored if she could prove that she herself had not emigrated. Her adversaries, the new owners, resorted to the device of getting her arrested as an English spy, but though she had made several voyages to England *viâ* Hamburg, she easily established her innocence. In 1800 they again procured her arrest, and she was consigned to the Temple. Dufort de Cheverny, who tells us thus much, does not give us the end of the story, but the lady's indomitable energy, coupled with her acquaintance with Josephine, probably secured her redress.

XII.
Paris Re-opened.

"Die Zwietracht fliegt, die Donnerstürme schweigen
   Gefesselt ist der Krieg,
  Und in den Krater darf man niedersteigen
   Aus dem die Lava stieg."
—SCHILLER.

XII.

PARIS RE-OPENED.

Fox — Rogers — Erskine — Mackintosh — Bentham — Romilly — Kemble—Watt—Aberdeen—High Life—Treasure-seekers.

WHEN Paris was re-opened to British visitors by the signature of preliminaries of peace, it became again, as Horace Walpole had said of it in 1763, "the way of all flesh." Ten years of abstinence had sharpened the appetite, and everybody was anxious to see how much the city had altered since the Revolution. People of fashion were curious to know whether its gaiety had revived. Politicians were eager to behold the young ruler whose career had already been so romantic, and whose star was evidently still in the ascendant. Madame de Stael felt sorely tempted to go and see these English visitors, but prudently refrained, for she had had a hint that her intimacy with Bernadotte on her previous stay in Paris had given offence to the First Consul. Necker, her father, offered, however, to go and smoothe the way for her. Anthony Merry, the English envoy, calculated that in the summer of 1802 there were 5000 of his countrymen in Paris, and that on Lord

Whitworth's arrival in the winter there remained 1700. Wordsworth, who went no farther than Calais, was indignant at this worship of Bonaparte.

> "Lords, lawyers, statesmen, squires of low degree,
> Men known and men unknown, sick, lame, and blind,
> Post forward all, like creatures of one kind,
> With first-fruit offerings crowd to bend the knee
> In France before the new-born Majesty."

Whitworth found this throng of visitors politically mischievous. "It is absolutely necessary that we should stick to our text," he wrote to George Hammond on March 24th, 1803, "in order to do away with the impression which some of our rascally countrymen have given. I have for this last fortnight shut my door to Lord Lauderdale and all those of his stamp with which this city swarms." The Duke of Bedford, however, who conferred with Danton at Paris in the winter of 1792, and was again there, "seems perfectly aware," said Whitworth, writing on May 4th, "of the character and projects of the First Consul, and of the necessity (although he exaggerates the danger to ourselves) of imposing some restraint upon him if possible. . . . He conducts himself very properly. I wish I could say as much of many of my countrymen and countrywomen." *

Fox was by far the most notable of these visitors. He was accompanied by Mr. (afterwards Lord) St.

---

* "England and Napoleon in 1803." By Oscar Browning.

John, and by his future biographer, Trotter, and he met his brother, General Fox, his nephew, Lord Holland, General Fitzpatrick,* and Lord Robert Spencer. (The two last were M.P.s for Tavistock.) He stayed, as already mentioned, at the hotel Richelieu, which had still an air of grandeur, and had a pretty garden. A caricature of the time represented Fox and his wife as prostrate in slavish adoration before Bonaparte. The truth, however, was, that the Consul's character inspired him with distrust, and that he felt much more in his element with Lafayette in his retreat at Lagrange, where Lally Tollendal, another disillusioned revolutionist, and a born orator, recited his French translation of Shakespere. Yet Fox and Lord Holland (as a youth he had seen something of the Revolution) dined with Bonaparte, who was so anxious to make a good impression on his guest that long afterwards at Elba he asked Lord Ebrington what Fox had thought of him, and being told that he was flattered by his reception, replied, " He had reason to be so ; he was everywhere received as a god, because he was known to be for peace." Fox, indeed, Trotter assures us, was more applauded at the theatre than Bonaparte himself. He went over the Louvre with Sir Benjamin West and Opie, saw Kosciusko and Sieyes, and took tea with Helen Williams. He

---

* Page to Queen Charlotte in 1761, Secretary at War, 1806; died 1813, aged sixty-six.

was collecting materials in the French archives for his life of James II., but he combined pleasure with business, and Lewis Goldsmith's *Paris Argus* spoke of him as dancing attendance at ladies' saloons, particularly Madame Recamier's and Madame Tallien's. He met the poet Rogers, and commissioned him, as a better judge of furniture than himself, to buy fire-irons in the Palais Royal arcades, the price not to exceed a couple of louis. Rogers, too, saw Bonaparte, but only at a review, when he thought " his profile very strong, and his face one dead tint of yellow."

Erskine, who was over with his son, visited the Court of Appeal, and was loaded with attentions, but strangely enough was chiefly intimate with Barère, the most contemptible of surviving Jacobins. Barère, indeed—whose future biographer, President Carnot's father, then lying in his cradle, was destined to dwell on his unwavering enmity to England as the redeeming point in his character—seems to have been lionised by British visitors, as unconscious as himself of his cardinal virtue. Sir Francis Burdett called on him, and perhaps learned from him the poverty of Paine, who was enabled by a present of 300 louis from Burdett and Bosville to pay his debts and embark for America. This good deed may be set off against the vanity which led Burdett, applauded at Calais as the friend of Fox, to reply "No, I am the friend of the people." Burdett had seen Paris in 1793, when he sedulously attended the clubs and the Convention. Returning to England, in August of that year he married Miss Coutts, whose two sisters had been educated at Paris in 1787. John Kemble also, introduced probably by Talma, repeatedly met Barère.

Erskine was presented by Bonaparte with his portrait, and was perhaps accompanied to the Tuileries by Alderman Combe, M.P. and ex-Lord Mayor of London. At any rate a caricaturist depicted the Consul receiving Fox, Erskine, and Combe in a very unceremonious fashion:

"Fox! ha, how old are you? A brewer, Lord Mayor! ha, great pomp. Mr. Brief! ha, a great lawyer, can talk well. There, you may go." *

Grotesque as this was, it was hardly more so than what actually happened at the reception of Mackintosh. Bonaparte, with that desire to be thought omniscient which made him "cram" for a visit to the Paris Library by getting up the question of the interpolated passage in Josephus, had made inquiries about his visitors, but forgetting which was which, or the order of presentation being inverted, the compliment prepared for Mackintosh on his "unanswerable answer to Burke" was offered to the friend who preceded him. "I have got your compliment," whispered the friend as he made

* "English Caricature and Satire on Napoleon." By John Ashton, 1884.

way for Mackintosh. Perhaps after all this was as well, considering that Mackintosh had altogether changed his opinion of the Revolution, and had two years previously written to George Moore—

"I abhor, abjure, and for ever renounce the French Revolution, with all its sanguinary history, its abominable principles, and for ever execrable leaders. I hope I shall be able [in forthcoming lectures] to wipe off the disgrace of having been once betrayed into an approbation of that conspiracy against God and man, the greatest scourge of the world, and the chief stain upon human annals." *

Mackintosh's revulsion of feeling, laudable as it was, had carried him a little too far, by making him forget that the crimes of the Revolution were in part the result of the old *régime*. Yet his corrected opinion was probably identical with that really held by Bonaparte himself, who, when married to Marie Antoinette's great-niece, would actually speak of poor Louis XVI. as "my uncle." Neither the Consul nor Mackintosh could foresee that a year later Mackintosh would be defending Peltier for libels on Bonaparte, who meanwhile had become life consul. Jeremy Bentham, by the way, exercised the citizenship conferred on him in 1792 by voting for that consulate. The man in whose eyes the English constitution was a mockery and delusion, thus helped to rivet the chains of despotism on France.

* "Life," by his son, ii. 167.

PARIS RE-OPENED. 247

Romilly, who had seen Paris in August 1789, and regarded the Jacobins as monsters, and Holcroft, whose daughter married Danton's nephew Merget, were also among the politicians who visited France. So, too, was William Taylor, of Norwich, who, though he had warmly sympathised with the Revolution, became very anti-Bonapartist. He was in Paris from March till the summer of 1802, Southey's brother Henry being his companion. Taylor had an introduction to Lafayette, his cousin John Dyson having taught Lafayette farming, and he there met Madame d'Arblay. He also dined with Holcroft and Paine, and made the acquaintance of Thomas Manning the Orientalist, at whose suggestion Lamb wrote his " Roast Pig." Tierney, too, spent the summer of 1802 at Boulogne, but, doubtful of the continuance of peace, prudently declined to hire his house for another season. John Kemble, who has been already mentioned, is said to have been considered wonderfully like Bonaparte, though his portrait suggests no resemblance. He went on to Madrid to study the Spanish stage.

James Watt revisited Paris for the first time since 1786, when he had been invited to report on the Marly aqueduct. His son, after his experiences of 1792, did not again see France. Then there was Sir Elijah Impey, who had awarded damages to Grand for his wife's intrigue with Sir Philip Francis. He was trying to recover property in the French funds, and was actually welcomed by the lady. His testimony, people supposed, was essential to her marriage with Talleyrand, insisted upon by Bonaparte, but Madame Grand had obtained in 1798 a divorce from Grand, for whom she procured a post at the Cape, where he died, virtually a British subject, in 1821. Lord Whitworth was strangely misinformed when, as a reason for his wife (the Duchess of Dorset) accepting Talleyrand's hospitality he wrote, "The lady who presides in his house bears his name, and is in fact married to him as far as the sanction of the Romish Church can make such a marriage lawful." No religious marriage had been or ever was allowed in Talleyrand's case. It was the civil marriage which was then impending.

Maria Edgeworth and her father were also in Paris, and had a singular adventure. After a four months' stay, devoted to literary pursuits, they were suddenly ordered to quit Paris in twenty-four hours and France in a fortnight. Edgeworth had been taken for a brother of the Abbé Edgeworth, Louis XVI.'s confessor and chaplain to the future Louis XVIII. On explaining that he was only a distant cousin, and had never seen him, the order was apparently revoked. Then there was Sir John Carr, whose trip to Paris formed the subject of the first of his many books of travel. Another embryo author was Colonel Thomas Thornton, who had a mind to see how French sport had been affected by the Revolution. In 1815 he returned, hired Chambord for two years of the Princesse de Wagram, and lived in thoroughly British style. He ultimately left a will in favour of the daughter of a married Frenchwoman, which at the instance of his legitimate family was set aside by the French tribunals.

Another chiel taking notes and printing them was the Rev. Stephen Weston, grandson of Bishop Weston of Exeter. In 1791 he had witnessed the 14th July celebration. In 1792 he had "run from Paris with fear and trembling, because she was possessed like a demoniac with a spirit of carnage, and reeking in the blood of August and September," but he now found it "swept and garnished, restored to its senses, and in its right mind." It was less altered, too, than he had expected. So fond of Paris was this somewhat flippant and sceptical clergyman, that in 1829, when turned of eighty, he went over again, assiduously frequenting theatres and other amusements, and had he not died the following year he would probably have paid another visit to see France under the new dynasty. A fellow-clergyman, Stephen Shepherd, of Gateacre, Lancashire, a friend of Roscoe's, seems to have been equally fond of the French capital. He had a letter of introduction to Helen Williams, and at her tea-table met Kosciusko, Carnot, a Neapolitan princess, and a Polish countess. He spent a most agreeable evening, but on his returning in 1814 he did not renew acquaintance with his hostess. Perhaps he could not countenance her *liaison* with the printer Stone, who, however, must have been the gentleman who in 1802 brought him his invitation.

Lord Aberdeen, not yet "the travelled thane, Athenian Aberdeen," but a very agreeable young man of eighteen according to George (afterwards Sir George) Jackson of the Embassy, was introduced to Bonaparte. He was the Prime Minister of 1853–5. Lord Camelford, a second cousin of Pitt's, and the best shot in England, was over in strict incognito.* Refused a passport, he went to Boulogne as an American, and thence to Paris as a valet, but afraid of the police discovering him, he went on to Vienna. "It is feared," wrote Jackson, "he should attempt some personal mischief," which implies symptoms of the mental derangement which in 1804 led to his fatal duel with his friend Captain Best.† St. George Caulfeild, an Irishman,

---

* It was he who made Horne Tooke M.P. for Old Sarum. In 1798 he was arrested on the point of starting for France, but manifestly having no treasonable designs—his object was secretly to examine the French Mediterranean ports—was discharged, but deprived of his naval command. According to Fauche Borel, the royalist spy, he went over to Calais in a fishing boat, was arrested, was confined in the Temple at Paris, and was liberated by bribing a turnkey with 2000 louis to inform Lord Grenville of his whereabouts. But a more probable version is that he went to Switzerland, and made a point of witnessing the engagements between the Russians and the French.

† His sister, Lady Grenville, lived till 1864, to the age of ninety-one, and attended a flower-show only two days before her death.

just of age, with £30,000 a year, kept open house in grand style, and was expecting his future mother-in-law and bride, Lady and Frances Crofton, so that the marriage might take place at Paris.

Miss Berry, with her friend Mrs. Damer, the amateur sculptress, found the north of France more prosperous, the south less so, than before the Revolution. She met at Paris in March 1802 Lord Henry Petty, the statesman who as Marquis of Lansdowne lived till 1863; Sir Charles Blagden, a writer on music and natural philosophy; the Dowager Duchess of Cumberland, and Mrs. Cosway, the artist, who introduced her to Bonaparte's mother. Mrs. Cosway illustrated a work on France by John Griffiths, and she was induced by Cardinal Fesch to open a school in Paris, but it did not succeed. Miss Berry was also presented to Bonaparte and Josephine. In the autumn she was back in Paris, and met Lady Foster, sister to Lord Bristol and future Duchess of Devonshire, concerning whom there were such strange reports. She did not see France again till 1816, but Mrs. Damer, who in 1802 promised Bonaparte a bust of Fox, fulfilled her pledge on May-day 1815, the Emperor presenting her in return with a splendid snuff-box bearing his portrait set in diamonds. Miss Linwood went over to exhibit her art needlework. The Duchess of Gordon gave great entertainments in Paris in 1802, and her daughter, the future Duchess of

Bedford, often danced with the young and handsome Eugène Beauharnais, Bonaparte's stepson. The Duchess was a warm admirer of the Consul, and pointing to his likeness, would say to Madame Lebrun, "Voilà mon zéro" (héros). Lady Cholmondeley, Lady Conyngham, Lady Elizabeth Monck, and Lady Foster, also attended Josephine's receptions, whereas Lady Clarendon was one of the visitors who declined to worship the rising sun. "Those people who chose to be presented at Napoleon's courts," says her diary,* "were invited to many magnificent dinners and assemblies given by the ministers, but as ourselves with a very few exceptions did not feel inclined to pay homage to Bonaparte, the theatres and the entertainments given by foreigners were mostly our resources." She, however, saw Josephine at a ball at the Ministry of Marine. Lady Hester Stanhope, whose father's second marriage had produced domestic friction, accompanied the Egertons in a long trip, which included Paris, but there is no record of her observations.

Titled visitors of the other sex included Lords Douglas (the late Duke of Hamilton), Spencer, Egremont, Pembroke, Cholmondeley, Conyngham, Mount-Edgecumbe, Falkland, Ossulston, Cahir, and Loftus (afterwards Marquis of Ely), and Lord Archibald Hamilton, some of whom must have been the "young lords" who at Lady Higginson's balls

* Lord Westmoreland's MSS. Historical MSS. Commission.

eagerly questioned Maurice Dupin, George Sand's father, respecting the French army. They may have been interested in him as the descendant of Marshal Saxe.

Some of the United Irishmen released in 1802 went over to Paris, in the expectation that the peace would be very short, and that French help might be obtained for another rising in Ireland. It would have been well for two of them if they had remained in France,* for Robert Emmet and Thomas Russell were executed on their return. Macnevin was more prudent. Despairing of French aid, he quitted the French army, went to America, and resumed the medical profession.

The recovery of property confiscated by the Revolution was the object of several visitors. Philippe d'Auvergne, a native of Jersey, went in quest of the duchy of Bouillon. Not sent to France, as commonly stated, to complete his education, but captured on board the dreaded cruiser *Arethusa* and taken to Paris, he was introduced to the Duc de Bouillon, the last descendant of Turenne, who recognised him as a kinsman, for the Jersey Auvergnes had been Huguenot refugees. The duke, childless and on ill terms with his next of kin, had a mania for discovering Auvergnes, and was charmed with the

* As also for Arthur Thistlewood, who paid visits to France between 1799 and 1802, and returned to England in the latter year. He headed the Cato Street conspiracy, and was executed in 1820.

young sailor's appearance and manner. He formally, in 1788, adopted him as his son, and he took the title as such of Prince de Bouillon, but the Revolution obliged both to fly, and the estates were confiscated. Philippe d'Auvergne then rejoined the English navy, but on the conclusion of peace, his adoptive father having apparently died, he went over to Paris to claim the restoration of the duchy. He was, however, imprisoned in the Temple as a spy, and was a week in close confinement. On the representations of the British Embassy he was released, but expelled. He had been offered the restoration of the estates if he would betray his royalist correspondents in Western France. He resumed his naval duties, commanded the Jersey squadron, and is said to have superintended the military and forged-assignat expeditions to the Norman coast. The treaty of Paris recognised his claims to the duchy, but the arbitrators appointed by the Congress of Vienna held his adoption to be invalid, and assigned the estates to the Prince de Rohan Montbazon. Philippe d'Auvergne consequently remained a British admiral, and died in 1816, at the age of 81.

Dr. (afterwards Archbishop) Troy, President of Maynooth, went over during the Amiens negotiations to plead for the restitution of the property of the Irish colleges, but Lord Cornwallis could not get for them better terms than for other British claimants. Walter Boyd, the banker who fled from Paris in 1792, was one of these. He had started a bank in London, had helped to float Pitt's loans, was M.P. for Shaftesbury, and in the prospect of restitution by the French Goverment had contracted heavy engagements, when the *coup d'état* of 1797 shattered his hopes, drove him again from Paris, and ultimately caused his bankruptcy. On the return of peace he hurried over to press his claims, and he was accompanied or followed by his London partner, Paul Benfield, the man held up to odium by Burke for his usurious loans to the Nabob of Arcot. It was natural enough that men on such a quest should be loath to leave without having effected their purpose, and both of them were surprised by the decree for the detention of all British subjects between sixteen and sixty years of age.

XIII.

Napoleon's Captives.

"I hope I am mistaken, but if I have well understood the French nation there will be much bloodshed, and a despotism rougher than that which they flatter themselves on having destroyed."—*Washington to G. Morris, October* 1789.

XIII.

NAPOLEON'S CAPTIVES.

Elgin—Yarmouth—Liberations—Refugees—Escapes—Life at Verdun—Release.

THE detentions of 1803 were so much a second edition of those of 1793, that this alone would justify me in regarding the Revolution as lasting till the fall of Napoleon. The sufferers, moreover, were more numerous, though they did not exceed a thousand. The French Government pretended, indeed, that there were eight or ten times as many, but this was to conceal its disappointment at the smallness of the haul. Charles Sturt, ex-M.P. for Bridport, and brother-in-law to Lord Shaftesbury, who was probably well-informed, assures us that the detention of British visitors had been contemplated by Napoleon for six weeks, and that he had ordered returns of their numbers, which were estimated at 7000. Sturt adds that only 700 were entrapped, and that 400 of these were small tradesmen, with a sprinkling of Irish and English refugees. The embargo placed on French shipping in British ports a day prior to the declaration of war was a measure strictly in accordance with precedent—indeed, Napoleon himself ordered a like embargo in Dutch and Italian ports—and the alleged capture of two merchantmen at sea before the declaration was a pure invention, yet these were the pleas on which the French decree was grounded. The pretence of the prisoners being liable to militia duty was so hollow that clergymen, manifestly exempt from such duty, obtained no better treatment than laymen. It would be unprofitable to debate who was to blame for the rupture. Miot de Mélito, a member of Napoleon's Council of State, and assuredly devoid of bias in favour of England, throws the chief blame on his master, and speaks of the detention of British subjects as "a violent measure, unusual even in the bitterest wars." He heard Napoleon before the rupture, at a meeting of the Council to settle the new coinage bearing his effigy, wander off into a tirade against everything English—national character, political institutions, even Shakespere and Milton fell under his lash.*

Napoleon himself, moreover, in conversation with Lord Ebrington at Elba, scarcely affected to defend the detentions. Ebrington urged that the embargo on shipping prior to the declaration of war was sanctioned by precedent, whereupon the Emperor replied—" Yes, you considered it right because it was to your advantage; other nations who lost by

* "Mémoires de Miot de Mélito," 1858.

it thought it wrong. I am sure that in your hearts you in England approved me for showing force of character. Do you not see I am a bit of a pirate like yourselves?" But although the measure was justified by one at least of Bonaparte's victims, Lord Yarmouth, it was certainly impolitic as well as lawless. I have not, indeed, discovered in the newspapers of the time such an outburst of indignation as might have been expected, but according to the Duke of Buckingham, Napoleon, who till then had had admirers in England, became thoroughly execrated. Some of the captives were studying at universities, others copying at the Louvre, then full of foreign spoils, others in search of health in Southern France. The detention was especially hard for travellers in Switzerland, who could not be aware of the fluctuations of diplomacy. Sir William Coll took flight in time from Geneva, and Miss Berry and Mrs. Damer from Lausanne, thanks to a friendly warning from Lord John Campbell. The two ladies were blamed for not giving the signal to others less favoured. Madame de Stael's confidence that the rumour of arrests was unfounded was near proving calamitous to her English friends at Geneva. One hardly knows whether to regard as an extenuating or an aggravating circumstance the apparent impartiality with which the blow fell alike on friends and foes, Gallophobes and Gallophils.

Even if the detention itself had been justifiable,

the trickery by which English visitors were lured into remaining would have been inexcusable. The *Argus*, a semi-official paper printed in English, commenting on the 10th May 1803 on the hurried departure of British subjects, assured them that they would be much better protected if they remained than they could have been by Lord Whitworth, for France was no longer ruled by a Robespierre or by a system of terror. The local authorities at Brussels, Nimes, and other places, had given assurances that even expulsion was unlikely, and that in any case ample time would be allowed for departure. Talleyrand, too, had told Lord Elgin (of marble celebrity) that he might safely stay in Paris. Elgin was simply passing through France on his way home from the Constantinople Embassy, and had in Italy obtained passports from the French consuls, yet he vainly pleaded diplomatic immunity. Even Lord Whitworth's staff suffered treatment on a parallel with Lord Gower's in 1792. James Talbot was twice stopped and detained some hours on his way to Calais. James Henry Mandeville,* not allowed to embark at Boulogne, returned to Paris. The Embassy chaplain and doctor, Hodgson and Maclaurin, were also refused permission to embark. Talleyrand, who may safely be acquitted of these vexatious measures, had to be appealed to before the entire

* Afterwards Minister to the Argentine Republic; born 1773, died 1861.

staff could get away, and Talleyrand himself could do nothing when Lord Hawkesbury expressed surprise and astonishment at so extraordinary and unprecedented a step as the detention of English visitors.*

Lord Elgin, though in precarious health, was conveyed to Lourdes, not yet a resort for pilgrims, and for some time his family were ignorant of what had become of him. In October 1803 a London physician was allowed to see him at Barèges, the result being permission to pass the winter at Paris, where Lady Elgin joined him; but on an incorrect report that General Boyer was imprisoned in Scotland —he was really on parole at Chesterfield—Elgin was ordered to be arrested and sent back to Lourdes. There was an offer to exchange him for Boyer, but the English Government could not "sanction the principle of exchanging persons made prisoners according to the acknowledged laws of war against any of its own subjects who have been detained in France in violation of the law of nations and of the pledged faith of the French Government." Elgin was ultimately allowed to live at Paris, where a son, very short-lived, was born to him in 1805. He was released in 1806, simultaneously with Lord Yarmouth, M.P. for Lisburn, whose case was even harder. He went to fetch his family, inquired at Calais whether he might safely land, and was

* "England and Napoleon in 1803."

answered in the affirmative, yet no sooner had he landed than ship, passengers, and crew were declared prisoners. He was interned at Verdun and elsewhere, but as he had been a boon companion of the Prince of Wales, the latter induced Fox to make representations in his favour, and Talleyrand, imagining that he was a favourite with Fox himself, not only liberated him but made him the bearer of overtures for peace. Elgin, Yarmouth, and General Abercromby sailed together from Morlaix in May 1806. Yarmouth was promptly sent back with a response, and Lord Lauderdale followed him, but the negotiations came to nothing. It is said that Napoleon not only had Lauderdale's papers searched by surprise, but sent an order to stop his departure; Fouché, however, intentionally delayed its execution until the bird had flown. Yarmouth, afterwards Marquis of Hertford, is the Lord Monmouth of "Coningsby" and the Lord Steyne of "Vanity Fair." His wife, Maria Fagniani, whose paternity was disputed by George Selwyn and the Duke of Queensberry, left him, according to Lady Hester Stanhope, for a Frenchman, and lived in Paris, but occasionally obtained a passport for England to make arrangements for the children. One of these, Lord Henry Seymour, was not only born but chiefly lived in France, was one of the eighteen members of the English Jockey Club at Paris in 1830, and was very eccentric. At the

Carnival of 1834 and 1835 he tried to introduce Italian customs by flinging comfits and coins.

Carnot, as President of the Institute, interceded for several scientists or scholars, and it was fortunate that Sir Joseph Banks, President of the Royal Society, was not only in correspondence with him but was considered friendly to France. James Forbes, the Orientalist, Montalembert's grandfather, who had just become an F.R.S., thus obtained his liberty. Alexander Hamilton, though not an F.R.S. till 1808, was also released. He was regarded as the only man on the Continent acquainted with Sanscrit, into which he initiated Frederic Schlegel, who in 1802 was on a visit to Paris with his wife, daughter of Moses Mendelssohn. Hamilton catalogued the Sanscrit manuscripts in the Paris library, and to this service doubtless owed his liberation. It was perhaps also as F.R.S. that Lord Shaftesbury, the late philanthropist's uncle, was liberated, or this may have been due to his friendship with Fox, which had procured him permission to remain at Paris. Dr. Charles Maclean, who had gone to Paris to advocate an international institution at Constantinople for the study and treatment of the plague, was released after some demur on proving that he had been ten years out of England. He considered himself fortunate, for though the detention was ostensibly limited to males between sixteen and sixty years of age, passports were refused to women, and to boys of ten or twelve who had no written certificates of their age. John Pinkerton, the geographer, Horace Walpole's friend, had leave to stay in Paris, and in 1805 obtained a passport. During his detention his French publisher sued Maltebrun for plagiarism, but unsuccessfully, for Pinkerton had himself adopted Maltebrun's fifth division of the globe, Oceania. His "Recollections of Paris" are of scant interest, the fear of domiciliary visits having deterred him from keeping a diary. He went back to Paris after the Restoration, and died there in 1826. Robert Hendry, a Glasgow chemist, owed his release to Napoleon's visit in 1806 to the calico factory at Jouy where he was assisting Oberkampf. The latter introduced Hendry to the Emperor, who could not do less than grant him a passport.

Lord Duncannon, afterwards Earl of Bessborough, Lord Lieutenant of Ireland in 1846–47, seems to have been released before November 1805, for he then married. General Sir Charles Shipley, Sir Thomas Hare, and a son of Lady Foster—probably the future diplomatist, Sir Augustus Foster—were likewise liberated. Greathead, the lifeboat inventor, and his wife, to whom Mrs. Siddons had been companion, were also released, and in December 1804 were at Berlin on their way home. Their son, Bertie Greathead, who had married a Frenchwoman, is said to have remained, and to have made such excellent copies of famous pictures that Bonaparte would not allow them to be sent out of France. On the young man's death, however, in 1804 they were forwarded to his father. "Formerly a famous democrat," Greathead, according to Sir George Jackson, had been "cured by his French treatment." Possibly the effect was the same on Stuart Kydd, one of the English radicals prosecuted in 1794, but discharged without trial after three years' detention. Ferguson, a mineralogist and F.R.S., was released in 1804. Sir Elijah Impey, the Duke and Duchess of Newcastle, the Dowager Marchioness of Donegal, and Sir John Morshead, were also released. Mrs. Tuthill, a great beauty, managed to present a petition to Napoleon while out hunting, and gallantly obliged him to concede her husband's release. Sir James de Bathe is said to have secured the Pope's good offices by representing that his absence made his children in England in danger of becoming Protestants, and the papal mediation was effectual.

Others got back to England by less straightforward means. Some shammed illness, some broke their parole, the inevitable result being that the French authorities were obdurate towards persons really ill, and were more stringent towards those whose word was their bond. Astley, of circus fame, had leave to go to Piedmont to introduce equestrianism there, but he made his way to London, where his amphitheatre had been burnt down. He, like Pinkerton, was doomed to end his days in Paris, and whereas all biographical dictionaries represent him as a native of Newcastle-under-Lyme, his tomb at Père Lachaise, which ought not to lie, states that he was born at Manchester. A clergyman could not be logically detained as belonging to the militia, yet the Rev. W. H. Churchill, of Colliton, Dorset, was arrested while on a journey to Lyons, and brought back to Paris. Junot disdainfully tore up the certificate which he presented as a title to benefit of clergy, and the officials, Churchill tells us, were most uncivil and insulting to the English, though Frenchmen generally were quite the reverse, and even, as d'Allonville states, facilitated escapes, out of indignation at so unjust a detention. Some of the English in Paris were sent to Fontainebleau, and several who had expressed their feelings too warmly were kept under duress there. In December 1803 those still remaining in Paris were ordered to Verdun. Churchill, refused permission to accompany his invalid brother to England, was threatened with incarceration in the Temple if he did not start for Verdun, and he had to feign illness. A French doctor prescribed for an "ulcerated throat," and in January, not apparently without bribery, he was allowed to leave with his brother.* His fellow-traveller, less fortunate, died a captive a year or two afterwards.

* "Journal of Mary Frampton," 1884.

Fanny Burney, albeit marriage with a French general had made her a French subject, cannot be passed over. Law de Lauriston, a collateral descendant of the famous financier, arranged, on his visit to London with the ratification of the treaty of Amiens, that his friend d'Arblay, after serving a year in St. Domingo, should retire from service, but an indiscreet letter to Bonaparte, signifying a resolution never to bear arms against his wife's country, resulted in his being cashiered. D'Arblay, however, resolved to stay a year in France in case Bonaparte's anger should cool down, and in April 1802 he sent for his wife and son to join him. When war broke out their return was impossible. Not till 1812, during the Emperor's absence in Russia, could a passport be procured for mother and child.

Sir Humphrey Davy, however, was not only awarded in 1809 the Institute prize of 60,000 francs for improvements in electricity, but was permitted to pass through France on his way to Italy, and several Englishmen were left unmolested. Sir Herbert Croft, who wrote the life of his friend Young for Dr. Johnson, and who was too late to succour two suicidal poets—Chatterton * in London, and Grainville, Bernardin St. Pierre's cousin, whose

---

* Croft sent Chatterton's sister £10 for the loan of the poet's MSS., but published them without her sanction. Southey held him up to odium for this breach of trust, and a handsome subscription was raised for the sister.

"Dernier Homme" is a prose poem, at Amiens—was arrested at Valenciennes, but speedily released, and remained in France from choice till his death. He became acquainted just after his liberation with Lady Mary Hamilton, now a widow, and was her satellite and pensioner for the rest of his life, occupying when not in Paris a cottage near her mansion in the environs of Amiens, for his English vicarage yielded him little if anything. He fancied himself a commentator, and the lady imagined herself a novelist, not only in her native language but in French. Nodier was for two years literary factotum to both, and claims the lion's share in their ostensible productions, not including, perhaps, the verses on the death of the lady's bullfinch, with which Croft responded to the dedication of one of her books. Heedless of political changes, this singular pair died in the same year, 1816, he eighty-five years of age, she seventy-seven. Croft's brother Richard, who succeeded to the baronetcy, was physician to Princess Charlotte, and committed suicide owing to the blame thrown on him for her death.

Richard Chenevix, the chemist and mineralogist, whose uncle or father Malmesbury found at Paris in 1796, and whom he had probably accompanied, seems to have also remained from choice, for as an F.R.S. he could certainly have obtained a passport. He contributed from 1798 to 1808 to the *Annales de Chimie*, and in 1803 he was awarded the Copley medal of the Royal Society. He married in 1812 the Comtesse de Ronault, and remained in France till his death in 1830. Anne Plumptre, daughter of a Huntingdonshire clergyman, and a friend of Mrs. Opie, protested that from 1801 to 1805 she was as free as in England, and when desirous of leaving obtained a passport with ease. Quintin Crauford, Talleyrand's whist player, Helen Williams, the printer Stone, and other permanent residents, were also undisturbed. Lewis Goldsmith, not yet acting as Thersites to the French Ajax, was in Paris till 1809, first as editor of the *Argus* and then as interpreter to the tribunals, though he represents himself as having been long anxious to obtain a passport. Goldsmith, however, was rather a refugee than a captive.

So also was Robert Watson, who had a singular history. Nephew of a Leith doctor, he was secretary to Lord George Gordon, is said to have been implicated in his riots, and became his biographer. In 1796 he was arrested for conspiracy, was two years in Newgate, and was then liberated. A reward of £400, however, was offered for his re-apprehension, and he escaped to France. In October 1798 the *Moniteur* announced the arrival at Nancy of "Lord Walson (*sic*), ecossais libre." He went on to Paris and issued an address to the British people, advocating a general rising and the reception of the French as deliverers. Lodging with Bonaparte's forest-keeper, he was introduced to the Consul, and gave him lessons in English, with what success is doubtful, for Napoleon's ability to read English newspapers and reviews at St. Helena is a disputed point. Watson became president of the Scotch college. At Rome in 1812 he made acquaintance with persons possessing documents respecting the Stuarts and the relations of the Vatican with them. He wrote to Lord Castlereagh, who commissioned him to buy the papers, but the Vatican, having learned their existence, had seized them. Negotiations ended in the Vatican retaining the papers affecting itself and in its giving up the others. Again living in London and falling into poverty, Watson committed suicide at the age of eighty-eight.*

For some years the British Government refused to entertain the idea of exchanging Frenchmen captured in legitimate warfare for the so-called hostages of 1803. In January 1805 there was some prospect of a cartel of exchange, not apparently to apply to this class, but it came to nothing. In April 1810 a British commissioner, Colin Alexander Mackenzie, arrived at Morlaix, and prolonged negotiations ensued. England had reluctantly agreed to an exchange of the hostages as well as of prisoners proper. The Earl of Beverley,† grandfather of the

---

* See inquest in the *Times*, November 22-23, 1838.

† Returning from Italy with his wife and daughters, he had been detained.

present Duke of Northumberland—the father of fourteen children, one of whom became Bishop of Carlisle—was to be exchanged for a French general, privy councillors and peers' sons for colonels or navy captains, baronets and knights for military or naval officers of lower rank, untitled gentlemen for captains of the line or navy lieutenants, tradesmen for subalterns, and servants or artisans for soldiers or sailors. It is easy to say that the concession made in 1810 might have been made seven years earlier, but in 1803 there were no French prisoners to be given up in exchange, and the length of the war could not be foreseen. The negotiations of 1810, however, broke down on the question of Hanoverians and Spaniards, and in November Mackenzie returned to England.

This must have been a cruel disappointment. All hope of release before the end of the war was at an end, and on both sides the temptation to breach of parole became very strong. In the autumn of 1812 the Transport Office issued a list of 590 attempted and 270 successful escapes by French officers. The *Moniteur* retaliated by a catalogue of 355 English escapes, which number, it argued, was proportionately much larger. First on the list stood Sir James Craufurd, consul at Rotterdam in 1788, and Secretary of Legation at Copenhagen in 1796. He might have left Calais in 1803, but chose to wait, and lost the chance. "The arrival of a lady

s

from Paris next day," sarcastically wrote Talbot to Whitworth, "explains the motive of his refusal [to leave], and brings consolation, I trust, to the love-sick prisoner." Lady Craufurd, daughter of General Gage, seems to have been safe in England or Scotland. In October 1804 Craufurd had permission to go to Aix-la-chapelle for two months, but he made his way to England, pleading in excuse his wife's illness and the loss of promotion. Let us hope that his wife thought him sufficiently punished for his attentions to the lady from Paris, especially as gallantry ran in the family, for his cousin Quintin, as we have seen, had the same failing.* Craufurd's fellow-diplomatist, Alexander Cockburn, was more scrupulous as to his parole. Consul at Hamburg, he was detained at Paris in May 1803, but his French creole wife, Yolande de Vignier, obtained an introduction to Josephine, and thus procured his release. His son, the future Chief Justice, whom we all remember well, was then lying in his cradle. Cockburn became minister to Colombia, and died in 1852, thirteen years after Craufurd.

Brooke, M.P. for Newton, Lancashire, followed the example of escaping. His clever French valet

* Shortly before Quintin Craufurd's death at Paris in 1819 his wife was prosecuted for defamation by Sir James, for relating in drawing-rooms that he had forced Quintin, pistol in hand, to settle £48,000 a year on him. The suit was dismissed. Quintin's servants afterwards prosecuted Sir James for defamation, apparently at their mistress's instigation.

having procured a passport for two merchants, Brooke left a large dinner party at Valenciennes, boldly drove through the town, and reached Cologne. Broughton, a Staffordshire baronet's son, escaped in the guise of a courier. Sir Beaumont Dixie escaped by pretending to be drowned while bathing, but was recaptured. Colonel Annesley, apparently the son and successor of Lord Annesley, who was on his honeymoon in May 1803, got away from Verdun in December 1811. Alexander Don, the future baronet, fled from Paris in February 1810. Philip Champion de Crespigny, brother of the first baronet—he was married at the Danish Embassy, Paris, in 1809, his bride having apparently gone over to share his detention—escaped from St. Germain in May 1811. He lived to be eighty-six, dying in 1851. Dr. Roget (nephew of Sir Samuel Romilly), the future author of the Bridgewater Treatise on Physiology, and of the Thesaurus of Synonyms, escaped in July 1803 from Geneva, his father's birthplace. He lived till 1869, and was just a nonogenarian.

It is but fair to say that the bulk of the 355 defaulters belonged to the mercantile marine, and were not hostages, but regular prisoners. Breach of parole was a rare exception among the aristocratic and professional captives, most of whom were liberated only by death or by Napoleon's fall. Thus the Marquis of Tweeddale died at Verdun in

1804, two months after his wife. Lady Style, widow of Sir Charles Style, and sister of Lord Powerscourt, expired at St. Omer in 1803. Her former detention in 1793 does not seem to have taught her the necessity of hasty flight ten years later. Sir John Coghill died in 1827. James Parry, ex-editor of the *Courier*, was a confirmed paralytic at Orleans when the rupture occurred, yet though, according to Lewis Goldsmith, he had previously been in the pay of France, neither past services nor physical decay procured him any indulgence. He was ordered to Verdun, and died there in 1805, a victim to lack of proper medical advice, and of money or influence for obtaining permission to go to Paris. James Payne, brother of the Pall Mall bookseller, and an eminent bibliographer, had stayed in Paris to assist in arranging the National Library, was detained, and died in 1809. Benfield, the banker, of whom I have already spoken, died in poverty in Paris in 1810. His youngest daughter later on married Grantley Berkeley. Boyd, Benfield's partner, beguiled his captivity by writing pamphlets on finance, and by arbitrating in a dispute between the French Government and Schweizer, a Swiss kinsman of Lavater. Boyd, styled by Schweizer "a man of great culture and recognised probity," partially retrieved his losses, sat again in Parliament, and died in 1837.

Hingston Tuckey, the navigator, was equally industrious, for he compiled three volumes of a maritime geography. Destined to die two years after his release, while exploring the river Congo, he was not a hostage, but a prisoner legitimately captured in 1805. So also was William Hamilton, a navy lieutenant, who was vice-consul or consul at Boulogne from 1822 to 1873, was knighted on his retirement, and died at Boulogne in 1877, at the age of eighty-eight, probably the last survivor of Napoleon's captives. The tradition in his adopted town is that his jailer's daughter at Verdun assisted him in an unsuccessful attempt to escape, and that he afterwards married her. Henry Grey MacNab, physician to the Duke of Kent, and professor of rhetoric at Glasgow University, likewise made France his home. He obtained leave to reside at Montpellier, pursued his studies in medicine and political economy, was enchanted with Robert Owen's educational theories, and remained in France till his death in 1823. Fraser Frisell, who has been already mentioned, and whose son-in-law is now a municipal councillor for Paris, must have known Lady Webb, wife of Sir Thomas Webb and sister of Lord Dillon, for she, too, was in the Chateaubriand and Récamier "set." Interned with her husband at Lyons, Lady Webb befriended a little English girl named Marianne, who about 1813 was found performing in the streets with a troop of mountebanks. It was supposed that the child had been lost or left behind by her parents when the war recommenced. She was sent to school, apprenticed, and became a nun. Her protectress, Lady Webb, was handsome, rather flighty, and gave balls at Lyons.

Among other hostages seemingly detained till 1814 were Lord de Blaquiere's son, who in 1812 succeeded to the title; Gustavus Hamilton, afterwards Lord Boyne; Lord Boyle, son of the Earl of Glasgow; Henry, son of Sir William Wolseley of Staffordshire,* Sir Thomas Lavie, and Colonel Phillips of the marines, who had accompanied Captain Cook round the world.

The rigour of the detention varied with the temper of the garrison commandants, and also, as must be owned, with the frequency or otherwise of attempts to escape. At Fontainebleau the captives were at first required simply to report themselves once a week and always to sleep in the town, a few days' absence, moreover, being winked at provided Paris was not visited. But subsequently they were forbidden to go more than a league, and had to answer the roll-call thrice a week. In December 1803 all the prisoners at Fontainebleau, Phalsbourg, and Marsal were transferred to Verdun and Charlemont. The presence of the wealthier class was so good for trade in the towns where they were quartered that an English newspaper compared them

---

* His brother Charles escaped from Spa; he was the "legislatorial attorney" of Birmingham in 1832.

to a flock of sheep whose fold was occasionally changed in order that the whole field, that is to say France, might be fertilised. Verdun, however, from its inland position, was the town most favoured in this respect. The hundred wealthy hostages indulged in horse-racing, cock-fighting, and amateur theatricals, in which last a Mr. Concanon was the most active, until he obtained permission to live at Vienna. The divorced wife of Lord Cadogan gave entertainments, and there were marriages in an unconsecrated building, the validity of which was disputed by reversioners to property. Some of the hostages got into prison for debt.

Captain Myles Byrne, an Irish refugee in the French service, relates that his Irish legionaries, marching to Boulogne in 1806, should have halted for a night at Verdun, but the commandant of the garrison, apprehensive of a collision, lodged them outside the town, through which they passed next morning before it was light enough for their green flag, inscribed "The Independence of Ireland," to be seen. When, however, the band struck up "Patrick's Day in the Morning," many windows were opened and gentlemen in their night-shirts peeped out, bewildered at hearing a Hibernian air. "The prisoners," Byrne says, "could ramble freely all day, but had to answer the roll-call at sunset." When his regiment stopped a night at Arras, the commandant deemed it prudent to make the English captives sleep for once in the citadel.* At Bitche some of them cut their names indelibly on the outer walls of the barrack, and a recent visitor has noticed well-known British patronymics.† Verdun, it should be mentioned, contained in 1804 700 Englishmen, 400 of them hostages, the rest soldiers and sailors, but by the end of 1805 only 150 hostages remained. They had two clubs, and in 1807 invited the townspeople to a masked ball. Some of the captives, as well civilians as soldiers, were without means, and had to be assisted by their comrades. At Valenciennes, Lord Barrington gave a good meal once a day at his house to his poor countrymen, and Lord Elgin subscribed 100 guineas to a fund for their relief. In 1807 the Birmingham Quakers started a subscription, and in 1811 London followed suit, but this was mainly, if not exclusively, for the prisoners proper. General Lord Blayney, captured in an engagement in Spain, was also commissioned to watch over their interests, and he travelled about France for this purpose.‡

Sturt, at first confined in the Temple, escaped from Meaux in 1810, and published in London his "Real State of France," which exposed the rapacity of General Wirion, commandant of Verdun. This pork-butcher's son levied blackmail on all indul-

---

* "Memoirs of Myles Byrne," Paris, 1863.
† Mr. Childers, in *Nineteenth Century*, May 1888.
‡ "Narrative of a Forced Journey through France," 1810-14.

gences, pleasures, and even vices. James Henry Lawrence,* a Knight of Malta, who also escaped, and in the same year published anonymously a "Picture of Verdun," gave full particulars of Wirion's shameless extortions. Permission even to walk out of the town was tariffed, much more permission to live in a villa outside. Wirion would coolly ask himself to dinner with his wealthy prisoners. A Dr. Madan also made a handsome profit by certifying to the indisposition of sluggards who shirked answering the early morning roll-call. The captives were a motley band. Some had gone to France to retrench, some to educate their children, a few to study the artistic plunder at the Louvre, others to avoid their creditors or engage in smuggling, others again to establish manufactories. There was no little gambling, on which Wirion levied his commission, but as a set-off there were subscription schools for young sailors and children, and other forms of beneficence. Lawrence speaks of the brutality of his gaolers. A navy lieutenant, Leviscourt, after being on parole in the town for several years, was confined in the citadel. Thus relieved from his parole, he attempted to escape, but was recaptured, threatened with death, and by sentence of court-martial was dragged by gendarmes through

* He had published books in German at Weimar and Berlin in 1793 and 1801, one of them a women's rights or rather anti-marriage novel, the "Empire of the Nairs," reprinted in London 1811.

the streets, a heavy cannon-ball chained to his leg. Lawrence while in captivity wrote a drama entitled *The Englishman at Verdun, or the Prisoner of Peace*, and after his escape he published it. He acknowledges that at Nimes the captives were well treated.*

Until 1810 the captives were posted up in home news by the *Argus*, the English newspaper in Paris started by Goldsmith and continued by Dutton. Its leading articles were virulently anti-British, but it reprinted military dispatches and parliamentary debates from the London journals, and it did not always satisfy Napoleon, who in 1807 sent orders to Fouché to have it better conducted. Its articles were attributed to Bodini, who in 1796 edited *Bell's Messenger*, was addicted to drink and extravagance, was expelled under the Alien Act, and going to France, was reader of English newspapers for Bonaparte. The *Argus* must have been a considerable expense to the French Government, and its original purpose of circulating in England had never been realised. Its disappearance must, however, have been felt as a privation by the captives, whose family correspondence underwent the scrutiny of a French official, Lenoir.† Visits to England, at least by ladies, were occasionally allowed. Mrs. Mary Bishop, a widow with four daughters, obtained

---

* See his "Picture of Verdun."

† According to Sturt, 4000 letters were detained for years at the French post-office.

a passport to England and back in 1813, on the plea of securing an inheritance, and according to her petition to Louis XVIII. after the Restoration, she was entrusted with a mission by royalists who afterwards ignored her claims to gratitude. Such visits were made *viâ* Morlaix and Plymouth. Savary, Napoleon's Minister of Police, boasts in his Memoirs not only of procuring the escape of French prisoners from England and of keeping spies there, but of permitting occasional visits in order thereby to fathom Bourbon intrigues.

The retreat from Moscow gave the captives the first tangible prospect of deliverance, yet for a time it aggravated their position. In January 1814 those interned at Verdun were ordered to Blois, as also those in Paris, but very few of the latter obtaining exemption. At Blois they were ordered on to Guéret. There news arrived of Napoleon's abdication, and they were released. Some of them left debts behind them which they apparently regarded as "spoiling the Egyptians," for in 1839 a deputation from Verdun had an audience of Lord Palmerston to solicit repayment of £140,000 due by the former captives. The creditors, it seems, had waited till 1837, or had made representations to the individual debtors, but from that date the French Government had urged their claim to repayment by the British Treasury. The deputation stated that the number of prisoners at Verdun was never below

1200 and frequently rose to 2000, that many of them held high rank in the army or in society, that credit and loans were given them from feelings of humanity, and that vouchers could be produced before a mixed commission. They suggested that the sum could be repaid out of the surplus of £9,000,000 remaining from the £60,000,000 paid by France to indemnify British sufferers, and they urged that French prisoners in England had been released conditionally on the discharge of their debts. The treaty of peace, indeed, required prisoners of war to pay their debts, but the English prisoners mostly quitted France without waiting for formal release or for the conclusion of peace. The deputation apparently effected nothing. It was obviously difficult for the English Government to create a precedent by liquidating private debts, and the Verdun creditors had to whistle for their money.

Paris was again flooded with English in the spring of 1815, but when Napoleon's arrival became imminent there was a perfect stampede. One of his first questions was whether there were many English. On being told that nearly all had left, he replied, "Ah, they recollect what I did before, but such things are not repeated." Their alarm, however, was very natural, and their flight the plainest dictate of prudence. He might not have laid hands on them before Waterloo, but had he returned a victor, who could have trusted to his moderation?

Conclusion.

THIS book, beginning with 1789 and ending with 1814, covers exactly twenty-five years of Englishmen's experiences in France. That quarter of a century was undoubtedly the most thrilling period of French history, and not a few of our countrymen witnessed the whole of it. Yet we can scarcely envy their lot, for perspective is necessary to appreciate the gravity of events, and the position of spectator had not merely inconveniences but dangers. To us, however, these spectators are interesting as a psychological study. They present as striking contrasts as the Frenchmen among whom they lived. We see generosity and selfishness, enthusiasm and mockery, patriotism and anti-patriotism, fanaticism and calculation, refinement and brutality, curiosity and apathy, jubilation and anguish, fraternal affection and fraternal hatred. We see servility and manliness, human nature at its best and at its worst, now touching the clouds, now grovelling in the mire. For individuals as for nations the Revolution was an ordeal drawing out the brightest and the darkest sides of human character. It was a forcing-house which stimulated

the growth of the finest flowers and of the most
noxious weeds. Men who in ordinary times would
have been commonplace, neither very good nor very
bad, were developed by it into heroes or demons.
Englishmen, indeed, never played more than a
secondary part, and had not the opportunity either
of soaring to such heights or sinking to such depths
as natives, yet the maxim *noscitur à sociis* is strik-
ingly applicable. A French proverb says, "Tell
me whom you like and I will tell you what you
are like." What Englishmen might have been is
evidenced by their hero-worship as well as to some
extent by their acts. Grieve was not only the
admirer but in his way the imitator of Marat, as
Arthur was of Robespierre, as Helen Williams was
of Madame Roland, *minus* her ambition and im-
patience of social superiority. The two O'Sullivans
realised the calumnious legend of André Chénier's
betrayal by his brother, and the two Badgers are
a parallel to Frenchmen who eagerly perished by
mistake for fathers or brothers. Pigott, however,
with his reforms in food and costume, is perhaps
sui generis. The Abbé Edgeworth, facing what he
believed to be certain death, towers head and shoul-
ders over his countrymen; but Money was ready
to risk his life for the King and his Swiss, though
the King was not his sovereign nor the Swiss his
countrymen; Helen Williams sheltered a proscript,
and scorned to bow the knee to Napoleon; even

Paine, in voting against Louis's death, displayed a moral courage for which his antecedents would not have prepared us.

If Englishmen failed to gauge the character of Napoleon, and placed themselves in his power, it was excusable, seeing that Frenchmen were equally mistaken. If they applauded the rise of a tyranny more grinding and relentless than the old monarchy over whose fall they had exulted, almost the whole French nation did the like. The long detention at Verdun and elsewhere was in its way as much a touchstone of character as the prisons of the Terror. There, too, we see frivolity and earnestness, some killing time in a fashion not always even harmless, others diligently utilising it. We see some earning their release, others obtaining it by daring or stratagem.

We end, as we began, with jubilation. The fall of Napoleon was as much a cause of rejoicing to Englishmen, in France or at home, as the fall of the Bastille had been. If, indeed, we can fuse into one picture these hundreds of our countrymen, we are reminded of a biography or novel in which the hero sets out under the happiest auspices, encounters all sorts of vicissitudes and dangers, and finally emerges into tranquillity and comfort.

APPENDIX.

T.

APPENDIX.

A.

Sir William Codrington's Imprisonment.

(See page 148.)

THIS letter, dated January 3, 1795, and received in London February 23, 1795, is fully confirmed, as to the noisomeness of the *Conciergerie* and the light-heartedness or apathy of the inmates, by Beugnot and other French prisoners:—

LIBERTÉ, EGALITÉ, FRATERNITÉ, OU LA MORT.

PARIS, 14 *Nivose*, 3me *année Républicaine*.

You may think, perhaps, that you have lived long enough to know how to date a letter, but I can show you that the wisest may learn.

You may also learn that I am all alive again; how that comes about I am at a loss to tell you, unless you have faith in predestination; and, after all, that is the best way of accounting for it, that my time was not come; otherwise I presume I should have accompanied many of my companions. However, all is well that ends well; but would it were ended! For though I have escaped one great storm, the weather still seems inclined to be squally. To finish a history of fifteen months would be rather a bore, and would carry me beyond the limits of my paper; therefore, if you please, we will abridge it as much as possible.

To begin, then, I was arrested because I was born in one kingdom instead of in another; and also it was taken much amiss that my countrymen should accept of a town that was very kindly offered to them.

As I was above two hundred leagues distant from the town in question, and that I had not been consulted whether the offer should have been accepted or refused, I thought they might as well have found some other person to have punished instead of me. However, I was conducted to a high tower upon the sea-shore built by William the Conqueror. I was there placed in a room where there was, sure enough, no glass to the windows, but that deficiency was made up by the number of bars. What added to the agreeableness of the *séjour* was, that it happened to be exactly at the equinox, so I could not complain for the want of air. After a few days' residence there, an officer came into my room and told me he was ordered to accompany me to my house (which was about a mile from the tower), in order for me to be present at the examination of my papers. I accordingly followed him, and when I got into the street I was surprised to find guards to escort me sufficient in number to have defended the castle had it been besieged by an enemy. In this stately manner I was conducted to my house and back again.

After a few days I was informed they had found nothing among my papers but family matters and an innocent correspondence. However, they were sent to the National Deputy, who was then at Rennes, who put a different construction upon my correspondence; and he ordered me to be conducted thither. I was then thrown into a prison more disagreeable in every respect than that which I had quitted. After a few days there arrived a person from St. Malo's with a petition in my favour, and signed also by the Municipality of St. Servan. The person who brought it got a reputable woman to present it to the Deputy. She had no sooner done it than he began abusing her in a most indecent manner, and threatened to send her to prison. She defended herself by saying she was not acquainted with the contents of the letter, and that it was left at her house by a person who did not leave his name. "I wish," says he, "I could find him out; I would commit him directly; and as for the Municipality, I will break them," says he, "as soon as I return thither, for he is a conspirator, and I have the proof in my hands," holding up a paper. When I found how the land lay, I desired to be heard, but that was refused me, and in a few days after I had a visit from a Commissary of War, together with a national one, who signified to me that I must prepare to set off for Paris, they having received orders to conduct me thither. At eleven o'clock at night there came a guard and conducted me to the Diligence, where I was chained like an assassin to two other unfortunate people, and after travelling night and day during four days and a half, we arrived at Paris, where the Commissary of War got out of the coach, thinking it beneath his dignity to be seen upon such an errand; and sure enough it was very unusual to send such a conductor upon such an occasion. But Carrier had swelled up my importance by calling me a milord, and *ci-devant* this and *ci-devant* t'other; and in order to keep up the ball he occasioned me to be accompanied in an extraordinary manner, that he might gain the more credit to himself.* Our two other conductors

---

* "Lord Codrington is in the prison of Rennes. Papers which I think very interesting have been seized upon him. I shall soon send him to the Revolutionary Tribunal." (Carrier's letter to the Convention, September 25, 1793.)

conveyed us to the fatal *Conciergerie*. The entrance therein (at that period) and death were nearly synonymous. From the compliments we met with upon the road, I never thought we should have got so far, or that we should have lived to have died honourable deaths. Our conductors never attempted to quell the populace except when they cried out, "Rascals and conspirators;" they then answered that there was but one.

However, after so long and fatiguing a journey I comforted myself with the hope of one good night's rest, but was sadly disappointed when the *concierge* told us there was no private room vacant, and that we must sleep in the straw-room; but, added he, "take care of your pocket-book and watches, for you will be among a den of thieves, who will rob you of all you have." With such consolation we entered into the prison court, where there were some hundreds of unfortunate people of all denominations. Being tired and hungry, we employed a commissary of the prison to get us something to eat. When it came we were obliged to make use of a low parapet wall for a table (as the straw-rooms are kept shut during the day, and those that inhabit them are obliged to stay in the open air all the day long, be the weather what it may). The people in the court took compassion upon us and lent us knives and forks, and informed us, also, that by applying to the superior turnkey in a *prevailing* manner we might possibly obtain a place in a room. That business was presently undertaken, and two of us procured the seventeenth part of a small apartment. The beds were placed so near together that one was obliged to get in at the feet; and though we paid for them apart, I was three weeks before I could get any sheets; and when at length I had them, I could with great facility have crept through them. But the room being very small, and the ceiling so very low, and so many persons stove in so narrow a compass, the air was so bad we could none of us sleep, at least not for more than an hour, often less, and sometimes not at all. As we were locked up every evening about five o'clock, and the door not opened till near ten the next morning, a tub was placed in the room. . . . We had in the room with us a tolerably good physician, who advised us to burn incense, &c., every night before we went to bed, in order to purify the air, and to take a mouthful of brandy every morning as soon as we got up, as a preventive against infection. We all of us rose in a morning with a great dryness in the throat or something of a soreness. At twelve o'clock every night we used to be visited by three or four turnkeys, with as many great dogs. With large staves they used to thump against the ceiling, open the windows, and with an iron hammer beat against the bars to see that all was safe and sound. Another visit we were also subject to that was still more unpleasant, though it came but seldom. When we used to hear the jingling of the keys upon our staircase in the evening, we were sure it was to summons some one of us to appear the next morning at the fatal tribunal. As soon as the door opened, each was apprehensive of the lot falling upon himself. The taking leave the next morning of the unfortunate person before he went to take his trial, with so little hopes of ever seeing him again, was another melancholy proceeding.

Four months I passed in this pleasing abode, having seen half my room companions quit me to take their final leave; and the half of that half have since shared the same fate. One day with another we used to reckon on five condemnations, and esteemed that sufficiently severe for those times, notwithstanding how much they had since increased upon that number.

Towards the latter part of my *séjour* we had thrown

in amongst us upwards of a hundred prisoners from Nantes, most of them opulent people, and some among them of a great age. They had travelled in a severe season for forty days together, and had been most miserably fed and lodged on their journey; twenty-five died upon the road; as many were put into the infirmary of the prison upon their arrival; the rest were put in the straw-rooms; for there was then no other vacancy, our numbers amounting at that time to about 650. But notwithstanding the precaution of placing the most unhealthy of them apart, still the disorder they brought with them was so violent and so infectious that it began to spread in the prison. As I preferred the chance of a short death to a lingering one, I made what interest I could to bring on my trial, contrary indeed to the advice of my counsel, who would have had me wait for the chance of more lenient measures. I, however, succeeded in my attempt. But before one appears at the tribunal one's accusation and papers are laid before a council of judges, and they determine whether or no there are sufficient grounds for accusation; and luckily for me, they determined that there were not.[*] By that means I escaped the severity of that fatal court.

Though guiltless, still as a subject of Great Britain I was doomed to confinement; but by the assistance of some friends I got to be transferred to a Maison de Santé [†] instead of to another prison. A servant who waited upon us and my hairdresser were both taken ill of the Nantes fever the day I left the place, and died a few days after. I had begun to droop the few last days; but it was amazing the instantaneous effect that the change of air had upon me, like a fish that had been out of water for some

[*] January 18, 1794.
[†] Kept by Mahay, Rue du Chemin Vert. Removed thither February 2, 1794.

time and thrown into it again. In less than two hours I felt quite a different person. I dined with some friend by the indulgence of my conductor, and ate with a very good appetite, which had quite failed me latterly. Awful as that abode was, you would scarcely believe, perhaps, that I have not been so cheerful since as I was there, nor have I since seen so many cheerful people. One would think that nature had formed one's nerves according to the different situations that they may be exposed to. *On se fait à tout*, and one may accustom oneself to bad fortune as one does to good.

We used frequently to breakfast and dine at each other's room, which time generally passed in mirth. Most of us thought we had but a short time allotted to us, and that it was better to enjoy that little as much as we could. I do not recollect, among the hundreds that I both saw and spoke to after their condemnation, that one single one of them, except Madame du Barri, showed any softness upon the occasion; and several seemed as cheerful as if nothing had happened to them.

After I had remained a few months at my new abode, where we were comfortable enough, things took another turn, and without beat of drum we were all conveyed in a hurry to another prison,* where we had not been long before we were visited by a part of the Municipality of Paris, attended by a numerous guard, and all ordered to our rooms, with sentinels placed at our doors to prevent our going-out. Each of us was visited by a municipal and his attendants, who as soon as they came into the room told us with a threat to deliver all our money, knives, forks, scissors, &c., &c., and that whoever hid the least matter demanded should immediately be sent to the *Conciergerie*. I was in a very small room and alone, and yet they passed above an hour with me, to the amazement

* Prison Coignard, May 3, 1794.

of my neighbours. They examined my trunks and my drawers a second time, to see if there were not false bottoms to them; they were mean enough to stoop to take the buckles out of one's shoes. This visit was soon followed by another, to examine if our garden was not convenient to make a burying-ground of. Though no small one, they did not find it big enough. They afterwards went to another prison, a few doors from us, where they found a part of the garden would suit them, and where they occasioned to be dug a great hole, in which in a very few days they stove in two thousand two hundred corpses, and afterwards proceeded to make another hole of the kind, which they palisaded round, and was in a field opposite our prison. Having been tried by the council and acquitted, I concluded I had been out of harm's way; but from the above proceedings and unpleasant reports that went about, we concluded we were all of us destined for the other world. But very luckily for us, Robespierre and many of his party were overthrown on the 9th, and they had fixed on the 11th for a general massacre in the prisons.

"Thus! thus! and no nearer!" say the seamen. After that event there was a general cry in favour of the prisoners, and many were daily set at liberty; by which means my habitation became so thinned of its inhabitants that they transferred us to another prison; but they forgot me in the scramble, and I remained there alone for some time, having the whole house to range in, and thirty men, who used to mount guard night and day, to watch my person. At length they found they had left me by myself, and that it was not absolutely necessary to harass such a number of men to guard a single harmless prisoner. They ordered me to follow my companions to the Luxembourg,* where I found G. O'Hara and his

* November 25, 1794.

suite, Temple Lutterill, and Swale. There were there many other English, but most of them of an inferior class.

As the decree for the arrest of the English had not been repealed, I saw but little chance of obtaining my liberty before a peace. However, it at length came by accident, and when I the least expected it. A friend of mine applied to a printer of his acquaintance to demand me as his journeyman. By that means, together with a little interest of friends, I slipped my neck out of the collar, after having remained near fifteen months in prison.*

I shall remain here during the winter, and perhaps for a longer term, as this place, all things considered, is the best to reside in as long as the war lasts.

I take the same opportunity of sending you this as the inhabitant of Davies Street took when she wrote to me in the beginning of last June, which I received but a few days since, the person to whom it was directed not daring to deliver it, or even to inquire after me, such was the severity of those times.

As this epistle, or rather narrative, is already too long, I shall not add to the length of it, especially as I think there is a degree of uncertainty of its ever reaching you. But that my packet may risk the less, I have confined my correspondence to females only, notwithstanding it is said that there never was a plot but that there was a woman in it. If such be their ideas in this country, I shall have taken some pains and have used much ink and paper for nothing, and had better have confined myself by merely saying, "If you are well, I am well, &c., &c. I am so, and hope you are so; so adieu!"—Affectionately yours, W. C.

Salut et fraternité. Pray remember me to all the family.

* December 2, 1794.

B.

Narrative of the English Benedictine Nuns, Rue de l'Alouette, Paris.

(From a MS. at Stoneyhurst College. See page 160.)

The community of Benedictines, established in the Rue de Champ de l'Alouette, in Paris, in the year 1652, remained under the protection of Divine Providence in the regular observance of their rules and constitutions, until the year 1792; in which year their convent, as well as all other religious establishments in France, were put "*en arrestation*," by reason of the Revolution, which began in the year 1788.

From this year until 1792 the community continued in alarm on this account, and at the same time were afflicted with much sickness among themselves. Their worthy superior, Mrs. Bond, was taken ill of her last sickness, which deprived the community of her at the beginning of their troubles; also in the same year died three choir religious, and in the beginning of the following year two lay sisters. At the end of this same year died also our most worthy friend and respected superior, who acted for the communities under the Archbishop. In this moment of distress at the death of our dear and lamented Mother Prioress the nuns were greatly terrified by a report that the people in the "Quartiers" intended to take up the body as soon as they could. The religious sent to the "Section" to beg that guards should be sent, and they were so. They patrolled the gardens in the night, and the nuns watched within. But nevertheless they found the only way to secure it was to open the grave and transport the body into another which they had made for that purpose during the night. It

APPENDIX. 301

was doubtful for what reason the people had this intention. This was in November, four months after the taking of the Bastille, which was the beginning of the depredations caused by the Revolution. The convent being in the neighbourhood of the Bastille, on its being set on fire, their sick, particularly the Reverend Mother Prioress, who then lay in a dying state, were greatly alarmed by the firing of guns, shoutings, drumming, &c., which continued day and night for some weeks. The smoke and blazing of the flames were terrifying to all, so that the nuns had much to do to support their courage and compose the minds of their sick. The Assembly of the States then gave orders for the church-doors of the convents to be shut, and this, indeed, the religious found very agreeable. But then came the mobs, consisting of the worst sort of people, who surrounded the convent. The nuns, not knowing what to do, sent out to them in a kind manner to know if they wished for any refreshment and it should be given to them. This pleased them, and after having taken plenty they dispersed, without using any violence.

Then came orders from the parish that no Mass was to be said in the church of the convent by any priest, except he had faculties from the "intruding curate." But this order the community positively refused to obey, saying they neither could nor would acknowledge any other authority than their own Archbishop, who was not then in Paris. And it is remarkable that they were not offended, but went away in a respectful manner and assured the nuns of their protection. Next came the curate of the parish, desiring that the usual preparations should be made, it being within the Octave of the Feast of Corpus Christi, when the procession is made to all the convents in each parish. The nuns said their church-doors were shut by the orders of the Municipality. He said he should have them opened again. They replied, if he intended to use force they could not help it, but as he was not their lawful superior and pastor, they could not open the doors.

The *curé* then went away, and sent a commissioner, who came in a very civil manner and asked if he could prevail upon them to have the church-doors opened. But he was answered "No." He then asked if they would hang the street with tapestry as usual. They said "Yes;" at this he seemed surprised that he should gain so much, and returned several times to ask if he had understood them right.

But as the police could demand this, they thought it better to do so. Some time after this the civil magistrates gave orders that all the church-doors belonging to the convents should be opened. And after this their church remained so till they were imprisoned in their own convent, which took place on October 3, 1793, at which time all the other churches in France were demolished. People then came from all parts of Paris to attend Mass in the nuns' church. Their friends began to be much alarmed for the safety of the religious on this account. But the common people insisted on it so much that the magistrates ordered the doors should remain open.

The first visit in which they entered the convent was in the autumn of the year 1793. A body of men, with their leader, demanded entrance, surrounded by a vast number of people. This visit was made to find French writings. But all had been previously destroyed, except one letter from a deputy, which they approved of. The second visit was on Holy Thursday, about two o'clock in the afternoon. This was to discover if there were any priests concealed; but not finding any, they went to search "the deposit," and after having inspected its contents, they permitted each religious to take out the parchment whereon her vows were written, and then put the seal of the "Grand Nation" on all the papers, contracts, registers, &c. The third visit was made on the 8th of September, in the same year (1793), at about two o'clock in the morning. After having visited the confessor's apartments, and sealed up his money, papers, &c., they then rang the bells in a very hasty manner, and continued to do so till they had alarmed the whole convent, saying the religious need not dress, but must open the doors immediately, as they, the administrators of the Great Nation, were come to search for writings, &c. When they entered, the sight, noise, and confusion were terrible to the nuns. They searched every cell, turned over all they pleased, and proceeded on in this violence till near five in the morning, when they permitted the nuns to leave them and go to the choir to say matins, some among them acknowledging it to be the Feast of the Nativity of the Blessed Virgin. The superior and another religious remained with the commissioners, and they went out, which was before six o'clock in the morning. The fourth visit was made on the 3rd of October, in the afternoon, and on this, the religious were all made prisoners, having been denounced as holding assemblies in their house. And when the inquiry had been held and the accusation found to be false, according to the orders from the "Departement" to place the community under arrest, they were placed under a guard, to be maintained at their expense. After making a strict search through the convent, and an inventory of all its effects, they departed about midnight. They returned next day, and after visiting the confessor's apartments, placed him also under a guard, at his expense.

Then came commissioners from the "Departement" to view the convent within and without, to fit it up for the reception of prisoners, whom; to tranquillise the nuns, they said should be only ladies of their own nation. In the beginning of November the *concierge*, or keeper of the prison, came to announce himself and show his powers in form. The first interview showed what the community had to expect; he said the confessor should be sent away to another prison, but that they would give us another. But the Rev. Mother Prioress, who had been selected at the death of Mrs. Bond, viz., Mrs. Theresa Johnson, replied that we would on no account receive any other if sent to us. He answered that in that case she should be sent to another prison.

On the 8th of November the prisoners began to enter; but till some time after the nuns continued their choir duties. The keeper informed the superior that the "Departement" were collecting from each church all the sacred vessels, and said that the "Section" sent orders for her to prepare for their coming. They came, and entered the church. The confessor had made all things ready, and left open the door of the tabernacle; they took away thence all the plate, as well as that which remained in the sacristy.

The nuns got from a friend a pewter chalice, &c., and the confessor said Mass on the 23rd of the same month. The fifth visit was to make a still more strict search for all the plate, &c.

They obliged the prioress to go out into the confessor's apartments, which were without of the enclosure, and there to make a declaration of all the plate she had, signifying that it would be a capital crime if she kept anything which belonged to the nation. They took the Remonstrance, Thuribles, silver figures from the crosses, spoons, &c., and everything they could find to be silver, and all the gold lace from the vestments. The community continued to have Mass said till the 25th of November, when the keeper informed them that they could no longer have Mass, and that he expected the "Commissaires" from the section. They came and called for the superior to attend them in the church, there to give them an account of all the copper and brass belonging to the church. This was a mere ceremony, as they then began to strip both the church and the choir. Their looks, dress, and actions were equally dreadful, and can only be compared to our ideas of infernal beings. They tore down the shrines, pictures, and crosses. With joy mixed with fury they kicked up and down the church what they threw down. They acted in a similar manner in the sacristy and chapter-house, where all the ornaments were kept, so that all was taken away and the large cupboards pulled down. On the 1st of December 1793 our worthy and much respected confessor, the Rev. Father John Placid Nailor, was taken away from the community and placed with several others in the Scotch college, which was also made a prison.

He had been for a long time in a very bad state of health, and could not attend on the community for some weeks, or if he did, it was with the assistance of his man, who brought him downstairs to the parlour grate, that in this time of distress he might be able to speak to the nuns and they to him. But having found benefit from blisters on his legs, he recovered so far as to be able to walk, although the blisters were never properly healed. In this suffering state the keeper left him no peace till he got him transferred. In a few weeks he was again taken from the prison at the Scotch college, and carried to his own convent, which belonged to the Benedictine monks at St. Edmund's, which was also now made a prison.

The good prior, the Rev. Mr. Parker, rendered him all the service in his power, and he remained there until December 1794, when he was set at liberty, at which time the community being transferred to their third prison, which was at the English Austin nuns, Rue des Fossés St. Victor in Paris, Mr. Nailor took lodgings in the seminary belonging to the Eudistes in Rue des Postes, which was then in the possession of the nation. But a lay brother hired it and let it out to priests and chosen lodgers, through which they had the means of having Mass, which he said daily until a few days before his death.

He came to the Fossés several times to see the community before he fell sick, and they were permitted to speak to him, the first time since their separation, through an iron grate in the street door in presence of the guard. But as the Rev. Mother Prioress was confined to her bed and could not walk, they obtained permission from the keeper that Mr. Nailor might be conducted by the keeper's wife into the community's apartments, and he made a short and farewell visit to them all. He returned home, and died on the 16th of January 1795.

To return to the before-named period, November 1793, when the community were placed under arrest in their own convent, Rue du Champ de l'Alouette.

The house began to be crowded with prisoners of both sexes, consisting chiefly of nobility—a German prince and his brother, a princess who, taken from the convent in the night with twelve or thirteen other prisoners to the prison of St. Pélagie, and in a few days were put to death. The Duke and Duchess de —— were confined with her in the convent, and attended her till she was carried away. Their sister, the Countess d'Albane, also was detained, with their daughter, the Duchess de Montmorency, with their child and attendant. In short, their number increased so rapidly that the keeper called for all the rooms, in which he placed the prisoners according to their rank.

In the council room and the library adjoining to it were four or five ladies. In the chapter house a family. In each room in the infirmary five or six ladies. In the novices' rooms seven bedsteads, one of iron for the Duke, who was so large a man that he could not enter at some of the room doors, and when the Duchess his daughter was ill he could not enter her chamber to visit her, because the doorway would not admit him. In the work-room were as many bedsteads as could stand. They were removed during the day, and all the gentlemen occupied it till late at night, when their beds were made. In the refectory as many beds were placed as could stand side by side; the same was the case in the cloisters and outhouses, and in this manner the whole enclosure was filled from top to bottom.

But it was a happy circumstance for the religious that their convent, being in a remote part of the city, was for that reason chosen as the more secure prison for the nobility; by which means there happened to be none in it but those from whom nuns experienced the best behaviour and on every occasion kindness and respect. And it is but justice to observe that the manner in which this portion of the French nobility behaved in such afflicting circumstances was truly Christian and edifying to those who were in prison with them. Several among them suffered death, and prepared themselves for it, having neither priests nor sacraments. A lady and her son eighteen years of age were brought in. She had lived too much in the dissipation of high life. She was observed to walk about alone and look very sad under her misfortunes. Sometimes she would cast up her eyes towards the windows of the nuns' cells when in the court, but as the religious kept themselves apart shut up in their cells, she could not speak to them as she seemed to wish to do. But one day she ventured to knock at one of the cell doors under the pretext of presenting the nun with a silk gown. In this interview she unfolded her heart and declared the afflicted state of her mind. Expecting shortly to be put to death, and being totally unprepared, having for a long time neglected her duty to God, she begged the nuns would assist her to implore Heaven on her behalf. Some days after was brought to the prison a very worthy and respectable priest, who was an uncle of this lady. He was a chanoine of the Church of St. Geneviève, and had disapproved much of his niece's conduct.

She finding this favourable opportunity, which she considered as sent from God, lost no time in making herself known to him, who was ignorant where she was. He gave her his assistance in such a manner that she was enabled to die in a very happy manner very shortly after. She was beheaded with her son and daughter and several others on the same day. The religious were now deprived of their church, choir, and every part of the convent except their cells and a small room in the infirmary. The gardens and burial-ground were likewise all occupied for the use of the prisoners, for whose convenience the graves were laid flat, and the chapel of the Blessed Virgin, which stood in the middle of the cemetery, taken down, all the crosses burnt, and the large gravestones carried off. They then made gravel walks over the graves and turned the whole into a pleasure garden, which was filled every day with gentlemen as well as ladies. The nuns, being still in the religious dress, remained as near together as possible, observing their regular duties as punctually as their situation would permit, surrounded by alarms and continually insulted by the keeper for appearing in the religious dress, so that they could not pass from room to room with safety. On the 29th of December they put off the religious habit.

From the time the religious were put under arrest, all their effects were put in sequestration, so that they could receive no rents; therefore, from the 3rd of October till the 24th of December 1793, the community had to maintain themselves from what small property remained in the house, which was merely sufficient to keep them alive. On the 24th of December the Commissioners came from the department, and brought for each nun 200 livres, from which sum they had to pay the guard. It being now the depth of winter, and every room taken from the community which had a chimney in it, the nuns were obliged by reason of the cold to confine themselves to their cells. . . .

[Here the MS. breaks off. On the 15th of July the nuns were removed in the night, in six coaches, to the Castle of Vincennes, locked up in narrow cells, unable to see out of their windows. Four months after, they were taken back to Paris in a cart, and brought to the Convent of the Austin nuns in the Fossés St. Victor, who were also prisoners in their own house. On the 1st of March 1795 they regained their liberty, and recovered part of their linen and furniture. By the sale of these they raised supplies for their journey, left Paris June 19th, and arrived in London July 5th, 1795. They settled in the same year at Marnhull in Dorsetshire, and eventually removed to Colwich, Staffordshire.]

C.

Narrative of English Benedictine Nuns of Cambray.

(From a MS. at Stoneyhurst College. See p. 221.)

In the summer of the year 1793, the allied armies being near the gates of Cambray, the religious were repeatedly ordered in the most threatening manner by the district of the above place to lay in provisions for six months against the siege which was then about to take place. We accordingly provided ourselves with such a stock of necessaries as our finances would allow us to purchase. From the commencement of the unhappy troubles we had been constantly alarmed by the visits or decrees of the agents in the Revolution, who were nowhere more outrageous than at Cambray, though our being conscious of not having given the least offence made us willing to flatter ourselves we were on that account in some degree of safety. However, on Sunday, October 13th, 1793, the district of Cambray sent four of their agents to fix the public seals on all papers and effects belonging to us.

These commissioners appeared at the convent at about half-past eight at night. We had retired to our cells, having to rise at midnight to perform matins, so that it was some time before our superior could open the enclosure door, at which they seemed not a little displeased.

The Rev. Mr. Walker, who from a motive of charity assisted us as spiritual director, was just recovering from a dangerous illness, and had retired to rest, but on hearing the general alarm, arose, and immediately came to comfort and encourage us. All being assembled, one of the men, who seemed the most cruel of the company, read a long paper, the purport of which was, that all effects belonging to us should be seized, and confiscated to the nation.

Mr. Walker began to expostulate, but their brutality soon silenced and astonished him; they then proceeded to fix the seals upon all the books, papers, &c., belonging to the superior and dame procuratrix, threatening them all the while how severely they should be punished in case they concealed even the smallest article of their property.

Having secured everything, they told us we were now to consider ourselves prisoners, and then wrote a long account of their own proceedings, at the close of which they added, by desire of the community, that the religious wished to remain prisoners in their own convent, under a guard, rather than be removed to any other place of confinement; this paper our superior and procuratrix signed. They left the convent about eleven o'clock at night to put the seals on everything in the out-buildings, an apartment in which was appointed for the use of the chaplain; this they performed with the most exact scrutiny. They arrested the Rev. Messrs. Walker and Higginson (the latter was a priest who, in consideration of the age and declining health of the former, had some months before been appointed to assist him).

To prevent these gentlemen from conversing with us, they immediately deprived us of all solace from them, by removing them the same night, though it was near twelve o'clock when they were hurried away. Mr. Walker was quite broken with grief, age, and infirmity. We had the affliction of seeing how very roughly and inhumanly he was treated, from our adjoining convent, and feared they were dragging him away for immediate execution, but Providence kindly reserved him to be our support and consolation in a future place of suffering. What we felt on this occasion may be more easily imagined than expressed. That night the above gentlemen were confined

in the Town House; next morning they were removed to
the Bishop's seminary, which formerly belonged to the
Jesuits, but it was at that time become what they termed
a *maison de détention.*

There they remained till the 20th of November 1793,
deprived of the most common necessaries, and were one
day and a half without any other food than a bit of
bread. They wrote to different innkeepers in the town,
and assured them of immediate pay for the scanty sub-
sistence they asked, but so offensive was the name of a
religious person to the greater part of Cambray, and the
few well-disposed so terrified at the cruelty and wicked-
ness of the times, that no answer was ever returned, nor
could they ever prevail on a barber to attend them for
any reward. At last a good woman who had lived with us
in quality of servant, hearing by chance of the pressing
distress of these gentlemen, had the courage, notwithstanding every difficulty and danger, to wait on them, and
procure for them the best victuals in her power. Mr.
Walker frequently said she had by her charitable assistance saved him from starving. To return to the community. From the moment the commissioners of the
district entered our house on the preceding Sunday, we
found ourselves strictly guarded, but were still made to
hope we might remain in our convent, as we had been
assured by members of the district in the most solemn
manner there was neither danger nor probability of our
being sent out. That this was all treachery we were
afterwards convinced, for the next day, Friday the 18th,
we were suddenly seized upon by a body of light guards,
part of whom surrounded the street door, whilst the
rest entered the convent, with a rabble crowd attending. A very brutal man sent by the district headed
them. When he came to the enclosure door, his first
question was, "Have you laid in provisions for six

months?" On being assured that had been done, he seemed for an instant at a loss what to say. After a short pause he gave orders that we should be totally out of the house in half a quarter of an hour; that he would not allow us to take either trunk or box, but only each person a small bundle. His manner of speaking appeared so strangely insulting, it threw us into the greatest terror, so that amidst the hurry and confusion of so sudden and unexpected a calamity, overwhelmed with sorrow in being turned out of our much beloved abode, and for want of time to collect together our few clothes, many came away with only what they had then on. At that afflicting moment, the future want of necessaries found little or no place in our distressed minds. We were almost stupefied with grief. The procuratrix petitioned to bring away a small book which contained a few memorandums very useful to herself, but the man whom she addressed tore the book from her hand, telling her instantly to fetch brandy for the hussars, which command she was obliged to obey, whilst this barbarous man was running about the house with a club in his hand to hasten and affright us to be gone.

Thus in less than half an hour we were completely out and dispossessed of our whole property, without being able to learn of any one what was to be our fate, but thought death would soon have followed, and expected to be despatched by the fatal guillotine. On approaching the street door we found a coach and two carts, each strongly guarded by a detachment of hussars on horseback with drawn swords. We were hurried away with much precipitation. The guards seemed greatly displeased at this barbarous usage—some of them even shed tears, and on the road, with the most feeling compassion, even lent their own cloaks to those religious who were in the uncovered carts, to shelter them in some degree from the intense cold.

Through the whole dismal journey of five days they contributed all in their power to soften and alleviate the hardships they saw us exposed to; but it was not in their ability to prevent the populace treating us with the most insulting language through whatever towns and villages we passed, and when we arrived at any place to spend the night we were guarded by the soldiers who kept the prison in which we happened to be lodged, amongst whom we sometimes met with a variety of hardships and scenes of brutality, insomuch that we always dreaded the approach of night. We were twenty in number and one novice when expelled the convent, viz:—

	Aged
Mary Anselm Ann	79
Jane Alexander Gordon	78
Elizabeth Sheldon	73
Margaret Burgess	72
Elizabeth Haggerstone	68
Mary Blyde	64
Teresa Walmesley	55
Louisa Hagan	53
Elizabeth Knight	51
Elizabeth Partington	49
Mary Partington	42
Margaret Barnwall	37
Agnes Robinson	32
Anne Shepherd	31
Helen Shepherd	29

Lay Sisters—

	Aged
Ann Pennington	60
Louisa Lefebvre	59
Magdalen Kimberley	48
Ann Cayton	44
Martha Fryar	32
Jane Milner (novice)	27

The hussars who conducted us did not for some time know where we were to be taken; they were strangers to the country, having themselves been sent for from some distance for the purpose of convoying prisoners from Cambray. They received orders every night where they were to proceed the following day. At last we found our appointed place of captivity was Compiègne, where, being distanced from every friend, we might from want of ability to act lose every means of recovering our property, which was then very considerable.

The first night we were lodged in a ruinous place called Bassone (Bapaume ?); it had the appearance of having been a convent, but was almost destroyed. The violence of the rabble on seeing us was so great that we were happy to be taken into any place like a house. The mayor of this town was a native of Cambray, and well known to us, one of his sisters having received her education amongst us; but he now appeared to know nothing of us, nor showed us the least indulgence. He was highly displeased at our being in the religious dress, and said the people of Cambray had acted against the law by not making every one shun a dress which the law had proscribed. The jailor of this prison seemed a quiet man, and his daughter was good enough to buy for us two faggots, some very brown bread, and a kettle of boiling water. We made tea, but sugar and milk were delicacies not to be thought of, or at least not obtained, besides being too much exhausted with grief and the fatigue endured that day to relish that then luxurious meal, so that the greater part not being disposed to eat, were glad to throw their wearied bodies on the floor, and spread a few bundles of clothes to stretch their languid limbs upon; even in that state we were frequently disturbed by the guards looking through the windows. Next night we passed at Peronne in the citadel. Here we were guarded by the National

Troops, whose brutality can hardly be described; nothing can be conceived more disagreeably offensive than their language and behaviour. A woman who appeared to belong to one of them molested us by every means she could study; still amidst all their cruel treatment we had the comfort to meet with some few friends.

A female, whose father in better times had been employed by us, had the courage to make her way into our prison; she and her husband procured for us bread, small beer, and a few boiled eggs, which were really a great treat, as some had not tasted anything for two days. We also found in this place a few bedsteads with dirty straw, which the soldiers had apparently slept on for some months; we did not at first choose to lie down on them, but excessive weariness in the end overcame that difficulty. Still no rest was to be had in this scene of horror; the soldiers were passing to and fro the greater part of the night, even through the room we occupied. Next morning, by means of a lady who was there in arrestation, we procured one cup of tea each before the guards came to summon us away in order to proceed on our dismal journey. On Sunday evening we rested at Ham; here was as usual a great stir among the people crying out "Aristocrats to the guillotine," but this language had now become too familiar to have quite its former effect upon us. The prison we were lodged in being situated in the environs of the town, we experienced less inconvenience from the rabble than usual, for not to be insulted in a great degree seemed an extraordinary favour. The governor of this place proved a very quiet man; he gave orders that we should have a commodious room to ourselves, allowed clean straw spread over the floor, and we felt happy to lie down upon it. That night passed without noise or interruption; next morning the governor paid us a civil visit. The woman who took care of this prison had lived in our neighbourhood at Cambray, and seemed much affected on seeing our present distress. It gave her particular concern to see us go off in carts, whilst all the other prisoners, a few men excepted, were provided with coaches to their separate destinations; she thought as many others that we were exposed in carts that we might lie more open to insult.

Monday evening we arrived at Noyon. Words cannot describe the terror we here felt: the carts had no sooner stopped in the middle of the market-place than thousands assembled in the most tumultuous manner around us; for nuns to appear in their religious dress was at that time the worst of crimes. Some talked of tearing us to pieces, others were for burying us alive with the proscribed dress, as they termed it. The guards who conducted us endeavoured repeatedly to speak in our favour, but so great was the noise and riot amongst the populace, whose numbers had in a short time increased to a dreadful degree, that not a word could be heard. Not only the streets, but the windows and house-tops were crowded with spectators. The hussars, finding it impossible to keep order, called up the soldiers quartered in the town, by whose assistance we were taken out of the carts half dead with fright, after being detained in the market-place near an hour amidst a variety of the most outrageous insults and threats. One instance may suffice to show the disposition of the people in our regard. One of our company, a very old lady, being taken out of the cart, finding herself unable to stand leant against the horse which stood next her, upon which the beast immediately kicked her; the rabble set up the most exulting shouts and clapped their hands for joy. The soldiers who came to assist ours, guarded us that night, and were extremely civil; from motives of compassion they conducted us to a decent inn instead of the common prison.

They also allowed us to call for whatever we chose; two officers belonging to them took particular care of us, the younger of whom could not refrain from tears. The head officers of the hussars also came to see us twice at the inn, and they did all in their power to comfort us; but nothing could now revive our broken spirits.

The thought of being exposed on the roads was too distressing to admit of consolation; their kindness was, however, in our present circumstances highly pleasing. Although it is some years since these events happened, yet the writer of this account declares her blood chills whenever she thinks on those dreadful days. Those who have experienced similar distress will excuse her for expressing herself so feelingly on the subject.

We left Noyon about nine o'clock on Tuesday morning, and had covered our veils with coloured handkerchiefs, and otherwise disguised our dress, that we might pass for French villagers, who wear no hats, and this precaution was of some use, for the people seemed at a loss what to make of us. About four in the afternoon we arrived at Compiègne, and here our guards left us, after having said much in our favour to the mayor and two other members of the district, whose charge it was to meet and receive prisoners attended by the National Guards. The hussars, our own friendly guards, who had all along shown us so much humanity, were natives of Normandy, most of them under twenty years of age. We were the more surprised at their charity, as they were very giddy and profane in their discourse to each other.

The prisoners brought from Cambray to Compiègne at that time were fifty-two in number, our community included. All were confined in one house; it had been a convent belonging to nuns of the Order of the Visitation, but was then a common prison. The gentlemen of the district of Compiègne frequently visited the place. Whenever they called upon us they asked a thousand questions, but upon the whole behaved with civility. The procurator syndic, observing us half starved and perishing with cold, had the goodness to write twice to Cambray to the municipality of that city, to desire they would return some part of our wearing apparel, but they never sent any. We had a room assigned us in the infirmary of the convent; the adjoining apartment was occupied by persons of all descriptions and ranks, their numbers increased daily—whole families were sometimes brought together. It seems this place had been fixed on in preference to Cambray because it was more within the reach of the assassins of Paris, who then deluged the streets of that capital with human blood. On the 25th of November 1793 a great number of prisoners were brought from Cambray, amongst whom were the Rev. Messrs. Walker and Higginson and the Hon. Thomas Roper. It is not easy to express the joy we felt on seeing Mr. Walker, for we had lost all hopes of ever seeing him again: he also seemed much affected. But this transient gleam of pleasure was not a little allayed by orders very soon given that we should by no means be allowed to converse with them, one of the members observing to his colleagues that if they were permitted to visit or see us, some part of religious worship might probably be kept up amongst us, which he said they were bound to root out entirely. After this we saw Mr. Walker, &c., but seldom, and always in fear. It certainly cost him much uneasiness to be obliged to pass his time with a set of men whose manners and conversation were shocking to every well-disposed person. Soon after this the very man who had with club in hand turned us out of our convent, was sent after us to the same prison, but was shortly after removed to Paris, where he ended a wretched life on the guillotine, which was the fate of many who had been particularly active in the Revolution. For a time the allowance was one pound of bread to each person per day, besides one good meal, the expense of which was to be defrayed by the prisoners conjointly, the rich paying for the poor, and strict orders were given that equality should be observed according to the new republican law.

About the beginning of June 1794, many of us fell sick, eight were confined to their beds at the same time, and the rest so much indisposed as to be scarcely able to help their dying sisters. A woman who provided us with milk took much compassion on us, and even assisted in taking care of the sick, but after a short time she fell ill herself, which unfortunately made others afraid to come near us. The disorder was a fever, proceeding, as the doctor who attended said, from great hardship and ill-usage. We had still only one room for the whole community, twenty-one in number, several of whom were now drawing near their end. Every person seemed to pity but none dare approach to help or comfort us, for the disease beginning to spread, each one trembled for himself.

It was now judged proper to allow an adjoining room, and the prisoners, who were about one hundred and sixty, were permitted to walk in the garden, a favour which till then had not been allowed.

Our windows were unnailed for benefit of fresh air, but it was in the middle of winter, and of course very damp and wet, so that this indulgence was of little or no real benefit. On the 12th of January, about two o'clock in the morning, the Rev. Mr. Walker felt himself very indisposed, but would not disturb Mr. Higginson, who slept in the same room, until his usual hour of rising. Amongst the prisoners was a physician from Cambray—a fortunate circumstance for the sick. He immediately declared Mr. Walker's case to be dangerous; his disorder increased rapidly, so as to alarm every one, for he was deservedly and universally esteemed. He fell into his agony the same evening, and breathed his last about two o'clock next morning, having been ill only twenty-four hours. His disorder was generally thought to be gout in the stomach, but the doctor who attended always affirmed that the many and great hardships he had undergone, together with want of food and requisites for a person of his age and declining health, had not a little contributed to hasten his death. This fatal catastrophe distressed us beyond expression; the circumstances we were then in made his loss still more deeply and severely felt and regretted.

He had for some years been as a father and exemplary friend to the community, having remained with us by choice in the very heat of the Revolution, when his life was particularly in danger—even at a time when he might, had he pleased, have lived comfortably in England.

During his long confinement he was never heard to let fall one word of complaint, although he suffered so much. He died as he had lived, a truly good religious, aged seventy-three. He had resided twenty years at Rome, and received distinguished tokens of esteem and favour from his late Holiness Pope Pius VI.

The last seventeen years of his life he had, with much honour to himself, and edification to his brethren, held the office of president general of the English Benedictine congregation.

The morning after Mr. Walker's decease, January 14th, whilst his corpse was unremoved, died Dame Anselm Ann, aged seventy-nine. The 21st of the same month also Dame Walmesley, aged fifty-five. About the same time

Dame Margaret Burgess and Anne Pennington, lay sister. She had been of particular service in taking care of the sick. Her disorder was a gangrene in her arm, which from the first threatened her life. No resource could the prison afford, nor would the commissioner who was over us, though in the prison, and thoroughly acquainted with her distressing state, allow anything to be procured from the town, so that twenty-four hours had elapsed before any material service could be obtained. In the meantime the mortification had spread prodigiously, and her life was despaired of. She expired on the 6th of January, aged sixty.

Towards the beginning of March the same year, the surviving part of the community began to recover, though very slowly. The district of Compiègne now began to treat their prisoners with great severity; many had been sent from Cambray, their whole property had been seized, though no allowance was made towards their maintenance. On the 6th of March three of the members from the district of Compiègne came to the prison, escorted by a detachment of the National Guards. The prisoners were all ordered to assemble in a large room: part of our community were still confined by sickness, so that few only could attend. All the prisoners stood like condemned criminals. The procurator syndic made a long harangue, putting all in mind they had hitherto been served with one meal per day, but that nothing had been advanced for so liberal a treatment, that the people of Compiègne were resolved to reimburse themselves one way or other.

The prisoners alleged they had already been stripped of everything and their houses plundered, that to think of forcing more from them was cruel in the extreme. These expostulations, true as they really were, had not the least effect; the above procurator again and again repeated, that if the sum of French livres he demanded was not collected amongst them and sent to the district before ten o'clock next morning, they should be punished with the greatest rigour. The prisoners being by no means able to furnish the demanded sum, were on the 11th of March stinted to coarse brown bread and water. Many of us were still unwell when this severe order came out—some were even confined to their beds.

Six red herrings, which we happened to have by us when this command was given, was all that we had for three days, not being allowed to buy anything, not even a little salt. A surgeon of Compiègne, who had attended us during sickness, was compassionate enough to go to the district when the members were assembled, to beg as a favour they would permit a little broth to be procured for Dame Alexander, who was near eighty years old, and had been confined to her bed six weeks of a fever which terminated in an imposthume; but this indulgence was not granted; all we profited by the well-intentioned charity of this good man was a heap of compliments of condolence from the mayor and other magistrates for grievances which they themselves inflicted.

Our wants growing every day greater, we applied at last to some of the inhabitants of Compiègne for needlework; but the windows of the room we occupied being partly made up, little could be done, so that in order to raise money to buy bread we contrived privately to sell, though at great loss, a few gold crosses, &c., which we happened to have about us when we left Cambray.

The magistrates, finding nothing could be obtained from the above place, were every day still more importunate with the prisoners for money, which they had not to give. One day they came to take away the beds, which consisted of each a mattress and one blanket, but a charitable friend advanced money on condition they would leave ours one month longer; at the expiration of which they came again, but another friend interposed, and thus we went on, always under apprehension of being obliged to lie on a few handfuls of straw.

On the 17th of May 1794, at eight o'clock in the morning, about twenty members of the district of Compiègne, and six or seven of Robespierre's agents from Arras, came to the prison, escorted by one hundred and twenty guards.

The prisoners were immediately ordered each one to their own quarters, and a guard with a drawn sword was stationed within our room, strictly charged to take care we did not open a window, nor leave the apartment for one moment, and above all that we burnt no papers.

Some of us turned pale and nearly fainted, which the mayor perceiving, with his usual good nature, ordered the guard to sheathe his sword. An officer soon after making his round, asked the guard why he had not his sword drawn? He answered because we were afraid, at which the officer scornfully said something about the guillotine, and with horrid imprecations commanded the guard instantly to unsheathe it. This terrified us still more.

Whilst in this situation we heard the jailor repeatedly calling the prisoners separately, the men first, then the women, to a lower room, but not any of them returned. In this distress we durst not even speak to one another through fear of the guard.

After the most cruel suspense of about nine hours, we were ordered down. It was then five in the evening; before we had descended half-way downstairs, counter orders were given, and only one or two persons who could speak French were to be admitted—the rest returned with the guard. The commissioners began to search the pockets of the two religious above-named, but the mayor checked them, so that they were less insolent to them than to some others. Nothing of value being found upon them, they were dismissed, and the whole tribe of rough fellows, about thirty in number, came up with them to the apartment where we all were; one of them was a fallen priest. He could speak a little English, and was a busy man on the present occasion, and chief orator. He addressed us in a manner which seemed most proper to terrify, enumerating the punishments which would certainly be inflicted if we concealed either writing or anything of value from them.

The procuratrix produced the little paper money she had; the community in general assured them that all their writings, &c., had been taken from them at Cambray.

After asking many questions, and talking in a low voice to each other, they withdrew, leaving on the table the little paper money which we had produced, yet we durst not offer to take it. They then proceeded to search all the prisoners' beds, shaking the straw and moving everything about the room, and seized the most trifling things they met with, even to a silver thimble. During this examination they tore the females' caps off their heads (some of whom were ladies of quality), unpinned their gowns, and searched them in the most cruel manner, If they found a crucifix or reliquary of gold or silver, they took it; if of an inferior metal, they broke it and sometimes returned the bits to its owner.

From the Rev. James Higginson and Hon. Thomas Roper (the latter of whom was a very serviceable companion in prison), they took two metal watches, from the former two gold repeating watches which had belonged to the Rev. Messrs. Walker and Walsh. This last mentioned gentlemen had ended his life with us during the early part of the Revolution.

Having now stripped the other prisoners of everything, of even the smallest value, they were returning to our apartment, when one of the prisoners addressed the mayor as follows: "Surely, sir, you are not going to search these poor nuns a second time! You know how barbarously they have been used by the people of Cambray, and at present you are well assured they live in the greatest poverty, having only the small pittance which they gain by the needle to maintain them." The mayor seemed pleased with the person who spoke, and after a short pause turned off, called the guard out of the apartment, and soon after left the prison, attended by the administrators of the district, &c.

This was one of the most suffering days we ever passed, though at that time we experienced many. The prisoners from this time were treated with still greater rigour than ever, and were now reduced to the utmost distress. Some passed days and weeks with no other food than bread and water, and few entertained even a hope of escaping public execution, yet this seemed to have little or no effect on the morals of many. They were for the most part very ill livers, though few days passed but one or other was taken out of the Compiègne prison to be thrown into the dungeon, there to be ready for execution, and there some remained till the death of Robespierre; others were taken out of prison and an end put to their existence by the fatal guillotine. About the middle of June 1794 sixteen Carmelite nuns were brought to Compiègne and lodged in a room which faced ours; they had not been long there before they were hurried off to Paris, without any previous notice, for no other crime than that an emigrant priest, who had been their chaplain, had written to them and made mention of a bishop, who was also an emigrant, desiring compliments to an elderly gentleman who was cousin to one of the community. This person unfortunately possessed considerable property, a crime not easily overlooked in those days. This venerable man was also conducted to

Paris with the nuns. A servant who attended him seemed ready to die with grief, and the good old gentleman shed tears at parting. The above religious quitted the Compiègne prison in the most saint-like manner. We saw them embrace each other before they set off, and they took an affectionate leave of us by the motion of their hands and other friendly gestures. On their way to the scaffold itself (as we were informed by an eye-witness of respectability and credit), they behaved with a firm and cheerful composure which nothing but a spotless conscience could inspire, resulting from a joyful hope and confidence in the blessed recompense that attended their sufferings in the cause of virtue. They repeated aloud on the scaffold the Litanies of the Blessed Virgin, until the fatal axe interrupted the voice of the last of this holy company. They suffered the 16th of July 1794.

One of the community happened to be absent when her sisters were taken to Paris; she concealed herself in different places during the life of the tyrant Robespierre.

After he ceased to exist, which event took place on the 28th of July 1794, she returned to Compiègne and frequently visited us.

She also favoured us with the names and ages of her deceased sisters, which are as follows:—

	Age		Age
Croisé	49	Brard	58
Froselle	51	Chretien	52
Hourrisset	52	Dufour	29
Le Donine	42	Fourcon	45
Libret	34	Fourcon	55
Touret	79	Bousset	52
Pidcourt	98	Nesolat	30
Brudeau	—	Mounier	—

Two or three days after the Carmelites were gone to Paris, the mayor and two members of the district of

Compiègne called upon us. We were still in our religious dress, which he had frequently urged us to change, but we always alleged that we had not money sufficient to furnish ourselves with clothes. The same day he returned to us again, called two of our company aside, and told them they must now absolutely put off that uniform, alluding to the habit, for that he durst no longer permit that prohibited dress; that should the people again become riotous, we should be more safe from their resentment in any other dress than the religious one. The truth was, he expected we should like the good Carmelites be soon conducted to Paris for execution, and was afraid he might be put to trouble if we were found in the conventual dress.

Being repeatedly assured we had not money to purchase clothes, he went himself to the apartment which those respectable ladies had occupied, and brought us some of the poor clothing they had left there; these he desired we would put on without delay. We were still in want of shoes: he very civilly said he would provide us with what we wanted, but one of the jailors standing by bluntly told us we should not long have occasion for shoes.

One day on leaving the room, the mayor, turning to the Rev. Mr. Higginson, in a low voice said, "Take care of your friends," meaning, prepare them for death, for he well knew Mr. Higginson had nothing else in his power. The next day the news became confirmed that the poor Carmelites had been put to death by the guillotine. The old clothes, which before appeared of small value, were now so much esteemed that we deemed ourselves unworthy to wear them; still, forced by necessity, we put them on, and these constituted the greater part of our mean apparel on our return to England. We yet keep them, a few excepted, which we have disposed of to particular friends. The prisoners of Compiègne were still pressed to pay off the old debt for the allowance of one meal per day which had been formerly given, as mentioned above, but now long since withdrawn, insomuch that during many months before we quitted this tedious confinement we were not even allowed bread unless we could pay for it. The two last months of the year 1794 and beginning of 1795 being extremely severe, we had much to suffer from wants of various kinds, especially of fuel and warm clothing, for no person had sufficient to keep herself, even the youngest of us, warm.

The room we inhabited was large and very cold, but no entreaties could obtain us more than one blanket each. The scarcity of provisions also increasing to a dreadful degree, bread was so hard to be procured that no inhabitant of the town was permitted to purchase more than a certain fixed allowance, which made a very scanty portion. Guards were placed at every baker's shop, and in their presence the bread was weighed out to each individual until the whole poor stock was distributed; but commonly there was not sufficient quantity to supply more than half the people, who were expecting to have each a little, so that no day passed without some tumult in the town. The bread in general was of the worst quality, yet we thought ourselves very fortunate when we could purchase a sufficient quantity to supply our large family. Very frequently after we had finished our meal we had not a morsel left for the next. The English throughout every part of France had repeatedly petitioned for some mitigation of their sufferings, and some had with becoming freedom pointed out the absurdity of detaining in confinement so many innocent sufferers, for the apprehension of whom there had never existed a pretext of justice. At last it was decreed that all foreigners should have for allowance two livres per day paper money. Bread was then sold at three livres per pound.

Besides its being irregularly paid, it was quite insufficient to subsist upon, in the state in which France then was, paper money being then reduced to a very low ebb.

We received the above for the first time on the 23rd of December 1794. Its value was then computed at twopence-halfpenny, or at most threepence, per day English.

Some time after this, the prisoners began to be treated with more lenity than they had yet experienced. The Rev. James Higginson and the Hon. T. Roper had liberty to go into the town; this was of much service to us, for the latter of these gentlemen proved himself indefatigable in using every means possible to procure for us victuals and fuel—he even carried wood himself, and ran from shop to shop to buy us bread. Still, notwithstanding this seeming liberty, the situation was very disagreeable, though the soldiers had no longer power to command us as formerly, yet the street door was open night and day, so that we could not step out of our room without meeting crowds of people. One part of the prison being turned into a guard house, all came in and went out at pleasure. The garden, too, was always taken up by the soldiers and rabble. About this time the Convention frequently ordered the prisoners of war to be sent from one town to another, to show them to the people; when these companies passed through Compiègne, they were always lodged in our place of confinement, and nothing distressed us more than on such occasions to meet with brave Englishmen in want of the most common necessaries of life; and at the same time treated with the most inhuman scorn and contempt by the French Jacobins, who were quite elated to have an Englishman in their power. Whenever the above prisoners arrived, all was noise and confusion, and we often expected nothing less than to see the house on fire, for the

APPENDIX.

weather being remarkably cold, they burnt everything they could lay hands on.

Seeing no prospect of an end to the miseries of an unhappy country, in which we had now long been sufferers, and provisions becoming daily more scarce and dear, so that it was now almost out of our power to procure them at any rate, we at last resolved to apply to Paris for passports to return to our native country.

The mayor of Compiègne privately advised us to take this step, and assured us of his assistance; accordingly a petition was drawn up and signed by the whole community. The mayor forwarded it to the Convention at Paris, and seconded it by a letter in our favour. About ten days after, our liberty was announced by the district of Compiègne. After this we endeavoured to procure (the good Carmelite above-mentioned assisting) sacred vessels and vestments, that we might have the happiness of assisting at one Mass, the only one during our eighteen months' confinement, and we were in the utmost alarm the whole time. To raise money for our journey, we contrived to draw privately from England by way of Hamburg, though at considerable loss. A most charitable gentleman, Edward Constable, Esq., of Burton, had two years before given us leave to call upon him for any money we might want in case of distress, which he seemed to foresee would happen. The horses being chiefly in use for the army, we found much difficulty to procure conveyance to Calais.

At last we quitted Compiègne, on the 24th of April 1795, in two carts. We took Cambray in our way, but had not courage to cast an eye upon our much-beloved but now lost convent.

On the 23rd of May 1795 we sailed from Calais, and on the 24th arrived in London.

Our return to England was no sooner known, than a

lady, still more distinguished by her extensive charities than by her station in life, sent the chaplain of her family (a clergyman of the Established Church of England) to inform us that, conceiving our situation at a common inn to be exceedingly inconvenient and unpleasant, she had provided a house at the west end of the town for us during our residence in London. Here she was the first person to visit and comfort us. Struck with such marks of divine bounty in our regard, we ceased not to put up our prayers in behalf of the immediate instrument of it and of her noble relatives.

[The nuns first settled at Wootton, near Liverpool, removed in 1808 to Stratford-on-Avon, and have now a convent at Stanbrook, Worcestershire.]

APPENDIX.

D.

Whyte, the Bastille Prisoner.

(See pp. 8–10.)

An article by M. Begis, in the *Intermédiaire*, April 10, 1889, based on researches among the Bastille papers in the Arsenal Library, clears up all those doubtful questions. James Francis Xavier Whyte, afterwards known as Count Whyte de Malleville, was born at Dublin in 1730. He went over to France, and became first a cornet in the Soubise volunteers, and then a captain in Lally Tollendal's Franco-Irish regiment. In 1767 he married at Paris. In 1781 he was incarcerated at Vincennes, at the instance of his family, on account of mental derangement. In 1784 he was transferred to the Bastille. In March 1789 he was declared *interdit*, that is to say, deprived of the management of his property. The two court pensioners, whom I conjectured to be his sisters, were evidently his daughters, and the proceedings against him were probably taken for their protection. The day after the fall of the Bastille, Whyte was placed in the asylum at Charenton, on the closing of which he was transferred, July 31, 1795, to another asylum, Petites Maisons. Whyte, while an object of pity, was thus in no way a victim of despotism. Of his six fellow-captives, four were forgers, a fifth was confined for indecency, and the sixth, like Whyte insane, had declared himself an accomplice in the attempted murder of Louis XV.

Œ.

English Prisoners, 1789–96.

IN PARIS.

(See p. 145.)

Alder, Daniel. At Luxembourg, June 15, 1794. Liberated Feb. 5, 1795.

Alison, Sophia, 28, wife of Berger. For stealing wool of a mattress. St. Pélagie and Madelonnettes. May 19, 1796.

Arthur, John James, 33, paper-hanger. Guillotined July 30, 1794. See p. 192.

Aston, Mary Anne, 45, Conceptionist nun. Oct. 13, 1793, to Feb. 27, 1795.*

Badger, Meunier, silk-spinner, Tours. At Luxembourg. Charged with having supplied cannons from his brother-in-law at London to the Vendean insurgents. Published a pamphlet while in prison, in which he challenged production of any evidence against him, mentioned his three motherless children, and urged that he had fought in the National Guard against the Vendeans.

Bagnal, Anne Theresa, Benedictine lay sister.

Baker, Caroline, 25, and two children. At Luxembourg and Austin convent. Oct. 15, 1793.

Baldwin, Samuel, 67, professor of languages. St. Pélagie and La Force. Oct. 15, 1793.

Barker, George. Liberated Nov. 17, 1793.

Barnston, Edward, 24, teacher of drawing and languages. Charged with possessing anti-revolutionary pamphlets. July 13, 1793, to Sept. 27, 1795. In twelve different prisons.

Baron, Elizabeth, 24, Conceptionist nun. Oct. 13, 1793, to Feb. 19, 1795.

Barton, Jane. At Luxembourg and Austin convent. Oct. 26, 1793.

---

* These dates apply to all the other nuns also.

Bayle, William, groom. At Scotch college and four other prisons, Oct. 30, 1793, to July 8, 1795.
Beeston, Theresa Anne, 47, boarder at Austin convent.
Bell, Mary, 48, Conceptionist nun. Died Oct. 1794.
Bishop, Elizabeth, 32, Austin nun. Died 1819, aged 57.
Bishop, Frances, 30, Austin nun, sister of above. Left the convent in 1836.
Blanchet, Mary Long, wife of, arrested for concealing a conspirator, and shielding him from national vengeance. At Austin convent, Feb. 13, 1794, to Aug. 6, 1794.
Blount, Mrs. Mary, and two daughters, of Chalgrove, Oxon., boarders at the Austin convent. Mrs. Blount was sister to the superior, Mrs. Canning. Liberated Jan. 1795. Her daughter Elizabeth married, 1802, Ralph Riddell, of Felton Park, Northumberland. The other daughter, Frances, and her mother, were still boarders at the convent in 1820.
Blount, Joseph, 14, son of the above. At Luxembourg, Oct. 11, 1793, to Dec. 15, 1794.
Bond, Andrew, surgeon. Captured at Toulon.
Bourk, Mary Adelaide, 17. At Conceptionist convent. Liberated Sept. 28, 1794.
Brindels, Helen, 53, Benedictine nun. At Vincennes and Austin convent. Died 1807.
Budge, ———, and his children. Jan. 3, 1794.
Burk, François Ursule, 17, sailor, native of L'Orient. On June 9, 1794, the charge against him was dismissed, and it was ordered that he should be detained till 21 years of age, but on July 23 he was again tried for prison plot at the Carmelites'. He was accused of saying that the English were brave; also that it was absurd to make citizens serve as soldiers when there were regular troops. He replied that he had said the Irish were brave; his father was one, and served France well. He was guillotined.
Burque, Marie Félicité Launay, 27, native of Paris, wife of an English doctor. Arrested Sept. 30, 1793. Guillotined July 7, 1794, for retaining titles of nobility, and possessing medallion of royal family.

Cameron, Anne Caroline, 40, native of Dunkirk, wife of Charles Pierre Gassien, notary. Tried for talk in favour of restoration of monarchy, Nov. 27, 1793, and acquitted.

Campbell, Archibald, major in 69th infantry. Captured at Toulon. At Luxembourg, Jan. 9, 1794.

Campbell, John, 58, rentier. At Luxembourg, Oct. 1, 1793, to Oct. 23, 1794.

Campbell, William, 54, Irish (qy. the actuary). Oct. 12, 1793, to Feb. 14, 1795.

Canning, Anne Mary, 43, daughter of Francis Canning, of Foxcote, Warwickshire, Austin nun, and superior of convent from 1808 till her death in 1820.

Carr, John Baptist, 21, émigré. Was sent in 1788 to England by his father (qy. Louis Alexander Carr, member of a Paris revolutionary committee in 1792) to learn commerce. Liberated June 30, 1795. See p. 213.

Caucey (?), Colin. At Luxembourg. Liberated Oct. 18, 1794.

Chambly, Charles Francis, 57, native of Louisburg, Canada, captain at Cayenne. Guillotined for prison plot at the Carmelites', July 23, 1794. See p. 180.

Châtellux, Mary Bridget Josephine Plunket, 34, widow of Marquis de Châtellux. At Austin convent, Nov. 30, 1793, to Nov. 28, 1794. See p. 157.

Chevenix, Richard. At Luxembourg. Liberated Dec. 4, 1794. See p. 228.

Clark, Jaerens (?), 64, Scotch. At Austin convent, Oct. 30, 1793, to Sept. 28, 1794.

Clarmont, John Charles. At Luxembourg and Scotch college. Oct. 10, 1793.

Clutterbuck, Charles, 38, professor of languages. At Luxembourg and Irish college, Oct. 13, 1793, to Oct. 3, 1794.

Codrington, Sir Wm., Bart., 56. Charged, Jan. 18, 1794, with dealings with the enemy. Acquitted, but to be detained till the peace. Liberated Dec. 2, 1794. See pp. 148, 291.

Collier, John. At Luxembourg and Scotch college. Oct.

12, 1793. (Indemnity awarded, 1820, to executrix of Sir George Collier.)

Cooper, Margaret, 69, lay sister at Benedictine convent. At Vincennes and Austin convent, Oct. 13, 1793, to Feb. 27, 1795. Died 1807.

Cowlechette, William. Feb. 21, 1792.

Darby, John Baptist (qy. Jonathan, of King's County). Had two sons in English army. At Carmelites, Oct. 8, 1793, to Sept. 30, 1794.

Day, Denis. Sent from Epernay to Paris, July 31, 1794.

Delany, Thomas, 17. Guillotined June 6, 1794. See p. 179.

Dillon, General Arthur. Guillotined for prison plot at Luxembourg, April 13, 1794. See p. 171.

Dollond, Miss, boarder at Austin convent.

Douglas, Abbé. Arrested, Dec. 1789, for complicity in the plot for the King's escape to Metz, but prosecution was dropped. Qy. brother of Charles Joseph Douglas, ex-captain in the Scotch Guard, one of the alleged Orleanist instigators of the mob march to Versailles.

Duffield, Anne, 46, Conceptionist nun.

Easter, John, artisan, wife Mary, and two daughters. At Luxembourg, Nov. 1793.

Edgeworth. See Firmont.

Edwards, Elizabeth, 43, Conceptionist nun.

Elven, Robert, servant to Captain Athol Wood. Brought from St. Malo to the Luxembourg, June 16, 1794.

Fermor, Frances Mary Agnes, 71, Austin nun. Died March 9, 1794. Niece of Arabella Fermor, heroine of Pope's "Rape of the Lock."

Finchet, Helena Mary Monica, 29, Austin nun. Niece of the chaplain, Hurst. Superior from 1828 to 1840. Died 1847.

Firmont, Elizabeth, sister to the Abbé Edgeworth. At Austin convent, Feb. 23, 1794, to Sept. 26, 1794. Still living in Paris in 1799. See p. 156.

Finith (Frith?), Margaret. At Luxembourg and Conceptionist convent. Oct. 15, 1793.

Fitzherbert, Mary Bernard, 49, Austin nun. Her brother's widow married George IV.

Fitzpatrick, Richard, Irish student. At Luxembourg. Liberated March 4, 1795.

Foster, John, gamekeeper to the Duc de Biron, his wife Mary Burnet, and his two daughters. At Luxembourg, July 21, 1794.

Fox, General. Scotch adventurer, first employed in France, next engaged in anti-Orange movement in Holland, then in Brabant rising; returned to France 1790, and was one of Lafayette's agents. May 22, 1795. Probably arrested on account of his tardiness in repressing the Jacobin insurrection of the 20th, when the President of the Convention had appointed him temporary general, and had bidden him meet force with force. When Féraud's head was held up to the President, the latter imagined at first that it was Fox's.

Framson, father and son. At Abbaye and Carmelites'.

Gall, Major, two daughters of. See p. 228.

Garnett, George. Liberated Sept. 29, 1794.

Gee, Anne Joseph, Benedictine nun. Died 1816.

Gee, Mary Placida, Benedictine nun.

Gem, Dr. Richard. At Luxembourg and Scotch college. Oct. 13, 1793. See p. 29.

Glynn, Magdalen, Benedictine postulant. Died 1811.

Godard ———. (Qy. one of the captors of the Bastille.) At Luxembourg and Scotch college. Oct. 13, 1793.

Godson, George, officer in 17th cavalry. At Abbaye, Oct. 16, 1793; liberated 1794.

Godson, James. At La Force and Luxembourg, Oct. 24, 1793, to Feb. 10, 1795.

Gordon, John, negro servant. Captured at Toulon. At Luxembourg, Jan. 9, 1794.

Graham, Admiral Mitchell. Son of Sir Reginald Graham, Bart., aide-de-camp to Duke of Marlborough. Appointed to naval captaincy, 1760. On becoming senior captain without ever having had any command, he was superannuated as admiral. Embarrassed circumstances made him retire to Paris with his second wife (Maria Rebecca Bowater) and their two children, John Bellingham, afterwards captain in the

APPENDIX. 339

Marines, and Maria. At Luxembourg and Scotch college. Died at Dreneux Infirmary, March 7, 1794.

Graham, William, doctor, prisoner at Toulon. At Luxembourg, Jan. 9, 1794.

Grant, Thomas, naval ensign. At Luxembourg, Jan. 9, 1794.

Grattan, Pierre, magistrate at Castel Sarrazin. Tried for dealings with the enemy, Oct. 13, 1794, and acquitted.

Green, Elizabeth, 59, superior of Conceptionist convent. Oct. 13, 1793, to Feb. 27, 1795.

Greenal, Elizabeth, 52, teacher. Liberated Feb. 27, 1795.

Greenay, Esther, 34, Benedictine nun. Oct. 13, 1793, to Feb. 27, 1795. Died 1807.

Grenville, Colonel Richard. At Abbaye and Luxembourg, Sept. 22, 1793, to Feb. 11, 1795. See p. 149.

Hagan, Theresa, Conceptionist nun. Died 1816.

Hailes, Frances, 33, Austin lay sister.

Hall, Theodore, 26, tradesman at Sens; born at Scury, Yonne; son of Thomas Hall. Guillotined along with Princess Elizabeth, May 9, 1794.

Hall, Thomas, father of above. Died before trial, Jan. 31, 1794.

Hall, ——, 14. Liberated July 21, 1795.

Haly, John. Liberated Feb. 17, 1795.

Hamilton, John, navy captain, native of Dublin. Sentenced, June 28, 1792, to eight years' imprisonment. Taken to Rochefort, Oct. 1, 1793.

Harris, ——, Benedictine. At Luxembourg. Liberated Dec. 10, 1764.

Harrop, Charles, 22, native of London, tradesman. At Scotch college and Carmelites'. Guillotined for prison plot at the Carmelites', July 23, 1794. See pp. 146, 181.

Hartwidge, Elizabeth, 37, Benedictine nun. Died 1823.

Harwood, Samuel, 42. At Luxembourg and Scotch college, Nov. 19, 1793, to Nov. 24, 1795.

APPENDIX.

Hawkins, William, landed at Calais from London. At Luxembourg, Jan. 6, 1794, to Jan. 25, 1794.

Hickson, Nicholas, Scotch, teacher of languages. At Scotch college and Luxembourg, Oct. 20, 1793, to Nov. 28, 1793.

Hill, William, groom. At Scotch college, Dec. 4, 1793, to Dec. 19, 1794.

Hinde, ———. At Madelonnettes, Luxembourg, and Scotch college. Oct. 19, 1793.

Howard. See Stafford.

Hunt, Edward, 33, servant. Oct. 12, 1793, to Sept. 25, 1794.

Hurst, William, 56, chaplain to Austin convent. At St. Pélagie and Luxembourg, Oct. 13, 1793, to Oct. 30, 1794.

Innes, Alexander, 43, superior of Scotch college. At St. Pélagie, Luxembourg, and Scotch college, Oct. 13, 1793, to Jan. 10, 1795.

James, John, 29. June 4, 1794, to Oct. 12, 1794.

James, Henry, 40, doctor, Nantes. Tried Sept. 14, 1794, with the other Nantes prisoners, and acquitted.

Jeffries, Molly, governess. At Austin convent, Jan. 26, 1794, to Feb. 27, 1795.

Jennings. See Kilmaine.

Jennings, Jacques, priest. At Luxembourg. Liberated Dec. 10, 1794.

Johnson, Anne, 41, superior of Benedictine convent. Died 1807.

Jones, Hugh, lodging-house keeper. At La Force and Benedictines', Oct. 11, 1793, to Dec. 8, 1794. See p. 50.

Joyce, Frances Charlotte, 14, and two sisters. At Austin convent, Port Royal, and Luxembourg, Oct. 11, 1793, to Dec. 8, 1794.

Kellett, Robert Augustine, 61, Benedictine monk. At Luxembourg, Oct. 11, 1793, to Dec. 13, 1794.

Kilmaine, General Charles Edward Paul Jennings, born at Dublin 1751, entered French service 1774, died at Paris 1799.

Kilmaine, Susan, 28 (qy. wife of General Kilmaine). Liberated Aug. 8, 1795.

APPENDIX. 341

Knowles, his wife and daughter. Jan. 11, 1794.

Lack, Anne, servant to Duc de Biron. At Luxembourg, July 21, 1794, to Nov. 19, 1794.

Laing. See Delany.

Lambert, Sir John Francis, Bart., 63, banker. At St. Pélagie, Nov. 3, 1793. Liberated, rearrested, and liberated. Said to have made a large sum by speculations in the English funds, having had through Madame de Pompadour early intelligence of the treaty of 1763. Died in England 1799. Compensation awarded in 1820 to his widow, Sophia Niepe, a Swiss (she married again, 1805), and to his sons' heirs.

Lamplow, Richard, sergeant. Captured at Toulon with O'Hara.

Lang, Francis George, 14, jockey. Arrested for uttering counterfeit notes, April 22, 1795.

Latham, Sarah Mary, 24, lay sister. At Austin convent.

Lancaster, Frances Louisa, 61, superior of the Austin nuns from 1765 to 1808.

Leberton, Andrew James Hyacinth, Irish. At Benedictines'.

Lepine, James, 27, teacher of languages, native of London. At La Force and Luxembourg, October 11, 1793, to Jan. 1, 1794.

Lepretre, Jane Charlotte Floyd, 57, widow, and two daughters, 23 and 21, Jan. 12, 1794, to Oct. 11, 1794.

Lewis, Mary, 68, Conceptionist nun. Died 1794.

Lloyd, Mary, 77, Conceptionist nun.

Lonergan, Anne Theresa, 28, Conceptionist nun.

Long. See Blanchet.

Lutton, potter. At Carmelites', April 1, 1794, to Aug. 15, 1794.

Luttrell, Temple, M.P. for Milborne Port, 1776, son of Lord Carhampton; married daughter of Sir Henry Gould, Justice of the Common Pleas. Arrested at Boulogne, Sept. 18, 1793. At Abbaye and Luxembourg, Oct. 24, 1793, to Feb. 14, 1795. Died at Paris, Jan. 14, 1803. See pp. 148, 299.

Lynch, John Baptist, Irish. Liberated Sept. 15, 1794.

Lynch, Nicholas, Irish priest. At Luxembourg and Scotch college. Oct. 16, 1793.

Lyster, Richard, 25, servant. At St. Lazare and Luxembourg, April 24, 1794, to Jan. 27, 1795.

Lyster, Robert, 26. At Luxembourg and Irish college, Oct. 17, 1793, to Dec. 22, 1793.

Lyster, William Robert, 33, manufacturer at Paris. At St. Lazare and Luxembourg, April 24, 1794, to 1795.

Macadré (Macarthy?), Louis George Martin, 28, of Soissons, inspector of military relays. Aug. 2, 1794, to Oct. 11, 1794. Had been imprisoned at Amiens, Nov. 1793.

Macdermott, Thomas, 42, Irish priest. Jan. 19, 1793, to Oct. 13, 1793. Opened a school at St. Germain, Jerome Bonaparte being one of his pupils.

Macdonald, Charles Edward Frederick Henry, 49, sub-lieutenant in Ogilvie's regiment. Guillotined July 12, 1794. See p. 181.

Macdonald, Eliza, 36, Benedictine nun.

M'Glahan, ———. At Luxembourg and Scotch college, Oct. 20, 1793, to Oct. 27, 1793.

M'Nab, Edward, farmer, ex-ensign in Royal Scotch. Liberated Oct. 15, 1794.

Macswiney, Catherine Elizabeth, 48. At Port Royal, Dec. 7, 1793, to Oct. 11, 1794.

Maddock, Mary. At Luxembourg and Conceptionist convent, Oct. 16, 1793, to Oct. 28, 1793.

Madgett, Nicholas, 36, Irish priest. Arrested as a spy, having landed with a passport in the name of William Hurst, May 24, 1794 to Nov. 24, 1795. See p. 230.

Malone, James, 25, Irish, servant to General Ward, at Carmelites'. Guillotined June 23, 1794. See p. 177.

Mandeville, ———, Irish. Arrested at Avesnes, Oct. 1793, because styled marquis, and sent to Paris. Qy. the Mandeville, captain in Dillon's regiment, 1789.

Martin, Mary Anne. Liberated Feb. 22, 1794.

Martin, William, 28, rentier. (Qy. advocate of universal weights and measures.) At Luxembourg, Oct. 1, 1793, to Nov. 2, 1794.

Matthews, John, secret negotiator, making journeys between London and Paris in 1793. Declared a prisoner at his hotel, Sept. 6, 1793.

May, Nicholas, printer. Jan. 4, 1794.

Meek, Emily, 59, servant. Oct. 11, 1793, to Dec. 10, 1794.

Miglia, Seraphine Penry, widow. At Carmelites', Feb. 4, 1794, to Nov. 5, 1794. Styled "Mrs. Myler," by Grace Elliot, who has apparently appropriated and embellished her prison experiences. See p. 147. A Count Miglia was shot by the French at Verona, 1797.

Minns, James, 47, Benedictine. At Benedictines' and Scotch college. Oct. 11, 1793.

Minns, Jane Elizabeth Anne Frances, 48, Conceptionist nun. Died Nov. 1794.

Moore, John James. (Qy. author of "Sailors' Vocabulary." At Luxembourg and Irish college, Oct. 10, 1793.

Moore, Sarah. At Luxembourg and Austin convent.

Mosse, Francis. At Luxembourg and Scotch college, Oct. 16, 1793.

Mosse, Isaac, 29, factory-worker. At Luxembourg, Scotch, and Carmelites', Oct. 16, 1793, to Oct. 22, 1794.

Mowatt, Harold, 25. At Scotch college and Luxembourg.

Mullony, Jacques, tradesman. Had escaped from the galleys. Arrested for forging assignats, July 9, 1793.

Murdoch, James, 29, wigmaker; native of Edinburgh; formerly valet to Prince Poniatowski. Guillotined June 6, 1794. See p. 180.

Murphy, Marie Louise, widow of Lenormant. At St. Pèlagie and Benedictine convent, Feb. 16, 1794. See p. 147.

Naylor, Joseph Placidus, 69, chaplain to Benedictine nuns. At Scotch college, Conceptionist convent, and Luxembourg. Liberated Nov. 22, 1794. Corresponded with Lord Rawdon, Lord Moira, and Samuel Wesley the composer (son of Charles Wesley)

Newton, William, 32, ex-captain of dragoons. At Luxembourg, Oct. 12, 1793. Guillotined June 6, 1794. See p. 179.

Nichols, Augustus. At Plessis, April 2, 1795.

O'Brennan, Pierre, 55, priest, native of Compiègne. Guillotined July 23, 1794. See p. 182.

O'Byrne, priest, Versailles. At Luxembourg, Oct. 6, 1793, to Oct. 6, 1794.

O'Connor, James, 27, Irish student. At Benedictines' and Luxembourg, May 11, 1793, to Dec. 12, 1793.

O'Hara, General Charles. Captured at Toulon. At Luxembourg, Jan. 10, 1794. Exchanged for General Rochambeau, Aug. 1795. See pp. 227–229.

O'Hoole, ——, Irish. Arrested for "*incivisme*" and incendiary talk.

O'Keefe, Eliza. At Austin convent. Liberated Feb. 22, 1795.

O'Kennedy, wife of Charron. At Plessis. Liberated Oct. 18, 1794.

Oliveira, Catherine Kearney, widow of, 49. Liberated Jan. 27, 1794.

O'Moran, General Jacques Ferdinand, 59. Arrested at Arras, Aug. 1793; brought to La Force, Paris, Jan. 6, 1794; guillotined March 6, 1794. See p. 177.

O'Neil, Richard. At Luxembourg, July 10, 1794, to Aug. 18, 1794.

Orrell, Elizabeth Anne, 38, Austin nun.

O'Sullivan, Jacques, 33, fencing master. Tried for complicity in Nantes massacres, and acquitted Dec. 16, 1794. See pp. 208–210.

Packman, Thomas, 17, groom, Scotch. At Luxembourg, Nov. 19, 1793.

Paine, Thomas, deputy. Arrested as a measure of general safety. At Luxembourg, Jan. 1, 1794; at Hotel des Fermes, with the other Girondin deputies, Aug. 20, 1794; liberated Nov. 3, 1794. See p. 87.

Parish, Sarah. At Luxembourg, Oct. 10, 1793.

APPENDIX. 345

Parker, Dorothy, 54, Conceptionist nun. Died Dec. 1798.
Parker, George. At Luxembourg and Irish college, Oct. 13, 1793.
Parker, Henry, 40, Benedictine. At Benedictines' and Luxembourg, Oct. 11, 1793, to Dec. 10, 1794.
Parkinson, Mary Louisa, 24, Benedictine nun. Died 1794.
Parkinson, Mary Gertrude, Benedictine nun. Died 1799.
Parr, Thomas and William, brothers. At Luxembourg.
Pattinson, Jane Anne, 27, Austin nun.
Perkins, Mary Bellamy, 43. Liberated Oct. 13, 1794.
Perry, Sampson, 44, author. At Scotch college and Luxembourg. See p. 151.
Picotte (Pigott?), John. At Madelonnettes, Irish college, and Luxembourg. Liberated Sept. 24, 1794. See p. 45.
Pitt, Benjamin. At Abbaye and Luxembourg, Sept. 8, 1793, to Feb. 14, 1795. See p. 150.
Pitt, Elizabeth Atlay, wife of. At Abbaye and Luxembourg, Oct. 24, 1793, to Feb. 17, 1795.
Pitt, Elizabeth, a nun. Arrested at Amiens, Oct. 4, 1793; liberated June 5, 1795. See p. 149.
Plunkett. See Châtellux.
Pope, Francis. Arrested for insulting a deputy. At Carmelites', June 26, 1794, to Sept. 16, 1794.
Prout, Pierre Serey, 32, boatman.
Puller, William, 32, groom. At Luxembourg, Oct. 1, 1793, to Feb. 6, 1795.
Quarterman, Joseph, Irish. Oct. 18, 1793; expelled from France, Oct. 24, 1794.
Quintin, John James, 17, baker. Arrested for theft of notes, April 22, 1794; conducted to Brest, Feb. 8, 1795.
Rice, John, 32, Irish, sub-dean at English seminary. At Carmelites', July 13, 1793, to Jan 10, 1794.
Richards, ——. Liberated Feb. 4, 1795.
Rivarol, Louise Mather Flint, wife of the royalist pamphleteer. Arrested as wife of *emigré*. At Luxembourg, Austin convent, and Port Royal, April 22, 1794, to July 23, 1794. Her father was a teacher of languages. She died 1821.

APPENDIX.

Rive (Reeve ?), John. At Luxembourg.
Roden, Patrick, 28, weaver, Irishman; deserter from the English army. Guillotined June 6, 1794. See p. 180.
Sackville, Mary Clementine, 83, Conceptionist nun.
St. Leger, Edmund, 41, doctor, Irishman. Tried Jan. 8, 1794, and acquitted. Was one of the three commissioners of inquiry sent to St. Domingo in Aug. 1791; returned June 1792.
Shaw, Joseph Francis. At St. Lazare and Luxembourg.
Shelley, Dorothy, 54, Austin nun.
Simpson, Elizabeth, 52, Conceptionist nun.
Slater, Edward, 36. One of the petitioners against the muster of 20,000 National Guards near Paris, but with a number of others retracted his signature, June 19, 1792. Liberated Oct. 13, 1794.
Sloper, ——, National Guard in the Sarthe. At Madelonnettes. Liberated Oct. 25, 1794.
Smith, ——, Caday, widow of. At Plessis. Liberated Nov. 16, 1794.
Smith, Elizabeth, wife of Cornet, 22. At St. Pélagie, Oct. 10, 1793, to Oct. 17, 1794.
Smith, Elizabeth, wife of Jarnac; Irish. At Carmelites', Feb. 4, 1793.
Smith, Margaret, wife of Thevenot, 49. At Luxembourg and Austin convent, Oct. 15, 1793, to Oct. 25, 1794.
Smith, Peter, 31, baker. At Port Royal and Carmelites'. Liberated Aug. 27, 1794.
Spack, Thomas, formerly partner with Knowles in the Hotel Britannique. At Conciergerie, March 12, 1794.
Spicer, Catherine, 59, Austin lay sister.
Stafford Howard, Anastasia, 72, Conceptionist nun. Qy. Lady Anastasia Stafford Howard (only surviving child of William, Earl of Stafford), who died at Paris 1807, aged 84.
Stafford, Anne Mary, 68, Conceptionist nun.
Stanley, Thomas Francis, 59, watchmaker. Member of the Luxembourg section, alleged to have appropriated articles belonging to persons arrested by him. At

Carmelites'. Liberated April 3, 1794; rearrested, transferred to Plessis, March 20, 1795.
Stapleton, Elizabeth, 51, Austin nun.
Stevens, Henry, author. At Abbaye, Carmelites', and Luxembourg, Oct. 10, 1793, to Jan. 27, 1795. See p. 152.
Stock, Elizabeth Winifred, 72, Conceptionist nun.
Stockton, Mary, 40, Austin nun.
Stone, John Hurford. At Luxembourg, Oct. 13, 1793, to Oct. 30, 1793. Rearrested with his wife at St. Lazare, April 24, 1794, and released next day. See p. 65.
Stonor, Mary Eugenia, 25, Austin nun. Superior 1820–28. Died 1848.
Strickland, John, 70. At Benedictines' and Luxembourg, Oct. 11, 1793, to Feb. 3, 1795.
Stuart, Catherine, ex-Carmelite. At Austin convent, Feb. 23, 1794, to Nov. 28, 1795.
Stuart, Elizabeth, chambermaid. At Carmelites', Feb. 4, 1794, to Aug. 27, 1794.
Stuart, Mary Eugenia, Benedictine nun.
Sutton, Sarah, seamstress. At Plessis. Liberated Oct. 18, 1795.
Swale, Thomas, Scotch (?). At Luxembourg, Nov. 19, 1793, to Dec. 14, 1794. See p. 299.
Taylor, ——, and wife. Liberated Feb. 17 and 22, 1794. Qy. brother-in-law of Paul Jones. See p. 49.
Thellusson, John Isaac, 29, Peter, 27, and Paul Louis, 36, bankers. Probably nephews of the Peter Isaac Thellusson of London, famous for his strange will of 1797.
Thicknesse, Elizabeth, 42, Conceptionist nun.
Thilly, Matthew James. At Luxembourg, Port Royal, and Plessis. Dec. 19, 1794.
Tompson, Agnes, 40, Austin lay sister.
Tone, Matthew, brother of Theobald Wolfe Tone. Landed at Dunkirk, Aug. 1794, intending to join French army. Imprisoned as a spy till May 1795, then went to America.
Towsey, Thomas, 44. At Luxembourg, Oct. 13, 1793, to Feb. 15, 1795.

APPENDIX.

Travis, Richard, 62. At Benedictines' and Luxembourg, Oct. 11, 1793.

Trent, Mary, 72, and her niece Alice, 15, who gave herself up in order to wait on her aunt. At Conceptionist and Austin convents, Oct. 13, 1793.

Turner, John, 28, Benedictine. At St. Pélagie, Benedictines', and Luxembourg, Sept. 16, 1793, to March 19, 1795.

Twadell, Robert, 25 (qy. Rev. Robert Tweddell, brother of archæologist), at Madelonnettes, Luxembourg, and Scotch college. Liberated Jan. 18, 1795.

Vaughan, Benjamin, M.P., arrested by order of Committee of General Safety. At Carmelites', June 2 to 30, 1794. See p. 93.

Walker, ——. Arrested for insurrection of Vendémiaire (Oct. 1795); two days in prison. Probably the Protestant gentleman who at the beginning of the Revolution warmly pleaded for the British Catholic communities, and contributed to their being (temporarily) left undisturbed. See the Abbé Edgeworth's letters.

Walpole, ——, Bataille, wife of. Liberated Sept. 12, 1794.

Walpole, Lady. At Carmelites', May 22, 1794. (Qy. Mrs. Atkyns. See p. 125.)

Walsh, Comtesse Isidore Félicité Lottin, 29. At St. Pélagie and Austin convent, March 9, 1794.

Walsh, John Baptist, superior of Irish college. Arrested in March 1792 on an unfounded charge of passing a forged note. Released with apologies after several hours' detention with criminals.

Walsh, William, Irish medical student. At St. Pélagie, Oct. 11, 1793, to Dec. 15, 1793.

Ward, General Thomas, 45. Arrested as a foreigner, Oct. 10, 1793. At Abbaye and Carmelites'. Guillotined July 23, 1794. See p. 176.

Wardell, William, 23, tradesman. At Luxembourg and Scotch college, Oct. 28, 1793, to Nov. 2, 1794.

Weld, ——. At Luxembourg and Irish college, Nov. 4, 1793.

White, Christopher, 20, manufacturer. In several prisons, Oct. 11, 1793, to Nov. 18, 1794.

White, Anne Gray, wife of, 43, Mary Anne, 16, and Elizabeth, 14. At Austin convent and Luxembourg, Oct. 11, 1793 to Nov. 18, 1794.

Whiteside, Margaret Agatha, 27, Conceptionist nun.

Whittingham, Mary, 43, Austin nun.

Wild, William, 37, groom. At Luxembourg, Irish college, and Benedictines'. Liberated Feb. 6, 1795.

Wildsmith, Elizabeth Madeline, 73, Conceptionist nun.

Williams, Helen, 50, and her daughters, Perlis (Persis ?), Helen Maria, and Cecilia. At Luxembourg, Oct. 11, 1793; at Conceptionist convent, Oct. 26, 1793. See p. 68.

Wilton, Anne and Henrietta, seamstresses, formerly servants. At Luxembourg and Conceptionist convent, Oct. 11, 1793, to Oct. 4, 1794.

Winnifrith, Dinah. At Luxembourg and Conceptionist convent, Oct. 11, 1793.

Wolf, Francis. At Luxembourg and Irish college, Oct. 10, 1793.

Wood, James Athol, navy lieutenant, captain of the ship for exchanging prisoners. Brought from St. Malo, June 15, 1794. In October 1794 he petitioned the Convention, representing that in March 1794, on reaching St. Malo with 200 French prisoners from the West Indies, Deputy Lecarpentier arrested him and his crew. They were three days without food, and five months in a cell. Wood appeared before the Committee of Public Safety, but Robespierre sent him to Hermann, who consigned him to the Abbaye. The Convention asked the Committee for an immediate report on the reasons of Wood's detention. Result was probably his release. Wood became an admiral, and was knighted. Died 1829.

Woolrich, Anne, 54, Conceptionist lay sister. Died Dec. 1794, in Austin convent.

Worsley, Scolastica Joseph, Benedictine nun. Died 1821.

Williams, Thomas. At Luxembourg and Irish college, Oct. 10, 1793, to Nov. 17, 1793.

APPENDIX.

IN THE PROVINCES.

Aylmer, Balthazar Andrew, 64, ex-captain in Berwick's regiment. Arrested at Boulogne, Sept. 5, 1793; released Sept. 18, 1793.

Badger, Louis, 35, silk weaver. Shot at Lyons, Dec. 4, 1793. See p. 207.

Badger, Pierre, 27, silk weaver. Shot at Lyons, Nov. 28, 1793. See p. 207.

Bayer, Captain John, and ten sailors. Shipwrecked in the cutter *Felix*, of Southampton, off Blainville (Manche). Forged assignats in their possession. Acquitted of intention to pass them, but to be detained till exchanged. See p. 213.

Beckford, ——, and his valet, of Boulogne. Imprisoned at Arras, April 1793, because Beckford had put the valet into a green livery, "a symbol of feudalism."

Bertram, Elizabeth, 52. One of the sisters of mercy at Boulogne ousted from the hospital for refusing the oath to the civil constitution of the clergy, and imprisoned.

Brunel, *v.* Kingdom.

Buckle, Andrew Francis, deserter from Walsh's regiment. Shot at Rochefort, March 24, 1793. See p. 213.

Bulkeley, William, "Brigand of Vendée." Shot at Angers, Jan. 2, 1794. See p. 211.

Carr, John Baptist, ex-canon, recusant priest. Guillotined at Poitiers, March 18, 1794. See p. 213.

Campbell, Fanny, of Paris. Qy. Canoness of Denain. Arrested as an *émigrée* in the Doubs, 1795 or 1796.

Collow, Thomas, merchant, Havre; Scotchman. Arrested at Havre, 1793; died there, 1803. See p. 224.

Connelly, James, 39. One of the Irish *recollets* at Boulay, Lorraine. Monastery closed Nov. 1793; Connelly arrested as a recusant priest, sent to Rochefort to be transported, but fell ill and died in hospital, Aug. 4, 1794.

Dawber, John, Benedictine monk, Dieulouard. On his release became tutor and chaplain to a French viscount. Returned to England in 1802, and died at Coventry.

Dillon, Pierre, of Bouquenais (Loire Inférieure). Guillotined at Nantes, April 2, 1794.

Eliot, Charles, of Rennes. Guillotined at Rennes, Oct. 28, 1793. See p. 213.

Elliott, Grace Dalrymple, daughter of —— Dalrymple, divorced wife of Dr. (afterwards Sir) John Elliott. Imprisoned at Versailles. Died at Ville d'Avray, near Paris, 1823. See p. 146.

Farrel, Maurice, Benedictine monk, Dieulouard, 37. Died in prison.

Fitzroy, Lady. Prisoner at Quimper in 1794, but latterly allowed to occupy a house in the neighbourhood, guarded by a sentinel. Showed great kindness to English prisoners of war. Liberated about 1796. See *Blackwood's Magazine*, Dec. 1831.

Frisell, J. Fraser. Imprisoned at Dijon, 1793-94. See p. 114.

Galmoy, Viscount (Piers Butler), 52, captain in Irish Grenadiers. Arrested at Boulogne, Sept. 21, 1793.

Gem, Dr. Richard. Imprisoned at Versailles, 1793-94. See p. 29.

Glynn, Martin, 66, recusant priest. Born in Ireland. Guillotined at Bordeaux for evading the law of deportation, July 19, 1794. See p. 213.

Goff, John Joseph, of Quimper. Guillotined as a deserter, at Auxonne, June 15, 1794. See p. 213.

Gordon, Margaret Rose, 61, nun, of Bollène (Vancluse), native of Montdragon. Guillotined at Orange, July 16, 1794. See p. 213.

Griffiths, Jane Grey, 36, widow, of Hallines. Guillotined at Arras. See p. 211.

Hickey, Gregory, 58, ex-lieutenant in Berwick's regiment. Arrested at Chantilly, Jan. 23, 1794.

Joseph, Joachim, sailor. Prisoner of war, convicted of passing forged assignats at St. Brieux. Sentenced to fifteen years' imprisonment. See p. 213.

Keating, Colonel Thomas, 52, of Amiens, and wife. Arrested Oct. 11, 1793.

King, Daniel,. 36, shipowner, Dunkirk. At Tobago in 1781, became a French citizen in 1785, but arrested as a foreigner, Oct. 18, 1793, and imprisoned at Arras and Amiens. See p. 224.

Kingdom, Sophia, 17, afterwards Lady Brunel. At Rouen. Liberated 1794. See p. 215.

Knowles, Mrs., innkeeper, Boulogne. Eighteen months a prisoner, with Parker (son-in-law ?). Servant-maid and granddaughter in charge of house.

Lesueur, Marie, of Jersey. Arrested at Flamainville (Manche) with 1700 francs in her possession intended for *émigrés*. On business visits to France remittances for refugee priests were entrusted to her. Convicted at Cherbourg of exporting specie, sentenced to six months' imprisonment, and then detained till May 12, 1795. See p. 213.

Martin, Joseph, sailor. Same charge and sentence as Joseph (Joachim).

Montagu, Lord and Lady. Qy. the *soi-disant* Viscount Montague who died 1797. Arrested at Boulogne, Oct. 1793.

O'Donnel, Jacques Bruno, Jacobite refugee, living near Blois. Imprisoned and property confiscated.

O'Meara, General, 40, of Irish extraction. Arrested at Dunkirk as an Irishman and an aristocrat, July 25, 1793. Defended Dunkirk against the Duke of York, Sept. 1793.

O'Moran, Eleanor, widow of General O'Moran. Arrested at Amiens, May 14, 1794.

O'Sullivan, Charles, 28. Guillotined at Angers, Dec. 31, 1793. See p. 208.

Paterson, Mrs., wife of Col. Daniel Paterson, governor of Quebec. At Boulogne, Oct. 1793.

Plunkett, Elizabeth, of Aire. Guillotined at Arras. See p. 212.

Potter, Christopher. Arrested at Chantilly, Sept. 10, 1793, but released same day. See p. 222.

Rodney, Lady (widow of Admiral) and daughters. At Fontainebleau. Returned to England, 1796.

Smith, Joseph, engineer. Shot at Lyons. See p. 206.

APPENDIX.

Smith, Philippe, blacksmith. Guillotined at Mulhouse, Dec. 23, 1793.

Smyth (Walter?). Had lived twelve years at Nancy. Arrested in April 1793 for complicity in an alleged plot with persons mostly unknown to him. (Qy. Smythe of Bambridge, brother of Mrs. Fitzherbert. See p. 228.)

Stapleton, Dr. Gregory, Poynter, Dr. William, and Plowden, Charles, of Douai college. Prisoners at Doullens. See p. 217.

Style, Lady. At Abbeville. See p. 276.

Thicknesse, Anne. At Abbeville. See p. 214.

Tuffnell, Mrs. (of Langleys, Essex?). At Abbeville.

Thomson, Charlotte, 40, native of Vienne, wife of François Laisin, *émigré*. Interrogated and property sequestrated, April 6, 1794. See p. 214.

Thomson, William, 39, native of Bordeaux. Charged with dealings with the enemy; declared the letters to have been written by his partner, Wittford, a Swede. Acquitted Feb. 26, 1794.

Wallop, Hon. H., son of Earl of Portsmouth. Died at Calais, Nov. 28, 1794.

Warburton, Capt. Samuel, 58, native of London. Shot at Lyons, Dec. 22, 1793. See p. 207.

Watson, Peter, 28, Dunkirk. In partnership with Daniel King. See p. 224.

F.

English Prisoners, 1803-14.

(See p. 259.)

Ancrum, Lady. Allowed to return. Died 1805. Her husband afterwards Marquis of Lothian.
Annesley, Colonel (afterwards General) Arthur, son of Lord A. Escaped from Verdun, 1805. Died 1849. See p. 275.
Arblay, Madame d'. Released 1812. See p. 269.
Astley, Philip, circus proprietor. Escaped. See p. 267.
Aufrere, Anthony, editor of the Lockhart Letters.
Barrington, Lord. Died 1813. See p. 280.
Benfield, Paul. Died 1810. See pp. 255, 276.
Berry, Admiral Sir Edward.
Bessborough, *v.* Duncannon.
Beverley, Lord, *v.* Lovaine.
Boyd, Walter, banker. See p. 276.
Boyle, Lord, son of Earl of Glasgow.
Boyne, *v.* Hamilton, G.
Brooke, Thomas, M.P. for Newton, Lancashire. High Sheriff of Cheshire, 1810. Escaped from Valenciennes, 1804. Died 1821. See p. 274.
Cadogan, Lady. See p. 279.
Chambers, Sir Robert, late Chief Justice at Calcutta. Died at Paris, May 9, 1803.
Churchill, Rev. W. H., of Colliton, Dorset. Released 1804. Died 1847. See p. 268.
Clavering, Sir Thomas (1771-1853).
Cockburn, Alexander. See p. 274.
Coghill, Sir John. See p. 276.
Concanon, Richard, of County Galway. Died 1810. See p. 279.
Craufurd, Sir James. Escaped 1804. See p. 273.
Crespigny, Philip de. Escaped from St. Germain, 1811. Died 1851. See p. 275.
Croft, Sir Herbert. See p. 269.

APPENDIX.

De Bathe, Sir James. See p. 267.
De Blaquiere, Hon. G., son of Lord de B. See p. 278.
Don, Alexander. Escaped from Paris, 1810. See p. 275.
Donegal, Dowager Marchioness of. See p. 267.
Duncannon, Lord, son of Earl of Bessborough. Released. See p. 266.
Dupré, William, of Jersey. Author of the "Lexicographia Neologica Gallica," 1801.
Eardley (qy. Sir John Eardley Wilmot. 1774–1845).
Edwards, Colonel William, father of H. Milne Edwards. Died at Paris 1823.
Elgin, Earl of. Released 1806. See p. 262.
Ferguson, ——, F.R.S., mineralogist. Published account of meteorite seen by him at Geneva, April 15, 1804. Released 1804.
Forbes, C. Interned at Tours.
Forbes, James, F.R.S., orientalist. Released. See p. 265.
Frisell, J. Fraser. See p. 277.
Goldsmith, Lewis. See p. 282.
Gower, Captain Leveson.
Greathead, Henry. See p. 266.
Green, William, M.P. for Dungarvan.
Hamilton, Alexander, orientalist. Released. See p. 265.
Hamilton, Hon. G., afterwards Viscount Boyne. At Fontainebleau, 1803.
Hare, Sir Thomas. Allowed to return. See p. 266.
Harrington, Earl of. At Valenciennes.
Hendry, Robert. Released 1806. See p. 266.
Impey, Sir Elijah. Released. See p. 267.
Jodrell, Francis and Captain Thomas. Escaped from Valenciennes, 1813. They waited on the commandant, told him they withdrew their parole, and then posted off. Francis was High Sheriff of Cheshire, 1813.
Kydd, Stuart, jurist. Escaped. Died 1811. See p. 267.
Lavie, Sir Thomas. See p. 278.
Lovaine, Lord, afterwards Duke of Northumberland (1775–1867). See p. 272.

APPENDIX.

Maclean, Charles, M.D. Released. See p. 265.
Macnab Dr. Henry Grey. See p. 277.
Masterson, John. In the Franco-Irish regiment before the Revolution. Interned at Brussels.
Morshead, Sir John, Lord Warden of the Stannaries. Died 1813. See p. 267.
Mountcashell, Lord and Lady.
Mulvey, Farell, M.D., author of "Sketches of the Character, Conduct, and Treatment of the Prisoners of War," 1818. Attempted to escape, but recaptured.
Osborn, ——, F.R.S.
Parry, James, ex-editor of the *Courier*. Died at Verdun, May 1805. See p. 276.
Phillips, Colonel of Marines. See p. 278.
Pinkerton, John, geographer. Released 1805. See p. 266.
Plumptre, Anne. See p. 271.
Robson, R. B., ex-M.P. for Okehampton. Interned at Nimes. Released Nov. 1803.
Roebuck, Edward, 51, and wife. At Amiens, May 1794.
Roget, Peter Mark. Escaped from Geneva, July 18, 1803. See p. 275.
Roper, Hon. Thomas. See p. 319, 325, 330.
Shaftesbury, Earl of. Released. Died in London 1811. See p. 265.
Shipley, General Sir Charles. Released. See p. 266.
Spencer, Lord. See pp. 243, 252.
Stack, General Edward, aide-de-camp to Louis XV.; entered English army after Revolution. Died at Calais, 1833.
Sturt, Charles, ex-M.P. for Bridport. Escaped. See p. 259.
Style, Lady Isabella, widow of Sir Charles. Died at St. Omer, 1808. See p. 276.
Thompson, ex-M.P. for Evesham. Interned at Orleans.
Tichborne, Sir Henry (1779-1845), and his brother James, (1784-1862). "The Claimant" pretended to be Sir James's son.
Tuckey, J. Hingston, navigator. See p. 277.
Tufton, Hon. Edward and Henry, brothers of Earl of Thanet.

APPENDIX.

Tweeddale, Marquis and Marchioness of. See p. 275.
Walhope. Died at Verdun, 1807.
Webb, Sir Thomas and Lady. See p. 277.
Woodford, ——, son of Sir Ralph W.
Wolseley, Charles and Henry, sons of Sir William. See p. 278.
Yarmouth, Earl of. Released 1806. See p. 263.

INDEX OF NAMES.*

ABERCROMBY, General, 264
Aberdeen, Lord, 250
Albany, Countess, 127-8
Anderson, Professor John, 51-2
Annesley, Hon. A., 275
Arblay, Madame d', 269
Arthur, J. J., 183, 192-7, 286
Astley, Philip, 267-8
Atkyns, Mrs., 125-6
Auckland, Lord, 230
Auvergne, Admiral P. d', 253-4

BADGER, L. and P., 207
Banks, Sir J., 53, 265
Barclay, Sir R., 237
Barlow, Joel, 10
Barrington, Lord, 280
Bayer, Captain, 213
Beckett, William, 52
Bedford, Duke of, 242
Bedford, Duchess of, 252
Benfield, Paul, 255, 276
Bennett, Lawrence, 222
Bentham, Jeremy, 53, 84, 92, 246
Bernet, *vide* Kirkham.
Berry, Miss, 251, 261
Bessborough, Lord, 266
Beverley, Lord, 272
Bishop, Mrs. M., 282
Blackden, Samuel, 49
Blackwell, T., 13

Blackwood, Sir H., 113-14
Blagden, Sir C., 251
Blayney, Lord, 280
Bode, Baron de, 216
Bosville, 244
Boyd, Walter, 31, 129, 255, 276
Boyne, Lord, 278
Braham, John, 231
Brettergh, R., 217
Brook, Thomas, 274
Broughton, 275
Brunel, Sir M. and Lady, 215-16
Buckle, A. F., 213
Bulkeley, William, 211
Burdett, Sir F., 244-5
Burges, Bland, 34, 64, 117
Burney, Fanny, *vide* Arblay.
Burns, Robert, 51
Byrne, Miles, 168, 279-80

CADOGAN, Lady, 279
Cahir, Lord, 252
Camelford, Lord, 32, 250
Campbell, Lord John, 261
Carondelet, *vide* Plunket, R.
Carr, Sir John, 248
Carr, John Baptist, 213
Cartwright, Major, 53
Caulfeild, St. George, 250
Chambly, C. F., 180
Châtellux, Marquise, 157-8

* See also Appendix E. and F., pp. 334, 354.

INDEX.

Chenevix, R., 228, 270-1
Cholmondeley, Lord and Lady, 105, 252-3
Christie, Thomas, 78-9, 98
Churchill, Rev. W. H., 268
Clarendon, Lady, 252
Clarkson, Thomas, 84, 115-16
Cobbett, William, 124-5
Cockburn, Alexander, 274
Codrington, Sir W., 40, 148, 291-9
Coghill, Sir J., 276
Coigley, James, 164
Coll, Sir William, 261
Collow, Thomas, 224
Combe, Alderman, 245
Concanon, Richard, 279
Constable, Edward, 331
Conyngham, Lord and Lady, 252-3
Cooper, Thomas, 45-8, 98
Coquerel, *vide* Williams, Cecilia.
Corby, 130
Cornwallis, Lord, 254
Cosway, Mrs., 251
Cotes, Captain James, 232
Craufurd, Sir James, 273-4
Craufurd, Quintin, 121-2
Crespigny, P. de, 275
Croft, Sir H., 269-70
Crofton, Lady and Miss, 251
Cumberland, Duchess of, 251

DAER, Lord, 84
Damer, Mrs., 107, 251, 261
Davies, Captain, 228
Davy, Sir H., 269
Dayrell, E. and Mrs., 237-8
De Bathe, Sir J., 267
De Blaquiere, G., 278
Delany, Thomas, 179-80
Devonshire, Duke and Duchess of, 105
Dillon, General A., 132, 171-5, 183
Dillon, General Theobald, 175
Disney-Ffytche, 124
Don, Alexander, 275

Donegal, Lady, 267
Dorset, Duke of, 7, 9, 25-7
Dorset, Duchess of, 248
Duplessis-Smith, 201
Duroure, Scipio, 199-200
Dutton, 282

EBRINGTON, Lord, 243, 260
Eden, *v*. Auckland.
Edwards, Bryan, 50, 224
Edwards, George, 53
Edgeworth, Abbé, 134-8, 248
Edgeworth, Elizabeth, 156
Edgeworth, R. L. and Maria, 248
Egremont, Lord, 252
Elgin, Lord, 262-3
Eliot, Charles, 213
Elliot, Hugh, 36
Elliott, Grace Dalrymple, 30, 146-7
Ely, Lord, 252
Emmet, Robert, 253
Erskine, Lord, 85, 244-5
Este, Rev. Charles, 228.

FALKLAND, Lord, 252
Ferguson, R. Cutlar, 31
Ferguson, —— F.R.S., 267
Ferris, Richard, 167-8
Fitzgerald, Lord E., 64, 98
Fitzgerald, Pamela, 64
Fitzgerald, Lord R., 27-8
Fitzpatrick, General, 243
Fitzsimons, Gerard, 165
Flood, 130
Forbes, James, 265
Foster, Lady, 251-2
Fox, C. J., 65, 73-4, 98, 142, 193, 242, 244, 251, 264
Fox, General, 243
Foxlowe, 222
Frampton, James, 109
Ffrench and Johnston, 223
Freeman-Shepherd, Mrs., 54-6
Frisell, J. Fraser, 114-15, 277

INDEX.

GALL, Major, 228
Gamble, 47, 53, 223
Gay, Nicholas, 50, 59
Gem, Dr. R., 29-30
Gerard, Sir R., 124
Glynne, Martin, 213
Godwin, Fanny, 75
Godwin, vide Wollstonecraft.
Goff, J. J., 213
Goldsmith, Lewis, 56, 244, 271, 282
Gordon, Duchess of, 251-2
Gordon, Margaret, 213
Gower, Earl, 28-34
Granville, Earl, 30
Greathead, H., 266-7
Grenville, General Richard, 149
Grieve, George, 187-92
Griffiths, Jane Grey, 211-12

HAMILTON, Alexander, 265
Hamilton, Lord Archibald, 252
Hamilton, Duke of, 252
Hamilton, Lady Mary, 178, 229, 270
Hamilton, Miss, v. Jouy.
Hamilton, Robert, 178, 229
Hamilton, William, 277
Hammond, George, 117, 242
Hare, Sir T., 266
Harrop, Charles, 146, 181
Hathway, 12
Hendry, Robert, 266
Hertford, vide Yarmouth.
Higginson, Lady, 252
Hippisley, Sir J. Cox, 27, 56
Hodgson, Rev. ——, 262
Hodgson, Joseph, 218
Holcroft, Thomas, 247
Holland, Lord, 243
Horne-Tooke, 78, 90, 98, 250
Hunter, William, 108-9
Huskisson, William, 29-31, 116
Hutchinson, J. Hely, 118
Hyde, Catherine, 126-7
Hyde de Neuville, 233

IMPEY, SIR E., 247, 267

JACKSON, SIR G., 250, 267
James II., 164-6
James, Captain C., 199
James, W. B., 198.
Jerningham, C., 123
Jenkinson, vide Liverpool.
Jones, vide Paul Jones.
Jones, Hugh, 50
Joseph, J., 213
Jouy, Madame, 178, 229
Joyce, Jeremiah ("Scientific Dialogues"), 99, 100

KAVANAGH, JOSEPH, 200-1
Kemble, Charles, 218
Kemble, John P., 219, 245, 247
Ker, 31, 129
Kerly, 129
Kerry, Lord, 4, 119-21
Kilmaine, Gen., 152-3
King, Daniel, 224
Kingdom, Sophia, vide Brunel.
Kirkham, Lydia, 58-9
Knowles, Mrs., 108
Kydd, Stuart, 267
Kynnersley, vide Bode.

LALLY-TOLLENDAL, 243
Lambert, Sir J., 4
Lansdowne, Lord, 90-2, 121
Lansdowne (Lord H. Petty), 251
Lauderdale, Lord, 67, 92, 131, 242, 264
Lavie, Sir T., 278
Lawrence, J. H., 281
Lesueur, Mary, 213-14
Leviscourt, 281-2
Lindsay, William, 34, 120
Lingard, Dr., 109-11, 218
Linwood, Miss, 251
Liverpool, Lord, 15, 16
Luttrell, Temple, 148-9, 299
Lytton, R. Warburton, 214

MAC CANNA, 163
Macdermott, 166
Macdonagh, Colonel, 17-19

INDEX.

Macdonald, C. and D., 99, 180-1
Mackenzie, C. M., 272
Mackintosh, Sir J., 78, 84, 98, 245-6
Maclaurin, Dr., 262
Maclean, Charles, 265
Macnab, Dr. H. G., 277
Macnevin, 253
Madan, Dr., 281
Madgett, Nicholas, 230
Malmesbury, Lord, 30, 57-8, 152, 228-29, 232
Malone, John, 177
Mandeville, J. H., 262
Manning, Sarah, 91
Manning, Thomas, 247
Manning, William, 91, 96
Massareene, Lord, 3-8, 20
Marsh, Richard, 220-1
Martin, Jos., 213
Mary Stuart's portrait, 219-20
Maxwell, Dr., 77-8
Merry, Anthony, 241
Merry, Robert, 99, 101
Miglia, Mrs., 147
Milne, 223
Mitford, 228
Moncrief, 182
Money, General John, 132-4
Monro, Capt. George, 35, 85, 99
Monck, Lady E., 252
Moore, Dr. John, 131
Morgan (Irish), 35
Morgan and Massy, 222
Morgan, Lady, 74
Morris, Gouverneur, 33, 49, 87, 89, 158
Morshead, Sir J., 267
Mountedgecumbe, Lord, 253
Muir, Thomas, 97
Murdoch, James, 180-2
Murdoch, John, 51
Murphy, Maria, 147

NAYLOR, Rev. J. P., 305-6
Nesham, Admiral, 112-13
Newcastle, Duke and Duchess of, 267

Newton, William, 179-80
Northumberland, *vide* Beverley.
Nuns: Aire, 221
,, Cambray, 221, 310
,, Dunkirk, 221
,, Gravelines, 222
,, . Paris, 155
,, Rouen, 221

O'BRENNAN, P., 182
O'Brien, 201
O'Connell, D., 99-100, 218
O'Hara, General, 227, 229
O'Moran, General, 177-8
Opie, 243
O'Reilly, 223
Ossulston, Lord, 252
O'Sullivan, Charles, 208-10
O'Sullivan, J. B., 208-10
Oswald, John, 76-7
Otway, Sylvester, *vide* Oswald.

PAINE, Thomas, 78, 83-9, 98-9, 101, 142, 150, 152, 176, 188, 229, 244, 247
Palmerston, Lord, 105-7, 283
Parry, James, 276
Paul Jones, 48-9
Payne, James, 276
Pembroke, Lord, 252
Penswick, 219
Perry, Sampson, 88, 97, 150-2
Phillips, Colonel, 273
Pigott, Robert, 39-44, 65
Pigott family, 44-5, 51
Pinkerton, John, 266
Piozzi, Madame, 101, 155-6
Pitt, Benjamin and Elizabeth, 150
Pitt, Elizabeth Joanna, 149-50
Playfair, William, 10-13
Playfair, Dr. James, 13
Plumptre, Anne, 271
Plunket, *vide* Châtellux.
Plunket, Elizabeth, 212-13
Plunket, Rose, 17-19
Potter, Chr., 56-8, 222
Poynter, William, 218

INDEX.

Power, H. M., 52
Price, Dr., 63, 78
Priestley, Dr. and William, 14–15, 65, 67, 84, 90, 98

RAYMENT, Robert, 47, 53, 99
Reynolds, Thomas, 124
Rigby, Dr., 16–21
Rivers, Lady, 108
Roden, Patrick, 180
Rodney, Lady, 228
Rogers, Samuel, 64, 117–18, 244
Roget, Dr., 275
Romilly, Sir S., 247
Roper, Hon. T., 319–30
Rose, Auguste, 41, 197–8
Rowan, A. H., 75
Russell, Thomas, 253
Rutledge, James, 3, 18

ST. JOHN, Lord, 243
Seymour, Henry, 122–3, 190
Seymour, Lord H., 264
Seymour, J. B., 52
Seymour family, 123
Shaftesbury, Lord, 259, 265
Sheares, H. and J., 99–100
Sheffield, Lord, 115
Shelburne, *vide* Lansdowne.
Shepherd, *vide* Freeman.
Shepherd, Rev. S., 249–50
Shipley, Sir C., 266
Smith, George S., 236
Smith, Joseph, 206–7
Smith, Lady, 229
Smith, Sir Robert, 98, 101, 229
Smith, Sir Sidney, 228, 230, 232–6
Smith, Spencer, 232, 235
Smith, William, 67, 92
Smythe, Walter, 228
Somers, 35
Southey, Henry, 247
Spencer, Lord Robert, 243, 252,
Stanhope, Lady Hester, 100, 252
Stanley of Alderley, Sir J., 116
Stapleton, Gregory, 217
Stevens, Henry, 152

Stone, J. H., 63–8, 70, 74, 92, 98, 197
Stone, William, 66–7, 89, 92
Storace, Signora, 231
Strathnavar, Lord, 34
Sturt, Charles, 259
Style, Lady, 276
Sullivan, Mrs., *vide* Craufurd.
Sutherland, *vide* Gower.
Sutherland, Countess of, 33–4
Swale, Thomas, 299.
Swinburne, Anne, 111
Swinburne, Captain, 157, 162, 227, 230, 232
Swinburne, Henry, 111
Swinburne, Mrs., 108
Swinton, Samuel, 50
Sykes, 16, 223–4

TALBOT, JAMES, 262
Tandy, Napper, 13
Tarleton, Sir B., 116
Taylor, Mrs., 49
Taylor, William, 247
Thicknesse, Mrs., 214–15
Thomson, Charlotte, 214
Thornton, Colonel T., 248–9
Thrale, *vide* Piozzi.
Tierney, George, 247
Tone, Wolfe, 73
Trotter, J. B., 243
Troy, Archbishop, 254
Tuckey, J. H., 277
Tuthill, Mrs., 267
Tweeddale, Lord and Lady, 275–6
Twiss, Richard, 129–30

VAUGHAN, BENJAMIN, 89–97
Vaughan family, 89–90, 96–7
Vickery, 52
Vitré, Denis de, 153–4

WADDINGTON, WILLIAM, 224
Walkingshaw, Clementine, 128–9
Walsh, 167
Warburton, Samuel, 207

Ward, R. Plumer, 177
Ward, Gen. Thomas, 176-7
Warner, Dr. John, 31-2
Watson, Robert, 271-2
Watson, Peter, 224
Watt, James, jun., 45-8
Watt, James, 247
Webb, Sir T. and Lady, 277-8
West, Sir B., 243
Westerman, Richard, 213
Weston, Rev. S., 249
White, Capt. J. F., 8-10
White, Miss, 164
Whitworth, Lord, 242-8, 262
Wilberforce, William, 84
Williams, Cecilia, 73

Williams, David, 84, 116-17
Williams, Helen M., 64, 66 68-75, 243-4, 249 50
Wilson, Capt., 51
Wollaston, Charles, 109
Wollstonecraft, Mary, 75
Wolseley, C. and H., 278
Wordsworth, William, 118-19, 242
Wright, Capt. J. W., 232, 236

Yarmouth, Lord, 263
Yorke, H. Redhead, 99-101, 179
Young, Arthur, 132, 222

THE END.

PRINTED BY BALLANTYNE, HANSON AND CO.
EDINBURGH AND LONDON.

LOW'S STANDARD NOVELS.

In small post 8vo, uniform, cloth extra, bevelled boards.
Price SIX SHILLINGS each, unless where otherwise stated.

By WILLIAM BLACK.
The Penance of John Logan. 10s. 6d.
Three Feathers.
A Daughter of Heth (19th Ed.)
Kilmeny.
In Silk Attire.
Lady Silverdale's Sweetheart.
Sunrise.
Strange Adventures of a House Boat.

By R. D. BLACKMORE.
Lorna Doone. 25th Edition. (Also an Illustrated Edition, 21s., 31s. 6d., and 35s.)
Springhaven. Illustrated Ed. 12s.
Alice Lorraine.
Cradock Nowell.
Clara Vaughan.
Cripps the Carrier.
Erema; or, My Father's Sin.
Mary Anerley.
Christowell: a Dartmoor Tale.
Tommy Upmore.

By THOMAS HARDY.
The Trumpet-Major.
Far from the Madding Crowd.
The Hand of Ethelberta.
A Laodicean.
Two on a Tower.
A Pair of Blue Eyes.
The Return of the Native.
The Mayor of Casterbridge.

By GEORGE MACDONALD.
Mary Marston.
Guild Court.
The Vicar's Daughter.
Adela Cathcart.
Stephen Archer.
Weighed and Wanting.
Orts.

By Mrs. J. H. RIDDELL.
Daisies and Buttercups: a Novel of the Upper Thames.
The Senior Partner.
Alaric Spenceley.
A Struggle for Fame.

By W. CLARK RUSSELL.
In crown 8vo. volumes, half leather binding. 3s. 6d. each.
Wreck of the "Grosvenor."
John Holdsworth (Chief Mate.)
A Sailor's Sweetheart.
The "Lady Maud."
Little Loo: a Tale of the South Sea.
The Sea Queen.
Jack's Courtship.
My Watch Below.
The Frozen Pirate.

By Mrs. BEECHER STOWE.
Old Town Folk.
We and Our Neighbours.
Poganuc People.

By Mrs. CASHEL HOEY.
A Golden Sorrow.
Out of Court.
A Stern Chase.

By JEAN INGELOW.
Sarah de Beranger.
Don John.
John Jerome. 5s.

By Mrs. MACQUOID.
Elinor Drygen.
Diane.

By Miss COLERIDGE.
An English Squire.

By Rev. E. GILLIAT, M.A.
A Story of the Dragonnades.

By JOSEPH HATTON.
Three Recruits, and the Girls they Left Behind Them.
The Old House at Sandwich.

By C. F. WOOLSON.
Anne.
For the Major. 5s.

By LEW. WALLACE.
Ben Hur: a Tale of the Christ.

London: SAMPSON LOW, MARSTON, SEARLE & RIVINGTON, Limited,
St. Dunstan's House, Fetter Lane, Fleet Street, E.C.

STANDARD BOOKS FOR BOYS.
FULLY ILLUSTRATED.

In very handsome cloth binding; crown 8vo, 2s. 6d.; gilt edges, 3s. 6d.

By W. H. G. KINGSTON.

DICK CHEVELEY: His Adventures and Misadventures.

HEIR OF KILFINNAN: A Tale of the Shore and Ocean.

SNOWSHOES AND CANOES; or, The Adventures of a Fur-Hunter in the Hudson's Bay Territory.

THE TWO SUPERCARGOES; or, Adventures in Savage Africa.

WITH AXE AND RIFLE ON THE WESTERN PRAIRIES; or, The Western Pioneers.

CAPTAIN MUGFORD; or, Our Salt and Fresh Water Tutors.

By G. A. HENTY.

JACK ARCHER: A Tale of the Crimea. With Plans of some of the Principal Battles;

THE CORNET OF HORSE: A Tale of Marlborough's Wars.

WINNING HIS SPURS: A Tale of the Crusades.

By BOUSSENARD.

THE CRUSOES OF GUIANA; or, The White Tiger.

THE GOLD-SEEKERS. A Sequel to the above.

By LOUIS ROUSSELET.

THE DRUMMER-BOY: A Story of the days of Washington.

THE KING OF THE TIGERS.

THE SON OF THE CONSTABLE OF FRANCE.

By E. MULLER.

NOBLE WORDS AND NOBLE DEEDS.

By G. MANVILLE FENN.

OFF TO THE WILDS: Being the Adventures of Two Brothers.

THE SILVER CAÑON: A Tale of the Western Plains.

By COL. SIR W. BUTLER, K.C.B.

RED CLOUD, THE SOLITARY SIOUX: A Tale of the Great Prairie.

By HARRY COLLINGWOOD.

The VOYAGE of the "AURORA."

UNDER THE METEOR FLAG: the Log of a Midshipman during the French Revolutionary War.

By J. PERCY GROVES.

CHARMOUTH GRANGE: A Tale of the 17th Century.

By B. HELDMANN.

THE MUTINY ON BOARD THE SHIP "LEANDER."

By LEON CAHUN.

THE BLUE BANNER; or, THE Adventures of a Mussulman, a Christian, and a Pagan in the time of the Crusades and Mongol Conquest.

THE ADVENTURES OF CAPTAIN MAGO. A Phœnician's Explorations round the Cape of Good Hope 1000 years B.C.

By MRS. DODGE.

HANS BRINKER; or, The Silver Skates.

ADVENTURES in NEW GUINEA: The Narrative of Louis Trégauce.

The earlier issues of this Series have met with most remarkable success, both in the United Kingdom and abroad, and have been patronised very largely for Prizes by the School Board for London, and by many important School Boards in the Provinces. The merit of the NEW VOLUMES justifies expectations of equal success for them.

London: **SAMPSON LOW, MARSTON, SEARLE & RIVINGTON, Limited,**
St. Dunstan's House, Fetter Lane, Fleet Street, E.C.

A LIST OF MANUALS ON
FOREIGN COUNTRIES AND BRITISH COLONIES.

Edited by F. S. PULLING, M.A., F.R.G.S., Exeter College, Oxford; formerly Professor in the Yorkshire College, Leeds.

The general aim of the Series is to present a clear and accurate idea of the actual state of the different countries in a sufficiently popular form to interest the general reader, while, at the same time, the works will prove eminently useful for educational purposes.

Each country is treated of by a writer who, from personal knowledge, is qualified to speak with authority upon the subject.

The volumes contain from 200 to 230 crown 8vo pages, Physical and Political Maps, and Illustrations. Price 3s. 6d. each.

"*Very useful and valuable series.*"—*Pall Mall Gazette.*

Egypt. By STANLEY LANE-POOLE.
France. By the Authoress of "Mademoiselle Mori."
Denmark and Iceland. By E. C. OTTÉ.
Russia. By W. R. MORFILL.
Japan. By S. MOSSMAN.
Greece. By LEWIS SERGEANT.
Austria-Hungary. By DAVID KAY.
The West Indies. By C. H. EDEN.
Peru. By CLEMENTS R. MARKHAM.

Australia. By J. F. VESEY FITZGERALD.
"An excellent number of the useful and valuable series."—*Pall Mall Gazette.*
"Solid, trustworthy information."—*Manchester Examiner.*
"A comprehensive, accurate, and reliable digest of the history and physical characteristics of Australia."—*Melbourne Age.*
Spain. By the Rev. WENTWORTH WEBSTER, M.A.
Sweden and Norway. By the Rev. F. H. WOODS, B.D.
Germany. By S. BARING-GOULD, Author of "Germany, Past and Present."

THE GREAT MUSICIANS.
A Series of Biographies of the Great Musicians.
Edited by Dr. FRANCIS HUEFFER.
Small Post 8vo, Cloth Extra, price 3s. each.

"In these dainty volumes, under the able superintendence of Mr. Hueffer, musical authorities of note describe the lives and criticise the masterpieces of the great musicians, conveying just such information as is most required, and thereby satisfying a desire which has lately been making itself more and more felt."—*Times.*

Mendelssohn. By W. S. ROCKSTRO.
Mozart. By Dr. F. GEHRING.
Handel. By Mrs. JULIAN MARSHALL.
Wagner. By the EDITOR. Second Edition, with additional matter, bringing the history down to the end of 1882.
Weber. By Sir JULIUS BENEDICT.
Schubert. By H. F. FROST.

Rossini and the Modern Italian School. By H. SUTHERLAND EDWARDS.
Purcell. By W. H. CUMMINGS.
English Church Composers. By WILLIAM ALEX. BARRETT, Mus. Bac. Oxon.; Vicar Choral of St. Paul's Cathedral.
John Sebastian Bach. By REGINALD LANE POOLE.
Schumann. By J. A. FULLER MAITLAND.
Haydn. By Miss TOWNSHEND.

London: SAMPSON LOW, MARSTON, SEARLE & RIVINGTON, Limited,
St. Dunstan's House, Fetter Lane, Fleet Street, E.C.

SECOND EDITION, NOW READY.

Imperial 32mo, marbled edges, cloth, 3s. 6d. ; roan, 4s. 6d.

LOW'S POCKET ENCYCLOPÆDIA:
A COMPENDIUM OF GENERAL KNOWLEDGE FOR READY REFERENCE.

Containing 1206 columns, upwards of 25,000 References, and numerous Plates.

REVIEWS OF THE PRESS.

"A useful little work."—*Athenæum.* "Very correct and truthworthy."—*Standard.*

"A marvel of concise condensation, in which the utmost possible use has been made of abbreviations and signs. There are over twelve hundred pages and twenty-two plates. A great deal of thought and ingenuity has evidently been expended on this compact little volume. The print, though small, is not too small. Altogether, it forms the neatest, smallest, and most useful Encyclopædia we have yet seen."—*Spectator.*

"'The Pocket Encyclopædia' is one of the most handy and complete volumes of its kind yet offered to the public. The 'Encyclopædia' contains just that class of information which is most frequently required ; and this is put in the most concise and accurate manner possible."—*Morning Post.*

"A marvellous amount of information has been crowded into the 600 pages of this book by the adoption of a complete system of signs and contractions, and the rigorous exclusion of every superfluous word. It is no hasty compilation, but a comprehensive work of reference of a very solid and useful character. The printing is clear and distinct, and as the volume can be readily carried in the pocket, will prove a valuable travelling companion."—*Daily Chronicle.*

"A wonderful little Encyclopædia . . . . a pefect marvel of condensation and arrangement. The author says he compiled it, in the first instance, for his own use, but there will be thousands of persons grateful that he has not kept it to himself. It is surprisingly varied in its contents, is most compact and handy in form, is beautifully clear in typography and illustrations, and is low in price. It is not enough to say that we know of nothing to surpass this miniature Encyclopædia—we know of nothing that approaches it."—*Glasgow Herald.*

"'The Pocket Encyclopædia' merits the highest commendation. It is a thoroughly useful and trustworthy work, and we shall be much surprised if it does not obtain an enormous sale. It is the handiest book of reference ever offered to the public."—*Court Circular.*

"For handy reference 'The Pocket Encyclopædia' will be found extremely useful."—*Scotsman.*

"This diminutive dictionary will provide the inquirer with brief answers to the innumerable questions arising amid the affairs of ordinary life. The printing and paper are all that can be desired, and the volume is as neat as it is useful, and we can warmly recommend it."—*Public Opinion.*

"A veritable *multum in parvo.* What Bellows's little Pocket Dictionary has done for the French Language—being a treasure of completeness and accuracy—this small book achieves very efficiently for general information on everything. Its store of facts is wonderfully graphic and extensive. Its information is well up to date. This new book is a welcome and cheap addition to the list of works of reference."—*Leeds Mercury.*

The ENCYCLOPÆDIA will be sent post free on receipt of P.O.O. by the Publishers.

London : **SAMPSON LOW, MARSTON, SEARLE & RIVINGTON,** Limited, St. Dunstan's House, Fetter Lane, Fleet Street, E.C.

A Catalogue of American and Foreign Books Published or Imported by MESSRS. SAMPSON LOW & CO. *can be had on application.*

St. Dunstan's House, Fetter Lane, Fleet Street, London,
September, 1888.

A Selection from the List of Books
PUBLISHED BY
SAMPSON LOW, MARSTON, SEARLE, & RIVINGTON,
LIMITED.

ALPHABETICAL LIST.

*A*BBOTT *(C. C.) Poaetquissings Chronicle.* 10s. 6d.

—— *Waste Land Wanderings.* Crown 8vo, 7s. 6d.
Abney (W. de W.) and Cunningham. Pioneers of the Alps. With photogravure portraits of guides. Imp. 8vo, gilt top, 21s.
Adam (G. Mercer) and Wetherald. An Algonquin Maiden. Crown 8vo, 5s.
Adams (C. K.) Manual of Historical Literature. Cr. 8vo, 12s. 6d.
Agassiz (A.) Three Cruises of the Blake. Illustrated. 2 vols., 8vo, 42s.
Alcott. Works of the late Miss Louisa May Alcott :—
    Eight Cousins. Illustrated, 2s.; cloth gilt, 3s. 6d.
    Jack and Jill. Illustrated, 2s.; cloth gilt, 3s. 6d.
    Jo's Boys. 5s.
    Jimmy's Cruise in the Pinafore, &c. Illustrated, cloth, 2s.; gilt edges, 3s. 6d.
    Little Men. Double vol., 2s.; cloth, gilt edges, 3s. 6d.
    Little Women. 1s. ⎫ 1 vol., cloth, 2s.; larger ed., gilt
    Little Women Wedded. 1s. ⎭ edges, 3s. 6d.
    Old-fashioned Girl. 2s.; cloth, gilt edges, 3s. 6d.
    Rose in Bloom. 2s.; cloth gilt, 3s. 6d.
    Silver Pitchers. Cloth, gilt edges, 3s. 6d.
    Under the Lilacs. Illustrated, 2s.; cloth gilt, 5s.
    Work : a Story of Experience. 1s. ⎫ 1 vol., cloth, gilt
    —— Its Sequel, "Beginning Again." 1s. ⎭ edges, 3s. 6d.
Alden (W. L.) Adventures of Jimmy Brown, written by himself. Illustrated. Small crown 8vo, cloth, 2s.
Aldrich (T. B.) Friar Jerome's Beautiful Book, &c. 3s. 6d.
Alford (Lady Marian) Needlework as Art. With over 100 Woodcuts, Photogravures, &c. Royal 8vo, 21s.; large paper, 84s.
Amateur Angler's Days in Dove Dale : Three Weeks' Holiday in 1884. By E. M. 1s. 6d.; boards, 1s.; large paper, 5s.

A

Andersen. Fairy Tales. An entirely new Translation. With over 500 Illustrations by Scandinavian Artists. Small 4to, 6*s.*

Anderson (W.) Pictorial Arts of Japan. With 80 full-page and other Plates, 16 of them in Colours. Large imp. 4to, £8 8*s.* (in four folio parts, £2 2*s.* each); Artists' Proofs, £12 12*s.*

Angler's Strange Experiences (An). By COTSWOLD ISYS. With numerous Illustrations, 4to, 5*s.* New Edition, 3*s.* 6*d.*

Angling. See Amateur, "British," "Cutcliffe," "Fennell," "Halford," "Hamilton," "Martin," "Orvis," "Pennell," "Pritt," "Senior," "Stevens," "Theakston," "Walton," "Wells," and "Willis-Bund."

*Annals of the Life of Shakespeare, from the most recent authori-*ties. Fancy boards, 2*s.*

Annesley (C.) Standard Opera Glass. Detailed Plots of 80 Operas. Small 8vo, sewed, 1*s.* 6*d.*

Antipodean Notes, collected on a Nine Months' Tour round the World. By Wanderer, Author of "Fair Diana." Crown 8vo, 7*s.* 6*d.*

Appleton. European Guide. 2 Parts, 8vo, 10*s.* each.

Armytage (Hon. Mrs.) Wars of Victoria's Reign. 5*s.*

Art Education. See "Biographies," "D'Anvers," "Illustrated Text Books," "Mollett's Dictionary."

Artistic Japan. Illustrated with Coloured Plates. Monthly. Royal 4to, 2*s.*

Attwell (Prof.) The Italian Masters. Crown 8vo, 3*s.* 6*d.*

Audsley (G. A.) Handbook of the Organ. Top edge gilt, 42*s.*; large paper, 84*s.*

—— *Ornamental Arts of Japan.* 90 Plates, 74 in Colours and Gold, with General and Descriptive Text. 2 vols., folio, £15 15*s.*; in specially designed leather, £23 2*s.*

—— *The Art of Chromo-Lithography.* Coloured Plates and Text. Folio, 63*s.*

—— *and Tomkinson. Ivory and Wood Carvings of Japan.* 84*s.* Artists' proofs (100), 168*s.*

Auerbach (B.) Brigitta. (B. Tauchnitz Collection.) 2*s.*

—— *On the Heights.* 3 vols., 6*s.*

—— *Spinoza.* 2 vols., 18mo, 4*s.*

*B*ADDELEY *(S.) Tchay and Chianti.* Small 8vo, 5*s.*

Baldwin (James) Story of Siegfried. 6*s*

—— *Story of the Golden Age.* Illustrated by HOWARD PYLE. Crown 8vo, 6*s.*

List of Publications. 3

Baldwin (James) Story of Roland. Crown 8vo, 6s.
Bamford (A. J.) Turbans and Tails. Sketches in the Unromantic East. Crown 8vo, 7s. 6d.
Barlow (Alfred) Weaving by Hand and by Power. With several hundred Illustrations. Third Edition, royal 8vo, £1 5s.
Barlow (P. W.) Kaipara, Experiences of a Settler in N. New Zealand. Illust., crown 8vo, 6s.
Barrow (J.) Mountain Ascents in Cumberland and Westmoreland. Crown 8vo, 7s. 6d.; new edition, 5s.
Bassett (F. S.) Legends and Superstitions of the Sea. 7s. 6d.

THE BAYARD SERIES.
Edited by the late J. HAIN FRISWELL.

Comprising Pleasure Books of Literature produced in the Choicest Style.

"We can hardly imagine better books for boys to read or for men to ponder over."—*Times.*
Price 2s. 6d. each Volume, complete in itself, flexible cloth extra, gilt edges, with silk Headbands and Registers.

The Story of the Chevalier Bayard.
Joinville's St. Louis of France.
The Essays of Abraham Cowley.
Abdallah. By Edouard Laboullaye.
Napoleon, Table-Talk and Opinions.
Words of Wellington.
Johnson's Rasselas. With Notes.
Hazlitt's Round Table.
The Religio Medici, Hydriotaphia, &c. By Sir Thomas Browne, Knt.
Coleridge's Christabel, &c. With Preface by Algernon C. Swinburne.
Ballad Poetry of the Affections. By Robert Buchanan.

Lord Chesterfield's Letters, Sentences, and Maxims. With Essay by Sainte-Beuve.
The King and the Commons. Cavalier and Puritan Songs.
Vathek. By William Beckford.
Essays in Mosaic. By Ballantyne.
My Uncle Toby; his Story and his Friends. By P. Fitzgerald.
Reflections of Rochefoucauld.
Socrates: Memoirs for English Readers from Xenophon's Memorabilia. By Edw. Levien.
Prince Albert's Golden Precepts.

A Case containing 12 Volumes, price 31s 6d ; or the Case separately, price 3s. 6d.

Baynes (Canon) Hymns and other Verses. Crown 8vo, sewed, 1s.; cloth, 1s. 6d.
Beaugrand (C.) Walks Abroad of Two Young Naturalists. By D. SHARP. Illust., 8vo, 7s. 6d.
Beecher (H. W.) Authentic Biography, and Diary. [*Preparing*
Behnke and Browne. Child's Voice: its Treatment with regard to After Development. Small 8vo, 3s. 6d.
Beyschlag. Female Costume Figures of various Centuries. 12 reproductions of pastel designs in portfolio, imperial. 21s.
Bickersteth (Bishop E. H.) Clergyman in his Home. 1s.
—— —— *Evangelical Churchmanship.* 1s.

A 2

Bickersteth (*Bishop E. H.*) *From Year to Year: Original Poetical Pieces.* Small post 8vo, 3s. 6d.; roan, 6s. and 5s.; calf or morocco, 10s. 6d.

——— *The Master's Home-Call.* 20th Thous. 32mo, cloth gilt, 1s.

——— *The Master's Will.* A Funeral Sermon preached on the Death of Mrs. S. Gurney Buxton. Sewn, 6d.; cloth gilt, 1s.

——— *The Reef, and other Parables.* Crown 8vo, 2s. 6d.

——— *Shadow of the Rock.* Select Religious Poetry. 2s. 6d.

——— *The Shadowed Home and the Light Beyond.* 5s.

Bigelow (*John*) *France and the Confederate Navy. An International Episode.* 7s. 6d.

Biographies of the Great Artists (*Illustrated*). Crown 8vo, emblematical binding, 3s. 6d. per volume, except where the price is given.

Claude le Lorrain, by Owen J. Dullea.
Correggio, by M. E. Heaton. 2s. 6d.
Della Robbia and Cellini. 2s. 6d.
Albrecht Dürer, by R. F. Heath.
Figure Painters of Holland.
Fra Angelico, Masaccio, and Botticelli.
Fra Bartolommeo, Albertinelli, and Andrea del Sarto.
Gainsborough and Constable.
Ghiberti and Donatello. 2s. 6d.
Giotto, by Harry Quilter.
Hans Holbein, by Joseph Cundall.
Hogarth, by Austin Dobson.
Landseer, by F. G. Stevens.
Lawrence and Romney, by Lord Ronald Gower. 2s. 6d.
Leonardo da Vinci.
Little Masters of Germany, by W. B. Scott.
Mantegna and Francia.
Meissonier, by J. W. Mollett. 2s. 6d.
Michelangelo Buonarotti, by Clément.
Murillo, by Ellen E. Minor. 2s. 6d.
Overbeck, by J. B. Atkinson.
Raphael, by N. D'Anvers.
Rembrandt, by J. W. Mollett.
Reynolds, by F. S. Pulling.
Rubens, by C. W. Kett.
Tintoretto, by W. R. Osler.
Titian, by R. F. Heath.
Turner, by Cosmo Monkhouse.
Vandyck and Hals, by P. R. Head.
Velasquez, by E. Stowe.
Vernet and Delaroche, by J. Rees.
Watteau, by J. W. Mollett. 2s. 6d.
Wilkie, by J. W. Mollett.

Bird (*F. J.*) *American Practical Dyer's Companion.* 8vo, 42s.

——— (*H. E.*) *Chess Practice.* 8vo, 2s. 6d.

Black (*Robert*) *Horse Racing in France: a History.* 8vo, 14s.

Black (*Wm.*) *Novels.* See "Low's Standard Library."

——— *Strange Adventures of a House-Boat.* 3 vols., 31s. 6d.

——— *In Far Lochaber.* 3 vols., crown 8vo., 31s. 6d.

Blackburn (*Charles F.*) *Hints on Catalogue Titles and Index Entries,* with a Vocabulary of Terms and Abbreviations, chiefly from Foreign Catalogues. Royal 8vo, 14s.

Blackburn (*Henry*) *Breton Folk.* With 171 Illust. by RANDOLPH CALDECOTT. Imperial 8vo, gilt edges, 21s.; plainer binding, 10s. 6d.

——— *Pyrenees.* Illustrated by GUSTAVE DORÉ, corrected to 1881. Crown 8vo, 7s. 6d. See also CALDECOTT.

Blackmore (R. D.) Lorna Doone. Édition de luxe. Crown 4to, very numerous Illustrations, cloth, gilt edges, 31s. 6d.; parchment, uncut. top gilt, 35s.; new issue, plainer, 21s.; small post 8vo, 6s.
────── *Novels.* See "Low's Standard Library."
────── *Springhaven.* Illust. by PARSONS and BARNARD. Sq. 8vo, 12s.
Blaikie (William) How to get Strong and how to Stay so. Rational, Physical, Gymnastic, &c., Exercises. Illust., sm. post 8vo, 5s.
────── *Sound Bodies for our Boys and Girls.* 16mo, 2s. 6d.
Bonwick. British Colonies. Asia, 1s.; Africa, 1s.; America, 1s.; Australasia, 1s. One vol., cloth, 5s.
Bosanquet (Rev. C.) Blossoms from the King's Garden: Sermons for Children. 2nd Edition, small post 8vo, cloth extra, 6s.
────── *Jehoshaphat; or, Sunlight and Clouds.* 1s.
Boussenard (L.) Crusoes of Guiana. Gilt, 2s. 6d.; gilt ed, 3s. 6d.
────── *Gold-seekers.* Sequel to the above. Illust. 16mo, 5s.
Boyesen (F.) Story of Norway. Illustrated, sm. 8vo, 7s. 6d.
Boyesen (H. H.) Modern Vikings: Stories of Life and Sport in Norseland. Cr. 8vo, 6s.
Boy's Froissart. King Arthur. Knightly Legends of Wales. Percy. See LANIER.
Bradshaw (J.) New Zealand of To-day, 1884-87. 8vo.
Brannt (W. T.) Animal and Vegetable Fats and Oils. 244 Illust., 8vo, 35s.
────── *Manufacture of Soap and Candles, with many Formulas.* Illust., 8vo, 35s.
────── *Metallic Alloys. Chiefly from the German of Krupp* and Wilberger. Crown 8vo, 12s. 6d.
Bright (John) Public Letters. Crown 8vo, 7s. 6d.
Brisse (Baron) Menus (366). A *ménu*, in French and English, for every Day in the Year. 2nd Edition. Crown 8vo, 5s.
British Fisheries Directory. Small 8vo, 2s. 6d.
Brittany. See BLACKBURN.
Browne (G. Lennox) Voice Use and Stimulants. Sm. 8vo, 3s. 6d.
────── *and Behnke (Emil) Voice, Song, and Speech.* N. ed., 5s.
Bryant (W. C.) and Gay (S. H.) History of the United States. 4 vols., royal 8vo, profusely Illustrated, 60s.
Bryce (Rev. Professor) Manitoba. Illust. Crown 8vo, 7s. 6d.
────── *Short History of the Canadian People.* 7s. 6d.
Burnaby (Capt.) On Horseback through Asia Minor. 2 vols., 8vo, 38s. Cheaper Edition, 1 vol., crown 8vo, 10s. 6d.

Burnaby (Mrs. F.) High Alps in Winter; or, Mountaineering in Search of Health. With Illustrations, &c., 14s. See also MAIN.
Burnley (J.) History of Wool and Woolcombing. Illust. 8vo, 21s.
Burton (Sir R. F.) Early, Public, and Private Life. Edited by F. HITCHMAN. 2 vols., 8vo, 36s.
Butler (Sir W. F.) Campaign of the Cataracts. Illust., 8vo, 18s.
—— *Invasion of England, told twenty years after.* 2s. 6d.
—— *Red Cloud; or, the Solitary Sioux.* Imperial 16mo, numerous illustrations, gilt edges, 3s. 6d.; plainer binding, 2s. 6d.
—— *The Great Lone Land; Red River Expedition.* 7s. 6d.
—— *The Wild North Land; the Story of a Winter Journey* with Dogs across Northern North America. 8vo, 18s. Cr. 8vo, 7s. 6d.

CABLE (G. W.) Bonaventure: A Prose Pastoral of Acadian Louisiana. Sm. post 8vo, 5s.
Cadogan (Lady A.) Illustrated Games of Patience. Twenty-four Diagrams in Colours, with Text. Fcap. 4to, 12s. 6d.
—— *New Games of Patience.* Coloured Diagrams, 4to, 12s. 6d.
Caldecott (Randolph) Memoir. By HENRY BLACKBURN. With 170 Examples of the Artist's Work. 14s.; large paper, 21s.
California. See NORDHOFF.
Callan (H.) Wanderings on Wheel and on Foot. Cr. 8vo, 1s. 6d.
Campbell (Lady Colin) Book of the Running Brook: and of Still Waters. 5s.
Canadian People: Short History. Crown 8vo, 7s. 6d.
Carleton (Will) Farm Ballads, Farm Festivals, and Farm Legends. Paper boards, 1s. each; 1 vol., small post 8vo, 3s. 6d.
—— *City Ballads.* Illustrated, 12s. 6d. New Ed. (Rose Library), 16mo, 1s.
Carnegie (A.) American Four-in-Hand in Britain. Small 4to, Illustrated, 10s. 6d. Popular Edition, paper, 1s.
—— *Round the World.* 8vo, 10s. 6d.
—— *Triumphant Democracy.* 6s.; also 1s. 6d. and 1s.
Chairman's Handbook. By R. F. D. PALGRAVE. 5th Edit., 2s.
Changed Cross, &c. Religious Poems. 16mo, 2s. 6d.; calf, 6s.
Chaplin (J. G.) Three Principles of Book-keeping. 2s. 6d.
Charities of London. See Low's.
Chattock (R. S.) Practical Notes on Etching. New Ed. 8vo, 10s. 6d.
Chess. See BIRD (H. E.).

Children's Praises. Hymns for Sunday-Schools and Services.
Compiled by LOUISA H. H. TRISTRAM. 4d.

Choice Editions of Choice Books. 2s. 6d. each. Illustrated by C. W. COPE, R.A., T. CRESWICK, R.A., E. DUNCAN, BIRKET FOSTER, J. C. HORSLEY, A.R.A., G. HICKS, R. REDGRAVE, R.A., C. STONEHOUSE, F. TAYLER, G. THOMAS, H. J. TOWNSHEND, E. H. WEHNERT, HARRISON WEIR, &c.

Bloomfield's Farmer's Boy.
Campbell's Pleasures of Hope.
Coleridge's Ancient Mariner.
Goldsmith's Deserted Village.
Goldsmith's Vicar of Wakefield.
Gray's Elegy in a Churchyard.
Keat's Eve of St. Agnes.
Milton's L'Allegro.
Poetry of Nature. Harrison Weir.
Rogers' (Sam.) Pleasures of Memory.
Shakespeare's Songs and Sonnets.
Tennyson's May Queen.
Elizabethan Poets.
Wordsworth's Pastoral Poems.

"Such works are a glorious beatification for a poet."—*Athenæum.*

Chreiman (Miss) Physical Culture of Women. A Lecture at the Parkes Museum. Small 8vo, 1s.

Christ in Song. By PHILIP SCHAFF. New Ed., gilt edges, 6s.

Chromo-Lithography. See AUDSLEY.

Cochran (W.) Pen and Pencil in Asia Minor. Illust., 8vo, 21s.

Collingwood (Harry) Under the Meteor Flag. The Log of a Midshipman. Illustrated, small post 8vo, gilt, 3s. 6d.; plainer, 2s. 6d.

——— *Voyage of the "Aurora."* Gilt, 3s. 6d.; plainer, 2s. 6d.

Cook (Dutton) Book of the Play. New Edition. 1 vol., 3s. 6d.

——— *On the Stage: Studies.* 2 vols., 8vo, cloth, 24s.

Cowen (Jos., M.P.) Life and Speeches. 8vo, 14s.

Cowper (W.) Poetical Works: A Concordance. Roy. 8vo, 21s.

Cozzens (F.) American Yachts. 27 Plates, 22 × 28 inches. Proofs, £21; Artist's Proofs, £31 10s.

Crew (B. J.) Practical Treatise on Petroleum. Illust., 8vo, 28s.

Crouch (A. P.) On a Surf-bound Coast. Crown 8vo, 7s. 6d.

Crown Prince of Germany: a Diary. 2s. 6d.

Cudworth (W.) Life and Correspondence of Abraham Sharp. Illustrated from Drawings. (To Subscribers, 21s.) 26s.

Cumberland(Stuart) Thought Reader's Thoughts. Cr. 8vo., 10s.6d.

——— *Queen's Highway from Ocean to Ocean.* Ill., 8vo, 18s.; new ed., 7s. 6d.

Cundall (Joseph) Annals of the Life and Work of Shakespeare. With a List of Early Editions. 3s. 6d.; large paper, 5s.; also 2s.

——— *Remarkable Bindings in the British Museum.*

Curtis (W. E.) Capitals of Spanish America.. Illust., roy. 8vo.

Cushing (W.) Initials and Pseudonyms. Large 8vo, 25s.; second series, large 8vo, 21s.

*Custer (Eliz. B.) Tenting on the Plains; Gen. Custer in Kansas
and Texas.* Royal 8vo, 18s.
Cutcliffe (H. C.) Trout Fishing in Rapid Streams. Cr. 8vo, 3s. 6d.

*DALY (Mrs. D.) Digging, Squatting, and Pioneering in
Northern South Australia.* 8vo, 12s.
D'Anvers. Elementary History of Art. New ed., 360 illus.,
cr. 8vo, 2 vols. (5s. each), gilt, 10s. 6d.
—————— *Elementary History of Music.* Crown 8vo, 2s. 6d.
Davidson (H. C.) Old Adam; Tale of an Army Crammer. 3
vols. crown 8vo, 31s. 6d.
Davis (Clement) Modern Whist. 4s.
Davis (C. T.) Bricks, Tiles, Terra-Cotta, &c. Ill. 8vo, 25s.
—————— *Manufacture of Leather.* With many Illustrations. 52s. 6d.
—————— *Manufacture of Paper.* 28s.
Davis (G. B.) Outlines of International Law. 8vo. 10s. 6d.
Dawidowsky. Glue, Gelatine, Isinglass, Cements, &c. 8vo, 12s. 6d.
Day of My Life at Eton. By an ETON BOY. 16mo. 2s. 6d.
Day's Collacon: an Encyclopædia of Prose Quotations. Imperial 8vo, cloth, 31s. 6d.
De Leon (E.) Under the Stars and under the Crescent. N. ed., 6s.
*Dethroning Shakspere. Letters to the Daily Telegraph; and
Editorial Papers.* Crown 8vo, 2s. 6d.
Dictionary. See TOLHAUSEN, "Technological."
Dogs in Disease. By ASHMONT. Crown 8vo, 7s. 6d.
Donnelly (Ignatius) Atlantis; or, the Antediluvian World.
7th Edition, crown 8vo, 12s. 6d.
—————— *Ragnarok: The Age of Fire and Gravel.* Illustrated,
crown 8vo. 12s. 6d.
—————— *The Great Cryptogram: Francis Bacon's Cipher in the
so-called Shakspere Plays.* With facsimiles. 2 vols., 30s.
Doré (Gustave) Life and Reminiscences. By BLANCHE ROOSEVELT. Illust. from the Artist's Drawings. Medium 8vo, 24s.
*Dougall (James Dalziel) Shooting: its Appliances, Practice,
and Purpose.* New Edition, revised with additions. Crown 8vo, 7s. 6d.
"The book is admirable in every way. .... We wish it every success."—*Globe.*
"A very complete treatise. .... Likely to take high rank as an authority on
shooting."—*Daily News.*
Dupré (Giovanni). By FRIEZE. With Dialogues on Art. 7s. 6d.

EDMONDS (C.) Poetry of the Anti-Jacobin. With additional matter. New ed. Illust., crown 8vo.
Educational List and Directory for 1887-88. 5s.

Educational Works published in Great Britain. A Classified Catalogue. Third Edition, 8vo, cloth extra, 6s.
Edwards (E.) American Steam Engineer. Illust., 12mo, 12s. 6d.
Eight Months on the Argentine Gran Chaco. 8vo, 8s. 6d.
Elliott (H. W.) An Arctic Province : Alaska and the Seal Islands. Illustrated from Drawings ; also with Maps. 16s.
Emerson (Dr. P. H.) Pictures of East Anglian Life. Ordinary ed., 105s. ; édit. de luxe, 17 × 13½, vellum, morocco back, 147s.
—————— *Naturalistic Photography for Art Students.* Crown 8vo.
—————— *and Goodall. Life and Landscape on the Norfolk* Broads. Plates 12 × 8 inches, 126s.; large paper, 210s.
English Catalogue of Books. Vol. III., 1872—1880. Royal 8vo, half-morocco, 42s. See also " Index."
English Etchings. Published Quarterly. 3s. 6d. Vol. VI., 25s.
English Philosophers. Edited by E. B. IVAN MÜLLER, M.A. Crown 8vo volumes of 180 or 200 pp., price 3s. 6d. each.
Francis Bacon, by Thomas Fowler. | Shaftesbury and Hutcheson.
Hamilton, by W. H. S. Monck. | Adam Smith, by J. A. Farrer.
Hartley and James Mill.
Esmarch (F.) Handbook of Surgery. Translation from the last German Edition. With 647 new Illustrations. 8vo, leather, 24s.
Etching. See CHATTOCK, and ENGLISH ETCHINGS.
Etchings (Modern) of Celebrated Paintings. 4to, 31s. 6d.
Evans (E. A.) Songs of the Birds. Analogies of Spiritual Life. New Ed. Illust., 6s.
Evelyn. Life of Mrs. Godolphin. By WILLIAM HARCOURT, of Nuneham. Steel Portrait. Extra binding, gilt top, 7s. 6d.

*F*ARINI *(G. A.) Through the Kalahari Desert.* 8vo, 21s.

Farm Ballads, Festivals, and Legends. See CARLETON.
Fawcett (Edgar) A Gentleman of Leisure. 1s.
Fenn (G. Manville) Off to the Wilds : A Story for Boys. Profusely Illustrated. Crown 8vo, gilt edges, 3s. 6d.; plainer, 2s. 6d.
—————— *Silver Cañon.* Illust., gilt ed., 3s. 6d. ; plainer, 2s. 6d.
Fennell (Greville) Book of the Roach. New Edition, 12mo, 2s.
Ferns. See HEATH.
Field (H. M.) Greek Islands and Turkey after the War. 8s. 6d.
Field (Mrs. Horace) Anchorage. 2 vols., crown 8vo, 12s.
Fields (J. T.) Yesterdays with Authors. New Ed., 8vo, 10s. 6d.
Fitzgerald (P.) Book Fancier. Cr. 8vo. 5s. ; large pap. 12s. 6d.

Fleming (Sandford) England and Canada: a Tour. Cr. 8vo, 6s.
Florence. See YRIARTE.
Folkard (R., Jun.) Plant Lore, Legends, and Lyrics. 8vo, 16s.
Forbes (H. O.) Naturalist in the Eastern Archipelago. 8vo. 21s.

Foreign Countries and British Colonies. Cr. 8vo, 3s. 6d. each

Australia, by J. F. Vesey Fitzgerald.
Austria, by D. Kay, F.R.G.S.
Denmark and Iceland, by E. C. Otté.
Egypt, by S. Lane Poole, B.A.
France, by Miss M. Roberts.
Germany, by S. Baring-Gould.
Greece, by L. Sergeant, B.A.

Japan, by S. Mossman.
Peru, by Clements R. Markham.
Russia, by W. R. Morfill, M.A.
Spain, by Rev. Wentworth Webster.
Sweden and Norway, by Woods.
West Indies, by C. H. Eden, F.R.G.S.

Foreign Etchings. From Paintings by Rembrandt, &c., 63s.; india proofs, 147s.
Fortunes made in Business. Vols. I., II., III. 16s. each.
Frampton (Mary) Journal, Letters, and Anecdotes. 8vo, 14s.
Franc (Maud Jeanne). Small post 8vo, uniform, gilt edges:—

Emily's Choice. 5s.
Hall's Vineyard. 4s.
John's Wife: A Story of Life in South Australia. 4s.
Marian; or, The Light of Some One's Home. 5s.
Silken Cords and Iron Fetters. 4s.
Into the Light. 4s.

Vermont Vale. 5s.
Minnie's Mission. 4s.
Little Mercy. 4s.
Beatrice Melton's Discipline. 4s.
No Longer a Child. 4s.
Golden Gifts. 4s.
Two Sides to Every Question. 4s.
Master of Ralston. 4s.

Also a Cheap Edition, in cloth extra, 2s. 6d. each.

Frank's Ranche; or, My Holiday in the Rockies. A Contribution to the Inquiry into What we are to Do with our Boys. 5s.
Freeman (J.) Lights and Shadows of Melbourne Life. Cr. 8vo. 6s.
French. See JULIEN and PORCHER.
Fresh Woods and Pastures New. By the Author of "An Amateur Angler's Days." 1s. 6d.; large paper, 5s.; new ed., 1s.
Froissart. See LANIER.
Fuller (Edward) Fellow Travellers. 3s. 6d.
—— *Dramatic Year* 1887-88 *in the United States.* With the London Season, by W. ARCHER. Crown 8vo.

GANE (D. N.) New South Wales and Victoria in 1885. 5s.

Gasparin (Countess A. de) Sunny Fields and Shady Woods. 6s.
Geary (Grattan) Burma after the Conquest. 7s. 6d.
Gentle Life (Queen Edition). 2 vols. in 1, small 4to, 6s.

THE GENTLE LIFE SERIES.

Price 6s. each ; or in calf extra, price 10s. 6d. ; Smaller Edition, cloth extra, 2s. 6d., except where price is named.

The Gentle Life. Essays in aid of the Formation of Character.
About in the World. Essays by Author of " The Gentle Life."
Like unto Christ. New Translation of Thomas à Kempis.
Familiar Words. A Quotation Handbook. 6s.
Essays by Montaigne. Edited by the Author of " The Gentle Life."
The Gentle Life. 2nd Series.
The Silent Hour: Essays, Original and Selected.
Half-Length Portraits. Short Studies of Notable Persons. By J. HAIN FRISWELL.
Essays on English Writers, for Students in English Literature.
Other People's Windows. By J. HAIN FRISWELL. 6s.
A Man's Thoughts. By J. HAIN FRISWELL.
The Countess of Pembroke's Arcadia. By Sir PHILIP SIDNEY. 6s.

Germany. By S. BARING-GOULD. Crown 8vo, 3s. 6d.
Gibbon (C.) Beyond Compare: a Story. 3 vols., cr. 8vo, 31s. 6d.
—— *Yarmouth Coast.*
Gisborne (W.) New Zealand Rulers and Statesmen. With Portraits. Crown 8vo, 7s. 6d.
Goldsmith. She Stoops to Conquer. Introduction by AUSTIN DOBSON; the designs by E. A. ABBEY. Imperial 4to, 48s.
Goode (G. Brown) American Fishes. A Popular Treatise. Royal 8vo, 24s.
Gordon (J. E. H., B.A. Cantab.) Four Lectures on Electric Induction at the Royal Institution, 1878-9. Illust., square 16mo, 3s.
—— *Electric Lighting.* Illustrated, 8vo, 18s.
—— *Physical Treatise on Electricity and Magnetism.* 2nd Edition, enlarged, with coloured, full-page, &c., Illust. 2 vols., 8vo, 42s.
—— *Electricity for Schools.* Illustrated. Crown 8vo, 5s.
Gouffé (Jules) Royal Cookery Book. New Edition, with plates in colours, Woodcuts, &c., 8vo, gilt edges, 42s.
—— Domestic Edition, half-bound, 10s. 6d.
Grant (General, U.S.) Personal Memoirs. 2 vols., 8vo, 28s. Illustrations, Maps, &c. 2 vols., 8vo, 28s.
Great Artists. See " Biographies."

Great Musicians. Edited by F. HUEFFER. A Series of Biographies, crown 8vo, 3s. each:—

Bach.	Mendelssohn.	Schubert.
English Church Composers. By BARRETT.	Mozart.	Schumann.
	Purcell.	Richard Wagner.
Handel.	Rossini.	Weber.
Haydn.		

Groves (J. Percy) Charmouth Grange. Gilt, 5s.; plainer, 2s. 6d.

Guizot's History of France. Translated by R. BLACK. In 8 vols., super-royal 8vo, cloth extra, gilt, each 24s. In cheaper binding, 8 vols., at 10s. 6d. each.

"It supplies a want which has long been felt, and ought to be in the hands of all students of history."—*Times.*

―――― *Masson's School Edition.* Abridged from the Translation by Robert Black, with Chronological Index, Historical and Genealogical Tables, &c. By Professor GUSTAVE MASSON, B.A. With Portraits, Illustrations, &c. 1 vol., 8vo, 600 pp., 5s.

Guyon (Mde.) Life. By UPHAM. 6th Edition, crown 8vo, 6s.

HALFORD (F. M.) Floating Flies, and how to Dress them. Coloured plates. 8vo, 15s.; large paper, 30s.

―――― *Dry Fly-Fishing in Theory and Practice.* Col. Plates.

Hall (W. W.) How to Live Long; or, 1408 Maxims. 2s.

Hamilton (E.) Recollections of Fly-fishing for Salmon, Trout, and Grayling. With their Habits, Haunts, and History. Illust., 6s.; large paper, 10s. 6d.

Hands (T.) Numerical Exercises in Chemistry. Cr. 8vo, 2s. 6d. and 2s.; Answers separately, 6d.

Hardy (Thomas). See LOW'S STANDARD NOVELS.

Hare (J. S. Clark) Law of Contracts. 8vo, 26s.

Harley (T.) Southward Ho! to the State of Georgia. 5s.

Harper's Magazine. Published Monthly. 160 pages, fully Illustrated, 1s. Vols., half yearly, I.—XVI., super-royal 8vo, 8s. 6d. each.

"'Harper's Magazine' is so thickly sown with excellent illustrations that to count them would be a work of time; not that it is a picture magazine, for the engravings illustrate the text after the manner seen in some of our choicest *éditions de luxe.*"—*St. James's Gazette.*

"It is so pretty, so big, and so cheap. ... An extraordinary shillingsworth— 160 large octavo pages, with over a score of articles, and more than three times as many illustrations."—*Edinburgh Daily Review.*

"An amazing shillingsworth ... combining choice literature of both nations."—*Nonconformist.*

Harper's Young People. Vols. I.-IV., profusely Illustrated with woodcuts and coloured plates. Royal 4to, extra binding, each 7s. 6d.; gilt edges, 8s. Published Weekly, in wrapper, 1d.; Annual Subscription, post free, 6s. 6d.; Monthly, in wrapper, with coloured plate, 6d.; Annual Subscription, post free, 7s. 6d.

Harrison (Mary) Skilful Cook. New edition, crown 8vo, 5*s*.
Hartshorne (H.) Household Medicine, Surgery, &c. 8vo. 21*s*.
Hatton (Frank) North Borneo. Map and Illust., &c. 18*s*.
Hatton (Joseph) Journalistic London: with Engravings and
 Portraits of Distinguished Writers of the Day. Fcap. 4to, 12*s*. 6*d*.
—— See also LOW'S STANDARD NOVELS.
Hawthorne (Nathaniel) Life. By JOHN R. LOWELL.
Heath (Francis George) Fern World With Nature-printed
 Coloured Plates. Crown 8vo, gilt edges, 12*s*. 6*d*. Cheap Edition, 6*s*.
Heath (Gertrude). Tell us Why? The Customs and Ceremo-
 nies of the Church of England explained for Children. Cr. 8vo, 2*s*. 6*d*.
Heldmann (B.) Mutiny of the Ship " Leander." Gilt edges,
 3*s*. 6*d*.; plainer, 2*s*. 6*d*.
Henty. Winning his Spurs. Cr. 8vo, 3*s*. 6*d*.; plainer, 2*s*. 6*d*.
—— *Cornet of Horse.* Cr. 8vo, 3*s*. 6*d*.; plainer, 2*s*. 6*d*.
—— *Jack Archer.* Illust. 3*s*. 6*d*.; plainer, 2*s*. 6*d*.
Henty (Richmond) Australiana: My Early Life. 5*s*.
Herrick (Robert) Poetry. Preface by AUSTIN DOBSON. With
 numerous Illustrations by E. A. ABBEY. 4to, gilt edges, 42*s*.
Hetley (Mrs. E.) Native Flowers of New Zealand. Chromos
 from Drawings. Three Parts, to Subscribers, 63*s*.
Hewitt (James A.) Church History in South Africa, 1795-1848,
 12mo, 5*s*.
Hicks (E. S.) Our Boys: How to Enter the Merchant Service. 5*s*.
—— *Yachts, Boats and Canoes.* Illustrated. 8vo, 10*s*. 6*d*.
Hitchman. Public Life of the Earl of Beaconsfield. 3*s*. 6*d*.
Hoey (Mrs. Cashel) See LOW'S STANDARD NOVELS.
Hofmann. Scenes from the Life of our Saviour. 12 mounted
 plates, 12 × 9 inches, 21*s*.
Holder (C. F.) Marvels of Animal Life. Illustrated. 8*s*. 6*d*.
—— *Ivory King: Elephant and Allies.* Illustrated. 8*s*. 6*d*.
—— *Living Lights: Phosphorescent Animals and Vegetables.*
 Illustrated. 8vo, 8*s*. 6*d*.
Holmes (O. W.) Before the Curfew, &c. Occasional Poems. 5*s*.
—— *Last Leaf: a Holiday Volume.* 42*s*.
—— *Mortal Antipathy,* 8*s*. 6*d*.; also 2*s*.; paper, 1*s*.
—— *Our Hundred Days in Europe.* 6*s*. Large Paper, 15*s*.
—— *Poetical Works.* 2 vols., 18mo, gilt tops, 10*s*. 6*d*.
Homer, Iliad I.-XII., done into English Verse. By ARTHUR
 S. WAY. 9*s*.
—— *Odyssey,* done into English Verse. By A. S. WAY.
 Fcap 4to, 7*s*. 6*d*.

Hopkins (Manley) Treatise on the Cardinal Numbers. 2s. 6d.
Hore (Mrs.) To Lake Tanganyika in a Bath Chair. Cr. 8vo, 7s. 6d.
Howard (Blanche W.) Tony the Maid; a Novelette. Illust., 12mo, 3s. 6d.
Howorth (H. H.) Mammoth and the Flood. 8vo, 18s.
Huet (C. B.) Land of Rubens. For Visitors to Belgium. By VAN DAM. Crown 8vo, 3s. 6d.
Hugo (V.) Notre Dame. With coloured etchings and 150 engravings. 2 vols., 8vo, vellum cloth, 30s.
Hundred Greatest Men (The). 8 portfolios, 21s. each, or 4 vols., half-morocco, gilt edges, 10 guineas. New Ed., 1 vol., royal 8vo, 21s.
Hutchinson (T.) Diary and Letters. Vol. I., 16s.; Vol. II., 16s.
Hygiene and Public Health. Edited by A. H. BUCK, M.D. Illustrated. 2 vols., royal 8vo, 42s.
Hymnal Companion to the Book of Common Prayer. By BISHOP BICKERSTETH. In various styles and bindings from 1d. to 31s. 6d. *Price List and Prospectus will be forwarded on application.*
Hymns and Tunes at St. Thomas', New York. Music by G. W. FARREN. Royal 8vo, 5s.

ILLUSTRATED Text-Books of Art-Education. Edited by EDWARD J. POYNTER, R.A. Illustrated, and strongly bound, 5s. Now ready:—

PAINTING.

Classic and Italian. By HEAD. | **French and Spanish.**
German, Flemish, and Dutch. | **English and American.**

ARCHITECTURE.

Classic and Early Christian.
Gothic and Renaissance. By T. ROGER SMITH.

SCULPTURE.

Antique: Egyptian and Greek.
Renaissance and Modern. By LEADER SCOTT.

Inderwick (F. A.; Q.C.) Side Lights on the Stuarts. Essays. Illustrated, 8vo.
Index to the English Catalogue, Jan., 1874, *to Dec.,* 1880. Royal 8vo, half-morocco, 18s.
Inglis (Hon. James; "Maori") Our New Zealand Cousins. Small post 8vo, 6s.
——— *Tent Life in Tiger Land: Twelve Years a Pioneer Planter.* Col. plates, roy. 8vo, 18s.
Irving (Henry) Impressions of America. 2 vols., 21s.; 1 vol., 6s.
Irving (Washington). Library Edition of his Works in 27 vols., Copyright, with the Author's Latest Revisions. "Geoffrey Crayon" Edition, large square 8vo. 12s. 6d. per vol. *See also* "Little Britain."

JAMES (C.) Curiosities of Law and Lawyers. 8vo, 7s. 6d.

Japan. See ANDERSON, ARTISTIC, AUDSLEY, also MORSE.

Jefferies (Richard) Amaryllis at the Fair. Small 8vo, 7s. 6d.

Jerdon (Gertrude) Key-hole Country. Illustrated. Crown 8vo, cloth, 2s.

Johnston (H. H.) River Congo, from its Mouth to Bolobo. New Edition, 8vo, 21s.

Johnstone (D. Lawson) Land of the Mountain Kingdom. Illust., crown 8vo.

Jones (Major) Heroes of Industry. Biographies with Portraits. 7s. 6d.

—— *Emigrants' Friend.* Guide to the U.S. N. Ed. 2s. 6d.

Julien (F.) English Student's French Examiner. 16mo, 2s.

—— *Conversational French Reader.* 16mo, cloth, 2s. 6d.

—— *French at Home and at School.* Book I., Accidence. 2s.

—— *First Lessons in Conversational French Grammar.* 1s.

—— *Petites Leçons de Conversation et de Grammaire.* 3s.

—— *Phrases of Daily Use.* Limp cloth, 6d.

—— *"Petites Leçons" and "Phrases"* in one. 3s. 6d.

KARR (H. W. Seton) Shores and Alps of Alaska. 8vo, 16s.

Keats. Endymion. Illust. by W. ST. JOHN HARPER. Imp. 4to, gilt top, 42s.

Kempis (Thomas à) Daily Text-Book. Square 16mo, 2s. 6d.; interleaved as a Birthday Book, 3s. 6d.

Kent's Commentaries: an Abridgment for Students of American Law. By EDEN F. THOMPSON. 10s. 6d.

Kerr (W. M.) Far Interior: Cape of Good Hope, across the Zambesi, to the Lake Regions. Illustrated from Sketches, 2 vols. 8vo, 32s.

Kershaw (S. W.) Protestants from France in their English Home. Crown 8vo, 6s.

King (Henry) Savage London; Riverside Characters, &c. Crown 8vo, 6s.

Kingston (W. H. G.) Works. Illustrated, 16mo, gilt edges, 3s. 6d.; plainer binding, plain edges, 2s. 6d. each.

Captain Mugford, or, Our Salt and Fresh Water Tutors.	Snow-Shoes and Canoes.
Dick Cheveley.	Two Supercargoes.
Heir of Kilfinnan.	With Axe and Rifle.

Kingsley (Rose) Children of Westminster Abbey: Studies in English History. 5s.
Knight (E. J.) Cruise of the "Falcon." New Ed. Cr. 8vo, 7s. 6d.
Knox (Col.) Boy Travellers on the Congo. Illus. Cr. 8vo, 7s. 6d.
Kunhardt (C. B.) Small Yachts: Design and Construction. 35s.
—— *Steam Yachts and Launches.* Illustrated. 4to, 16s.

LAMB (Charles) Essays of Elia. Illustrated by C. O. MURRAY. 6s.
Lanier's Works. Illustrated, crown 8vo, gilt edges, 7s. 6d. each.
  Boy's King Arthur.
  Boy's Froissart.
  Boy's Knightly Legends of Wales.
  Boy's Percy: Ballads of Love and Adventure, selected from the "Reliques."
Lansdell (H.) Through Siberia. 2 vols., 8vo, 30s.; 1 vol., 10s. 6d.
—— *Russia in Central Asia.* Illustrated. 2 vols., 42s.
—— *Through Central Asia; Russo-Afghan Frontier, &c.* 8vo, 12s.
Larden (W.) School Course on Heat. Second Ed., Illust. 5s.
Laurie (André) Selene Company, Limited. Crown 8vo, 7s. 6d.
Layard (Mrs. Granville) Through the West Indies. Small post 8vo, 2s. 6d.
Lea (H. C.). History of the Inquisition of the Middle Ages. 3 vols., 8vo, 42s.
Lemon (M.) Small House over the Water, and Stories. Illust. by Cruikshank, &c. Crown 8vo, 6s.
Leo XIII.: Life. By BERNARD O'REILLY. With Steel Portrait from Photograph, &c. Large 8vo, 18s.; *édit. de luxe*, 63s.
Leonardo da Vinci's Literary Works. Edited by Dr. JEAN PAUL RICHTER. Containing his Writings on Painting, Sculpture, and Architecture, his Philosophical Maxims, Humorous Writings, and Miscellaneous Notes on Personal Events, on his Contemporaries, on Literature, &c.; published from Manuscripts. 2 vols., imperial 8vo, containing about 200 Drawings in Autotype Reproductions, and numerous other Illustrations. Twelve Guineas.
Library of Religious Poetry. Best Poems of all Ages. Edited by SCHAFF and GILMAN. Royal 8vo, 21s.; cheaper binding, 10s. 6d.
Lindsay (W. S.) History of Merchant Shipping. Over 150 Illustrations, Maps, and Charts. In 4 vols., demy 8vo, cloth extra. Vols. 1 and 2, 11s. each; vols. 3 and 4, 14s. each. 4 vols., 50s.
Little (Archibald J.) Through the Yang-tse Gorges: Trade and Travel in Western China. New Edition. 8vo, 10s. 6d.

Little Britain, The Spectre Bridegroom, and *Legend of Sleepy Hollow.* By WASHINGTON IRVING. An entirely New *Édition de luxe.* Illustrated by 120 very fine Engravings on Wood, by Mr. J. D. COOPER. Designed by Mr. CHARLES O. MURRAY. Re-issue, square crown 8vo, cloth, 6s.

Longfellow. Maidenhood. With Coloured Plates. Oblong 4to, 2s. 6d.; gilt edges, 3s. 6d.

────── *Courtship of Miles Standish.* Illust. by BROUGHTON, &c. Imp. 4to, 21s.

────── *Nuremberg.* 28 Photogravures. Illum. by M. and A. COMEGYS. 4to, 31s. 6d.

Lowell (J. R.) Vision of Sir Launfal. Illustrated, royal 4to, 63s.

────── *Life of Nathaniel Hawthorne.* Small post 8vo, ..

Low's Standard Library of Travel and Adventure. Crown 8vo, uniform in cloth extra, 7s. 6d., except where price is given.
1. **The Great Lone Land.** By Major W. F. BUTLER, C.B.
2. **The Wild North Land.** By Major W. F. BUTLER, C.B.
3. **How I found Livingstone.** By H. M. STANLEY.
4. **Through the Dark Continent.** By H. M. STANLEY. 12s. 6d.
5. **The Threshold of the Unknown Region.** By C. R. MARKHAM. (4th Edition, with Additional Chapters, 10s. 6d.)
6. **Cruise of the Challenger.** By W. J. J. SPRY, R.N.
7. **Burnaby's On Horseback through Asia Minor.** 10s. 6d.
8. **Schweinfurth's Heart of Africa.** 2 vols., 15s.
9. **Through America.** By W. G. MARSHALL.
10. **Through Siberia.** Il. and unabridged, 10s. 6d. By H. LANSDELL.
11. **From Home to Home.** By STAVELEY HILL.
12. **Cruise of the Falcon.** By E. J. KNIGHT.
13. **Through Masai Land.** By JOSEPH THOMSON.
14. **To the Central African Lakes.** By JOSEPH THOMSON.
15. **Queen's Highway.** By STUART CUMBERLAND.

Low's Standard Novels. Small post 8vo, cloth extra, 6s. each, unless otherwise stated.
A Daughter of Heth. By W. BLACK.
In Silk Attire. By W. BLACK.
Kilmeny. A Novel. By W. BLACK.
Lady Silverdale's Sweetheart. By W. BLACK.
Sunrise. By W. BLACK.
Three Feathers. By WILLIAM BLACK.
Alice Lorraine. By R. D. BLACKMORE.
Christowell, a Dartmoor Tale. By R. D. BLACKMORE.
Clara Vaughan. By R. D. BLACKMORE.
Cradock Nowell. By R. D. BLACKMORE.
Cripps the Carrier. By R. D. BLACKMORE.
Erema; or, My Father's Sin. By R. D. BLACKMORE.
Lorna Doone. By R. D. BLACKMORE. 25th Edition.
Mary Anerley. By R. D. BLACKMORE.
Tommy Upmore. By R. D. BLACKMORE.

Low's Standard Novels—continued.

Bonaventure. By G. W. CABLE.
An English Squire. By Miss COLERIDGE.
Some One Else. By Mrs. B. M. CROKER.
Under the Stars and Stripes. By E. DE LEON.
Halfway. By Miss BETHAM-EDWARDS.
A Story of the Dragonnades. By Rev. E. GILLIAT, M.A.
A Laodicean. By THOMAS HARDY.
Far from the Madding Crowd. By THOMAS HARDY.
Mayor of Casterbridge. By THOMAS HARDY.
Pair of Blue Eyes. By THOMAS HARDY.
Return of the Native. By THOMAS HARDY.
The Hand of Ethelberta. By THOMAS HARDY.
The Trumpet Major. By THOMAS HARDY.
Two on a Tower. By THOMAS HARDY.
Old House at Sandwich. By JOSEPH HATTON.
Three Recruits. By JOSEPH HATTON.
A Golden Sorrow. By Mrs. CASHEL HOEY. New Edition.
A Stern Chase. By Mrs. CASHEL HOEY.
Out of Court. By Mrs. CASHEL HOEY.
Don John. By JEAN INGELOW.
John Jerome. By JEAN INGELOW. 5s.
Sarah de Berenger. By JEAN INGELOW.
Adela Cathcart. By GEORGE MAC DONALD.
Guild Court. By GEORGE MAC DONALD.
Mary Marston. By GEORGE MAC DONALD.
Stephen Archer. New Ed. of "Gifts." By GEORGE MAC DONALD.
The Vicar's Daughter. By GEORGE MAC DONALD.
Orts. By GEORGE MAC DONALD.
Weighed and Wanting. By GEORGE MAC DONALD.
Diane. By Mrs. MACQUOID.
Elinor Dryden. By Mrs. MACQUOID.
My Lady Greensleeves. By HELEN MATHERS.
Spell of Ashtaroth. By DUFFIELD OSBORNE. 5s.
Alaric Spenceley. By Mrs. J. H. RIDDELL.
Daisies and Buttercups. By Mrs. J. H. RIDDELL.
The Senior Partner. By Mrs. J. H. RIDDELL.
A Struggle for Fame. By Mrs. J. H. RIDDELL.
Frozen Pirate. By W. CLARK RUSSELL.
Jack's Courtship. By W. CLARK RUSSELL.
John Holdsworth. By W. CLARK RUSSELL.
A Sailor's Sweetheart. By W. CLARK RUSSELL.
Sea Queen. By W. CLARK RUSSELL.
Watch Below. By W. CLARK RUSSELL.
Strange Voyage. By W. CLARK RUSSELL.
Wreck of the Grosvenor. By W. CLARK RUSSELL.
The Lady Maud. By W. CLARK RUSSELL.
Little Loo. By W. CLARK RUSSELL.
Bee-man of Orn. By FRANK R. STOCKTON.
My Wife and I. By Mrs. HARRIET B. STOWE.

Low's Standard Novels—*continued.*
  The Late Mrs. Null. By FRANK R. STOCKTON.
  Hundredth Man. By FRANK R. STOCKTON.
  Old Town Folk. By Mrs. HARRIET B. STOWE.
  We and our Neighbours. By Mrs. HARRIET B. STOWE.
  Poganuc People, their Loves and Lives. By Mrs. STOWE.
  Ulu: an African Romance. By JOSEPH THOMSON.
  Ben Hur: a Tale of the Christ. By LEW. WALLACE.
  Anne. By CONSTANCE FENIMORE WOOLSON.
  East Angels. By CONSTANCE FENIMORE WOOLSON.
  For the Major. By CONSTANCE FENIMORE WOOLSON. 5s.
  French Heiress in her own Chateau.

Low's Series of Standard Books for Boys. With numerous
  Illustrations, 2s. 6d.; gilt edges, 3s. 6d. each.
  Dick Cheveley. By W. H. G. KINGSTON.
  Heir of Kilfinnan. By W. H. G. KINGSTON.
  Off to the Wilds. By G. MANVILLE FENN.
  The Two Supercargoes. By W. H. G. KINGSTON.
  The Silver Cañon. By G. MANVILLE FENN.
  Under the Meteor Flag. By HARRY COLLINGWOOD.
  Jack Archer: a Tale of the Crimea. By G. A. HENTY.
  The Mutiny on Board the Ship Leander. By B. HELDMANN.
  With Axe and Rifle on the Western Prairies. By W. H. G.
    KINGSTON.
  Red Cloud, the Solitary Sioux: a Tale of the Great Prairie.
    By Col. Sir WM. BUTLER, K.C.B.
  The Voyage of the Aurora. By HARRY COLLINGWOOD.
  Charmouth Grange: a Tale of the 17th Century. By J.
    PERCY GROVES.
  Snowshoes and Canoes. By W. H. G. KINGSTON.
  The Son of the Constable of France. By LOUIS ROUSSELET.
  Captain Mugford; or, Our Salt and Fresh Water Tutors.
    Edited by W. H. G. KINGSTON.
  The Cornet of Horse, a Tale of Marlborough's Wars. By
    G. A. HENTY.
  The Adventures of Captain Mago. By LEON CAHUN.
  Noble Words and Noble Needs.
  The King of the Tigers. By ROUSSELET.
  Hans Brinker; or, The Silver Skates. By Mrs. DODGE.
  The Drummer-Boy, a Story of the time of Washington. By
    ROUSSELET.
  Adventures in New Guinea: The Narrative of Louis Tregance.
  The Crusoes of Guiana. By BOUSSENARD.
  The Gold Seekers. A Sequel to the Above. By BOUSSENARD.
  Winning His Spurs, a Tale of the Crusades. By G. A. HENTY.
  The Blue Banner. By LEON CAHUN.

Low's Pocket Encyclopædia: a Compendium of General Know-
  ledge for Ready Reference. Upwards of 25,000 References, with
  Plates. New ed., imp. 32mo, cloth, marbled edges, 3s. 6d.; roan, 4s. 6d.

Low's Handbook to London Charities. Yearly, cloth, 1s. 6d.; paper, 1s.

M^cCORMICK (R.). *Voyages in the Arctic and Antarctic Seas in Search of Sir John Franklin*, &c. With Maps and Lithos. 2 vols., royal 8vo, 52s. 6d.

Mac Donald (George). See LOW'S STANDARD NOVELS.

Macdowall (Alex. B.) Curve Pictures of London for the Social Reformer. 1s.

McGoun's Commercial Correspondence. Crown 8vo, 5s.

Macgregor (John) "Rob Roy" on the Baltic. 3rd Edition, small post 8vo, 2s. 6d.; cloth, gilt edges, 3s. 6d.

—— *A Thousand Miles in the "Rob Roy" Canoe.* 11th Edition, small post 8vo, 2s. 6d.; cloth, gilt edges, 3s. 6d.

—— *Voyage Alone in the Yawl "Rob Roy."* New Edition, with additions, small post 8vo, 5s.; 3s. 6d. and 2s. 6d.

Mackay (C.) Glossary of Obscure Words in Shakespeare. 21s.

Mackenzie (Sir Morell) Fatal Illness of Frederick the Noble. Crown 8vo, limp cloth, 2s. 6d.

Mackenzie (Rev. John) Austral Africa: Losing it or Ruling it? Illustrations and Maps. 2 vols., 8vo, 32s.

McLellan's Own Story: The War for the Union. Illust. 18s.

McMurdo (Edward) History of Portugal. 8vo, 21s.

Macquoid (Mrs.). See LOW'S STANDARD NOVELS.

Magazine. See ENGLISH ETCHINGS, HARPER.

Maginn (W.) Miscellanies. Prose and Verse. With Memoir. 2 vols., crown 8vo, 24s.

Main (Mrs.; Mrs. Fred Burnaby) High Life and Towers of Silence. Illustrated, square 8vo, 10s. 6d.

Manitoba. See BRYCE.

Manning (E. F.) Delightful Thames. Illustrated. 4to, fancy boards, 5s.

Markham (Clements R.) The Fighting Veres, Sir F. and Sir H. 8vo, 18s.

—— *War between Peru and Chili*, 1879-1881. Third Ed. Crown 8vo, with Maps, 10s. 6d.

—— See also "Foreign Countries," MAURY, and VERES.

Marshall (W. G.) Through America. New Ed., cr. 8vo, 7s. 6d.

Marston (W.) Eminent Recent Actors, Reminiscences Critical, &c. 2 vols. Crown 8vo, 21s.

Martin (J. W.) Float Fishing and Spinning in the Nottingham Style. New Edition. Crown 8vo, 2s. 6d.

Matthews (J. W., M.D.) Incwadi Yami: Twenty years in South Africa. With many Engravings, royal 8vo, 14s.
Maury (Commander) Physical Geography of the Sea, and its Meteorology. New Edition, with Charts and Diagrams, cr. 8vo, 6s.
—— *Life.* By his Daughter. Edited by Mr. CLEMENTS R. MARKHAM. With portrait of Maury. 8vo, 12s. 6d.
Men of Mark: Portraits of the most Eminent Men of the Day. Complete in 7 Vols., 4to, handsomely bound, gilt edges, 25s. each.
Mendelssohn Family (The), 1729—1847. From Letters and Journals. Translated. New Edition, 2 vols., 8vo, 30s.
Mendelssohn. See also "Great Musicians."
Merrifield's Nautical Astronomy. Crown 8vo, 7s. 6d.
Merrylees (J.) Carlsbad and its Environs. 7s. 6d.; roan, 9s.
Milford (P.) Ned Stafford's Experiences in the United States. 5s.
Mills (J.) Alternative Elementary Chemistry. Illust., cr. 8vo.
—— *Alernative Course in Physics.*
Mitchell (D. G.; Ik. Marvel) Works. Uniform Edition, small 8vo, 5s. each.

Bound together.	Reveries of a Bachelor.
Doctor Johns.	Seven Stories, Basement and Attic.
Dream Life.	Wet Days at Edgewood.
Out-of-Town Places.	

Mitford (Mary Russell) Our Village. With 12 full-page and 157 smaller Cuts. Cr. 4to, cloth, gilt edges, 21s.; cheaper binding, 10s. 6d.
Moffatt (W.) Land and Work; Depression, Agricultural and Commercial. Crown 8vo, 5s.
Mohammed Benani: A Story of To-day. 8vo, 10s. 6d.
Mollett (J. W.) Illustrated Dictionary of Words used in Art and Archæology. Illustrated, small 4to, 15s.
Moloney (Governor) Forestry of West Africa. 10s. 6d.
Money (E.) The Truth about America. New Edition. 2s. 6d.
Morlands, The. A Tale of Anglo-Indian Life. By Author of "Sleepy Sketches." Crown 8vo, 6s.
Morley (Henry) English Literature in the Reign of Victoria. 2000th volume of the Tauchnitz Collection of Authors. 18mo, 2s. 6d.
Mormonism. See "Stenhouse."
Morse (E. S.) Japanese Homes and their Surroundings. With more than 300 Illustrations. Re-issue, 10s. 6d.
Morten (Honnor) Sketches of Hospital Life. Cr. 8vo, sewed, 1s.
Morwood. Our Gipsies in City, Tent, and Van. 8vo, 18s.
Moxon (Walter) Pilocereus Senilis. Fcap. 8vo, gilt top, 3s. 6d.
Muller (E.) Noble Words and Noble Deeds. Illustrated, gilt edges, 3s. 6d.; plainer binding, 2s. 6d.

Murray (*E. C. Grenville*) *Memoirs*. By his widow. 2 vols.
Musgrave (*Mrs.*) *Miriam*. Crown 8vo.
Music. See "Great Musicians."

*N*APOLEON *and Marie Louise: Memoirs*. By Madame DURAND. 7*s.* 6*d.*
Nethercote (*C. B.*) *Pytchley Hunt*. New Ed., cr. 8vo, 8*s.* 6*d.*
New Zealand. See BRADSHAW.
New Zealand Rulers and Statesmen. See GISBORNE.
Nicholls (*J. H. Kerry*) *The King Country: Explorations in New Zealand*. Many Illustrations and Map. New Edition, 8vo, 21*s.*
Nisbet (*Hume*) *Life and Nature Studies*. With Etching by C. O. MURRAY. Crown 8vo, 6*s.*
Nordhoff (*C.*) *California, for Health, Pleasure, and Residence*. New Edition, 8vo, with Maps and Illustrations, 12*s.* 6*d.*
Norman (*C. B.*) *Corsairs of France*. With Portraits. 8vo, 18*s.*
Northbrook Gallery. Edited by LORD RONALD GOWER. 36 Permanent Photographs. Imperial 4to, 63*s.*; large paper, 105*s.*
Nott (*Major*) *Wild Animals Photographed and Described*. 35*s.*
Nursery Playmates (*Prince of*). 217 Coloured Pictures for Children by eminent Artists. Folio, in coloured boards, 6*s.*
Nursing Record. Yearly, 8*s.*; half-yearly, 4*s.* 6*d.*; quarterly, 2*s.* 6*d.*; weekly, 2*d.*

O'BRIEN (*R. B.*) *Fifty Years of Concessions to Ireland*. With a Portrait of T. Drummond. Vol. I., 16*s.*, II., 16*s.*
Orient Line Guide Book. By W. J. LOFTIE. 5*s.*
Orvis (*C. F.*) *Fishing with the Fly*. Illustrated. 8vo, 12*s.* 6*d.*
Osborne (*Duffield*) *Spell of Ashtaroth*. Crown 8vo, 5*s.*
Our Little Ones in Heaven. Edited by the Rev. H. ROBBINS. With Frontispiece after Sir JOSHUA REYNOLDS. New Edition, 5*s.*
Owen (*Douglas*) *Marine Insurance Notes and Clauses*. New Edition, 14*s.*

*P*ALLISER (*Mrs.*) *A History of Lace*. New Edition, with additional cuts and text. 8vo, 21*s.*
—— *The China Collector's Pocket Companion*. With upwards of 1000 Illustrations of Marks and Monograms. Small 8vo, 5*s.*
Parkin (*J.*) *Antidotal Treatment of Epidemic Cholera*. 3*s.* 6*d.*
—— *Epidemiology in the Animal and Vegetable Kingdom*. Part I., crown 8vo, 3*s.* 6*d.*; Part II., 3*s.* 6*d.*
—— *Volcanic Origin of Epidemics*. Popular Edition, crown 8vo, 2*s.*

*Payne (T. O.) Solomon's Temple and Capitol, Ark of the Flood
and Tabernacle* (four sections at 24s.), extra binding, 105s.
Pennell (H. Cholmondeley) Sporting Fish of Great Britain
15s. ; large paper, 30s.
—— *Modern Improvements in Fishing-tackle.* Crown 8vo, 2s.
Perelaer (M. T. H.) Ran Away from the Dutch; Borneo, &c.
Illustrated, square 8vo, 7s. 6d.
Pharmacopœia of the United States of America. 8vo, 21s.
Philpot (H. J.) Diabetes Mellitus. Crown 8vo, 5s.
—— *Diet System.* Tables. I. Diabetes; II. Gout;
III. Dyspepsia; IV. Corpulence. In cases, 1s. each.
Plunkett (Major G. T.) Primer of Orthographic Projection.
Elementary Solid Geometry. With Problems and Exercises. 2s. 6d.
Poe (E. A.) The Raven. Illustr. by DORÉ. Imperial folio, 63s.
Poems of the Inner Life. Chiefly Modern. Small 8vo, 5s.
Polar Expeditions. See MCCORMICK.
Porcher (A.) Juvenile French Plays. With Notes and a
Vocabulary. 18mo, 1s.
Porter (Admiral David D.) Naval History of Civil War.
Portraits, Plans, &c. 4to, 25s.
Porter (Noah) Elements of Moral Science. 10s. 6d.
Portraits of Celebrated Race-horses of the Past and Present
Centuries. with Pedigrees and Performances. 4 vols., 4to, 126s.
Powles (L. D.) Land of the Pink Pearl: Life in the Bahamas.
8vo, 10s. 6d.
Poynter (Edward J., R.A.). See " Illustrated Text-books."
Pritt (T. E.) North Country Flies. Illustrated from the
Author's Drawings. 10s. 6d.
Publishers' Circular (The), and General Record of British and
Foreign Literature. Published on the 1st and 15th of every Month, 3d.
Pyle (Howard) Otto of the Silver Hand. Illustrated by the
Author. 8vo, 8s. 6d.

RAMBAUD. History of Russia. New Edition, Illustrated.
3 vols., 8vo, 21s.
Reber. History of Mediæval Art. Translated by CLARKE.
422 Illustrations and Glossary. 8vo, .
Redford (G.) Ancient Sculpture. New Ed. Crown 8vo, 10s. 6d.
Reed (Sir E. J., M.P.) and Simpson. Modern Ships of War.
Illust., royal 8vo, 10s. 6d.
Richards (W.) Aluminium: its History, Occurrence, &c.
Illustrated, crown 8vo, 12s. 6d.

Richter (Dr. Jean Paul) Italian Art in the National Gallery.
4to. Illustrated. Cloth gilt, £2 2s.; half-morocco, uncut, £2 12s. 6d.
────── See also LEONARDO DA VINCI.
Riddell (Mrs. J. H.) See LOW'S STANDARD NOVELS.
Robertson (Anne J.) Myself and my Relatives. New Edition, crown 8vo, 5s.
Robin Hood; Merry Adventures of. Written and illustrated by HOWARD PYLE. Imperial 8vo, 15s.
Robinson (Phil.) In my Indian Garden. New Edition, 16mo, limp cloth, 2s.
────── *Noah's Ark. Unnatural History.* Sm. post 8vo, 12s. 6d.
────── *Sinners and Saints: a Tour across the United States of America, and Round them.* Crown 8vo, 10s. 6d.
────── *Under the Punkah.* New Ed., cr. 8vo, limp cloth, 2s.
Rockstro (W. S.) History of Music. New Edition. 8vo, 14s.
Roland, The Story of. Crown 8vo, illustrated, 6s.
Rolfe (Eustace Neville) Pompeii, Popular and Practical. Cr. 8vo, 7s. 6d.
Rome and the Environs. With plans, 3s.
Rose (F.) Complete Practical Machinist. New Ed., 12mo, 12s. 6d.
────── *Key to Engines and Engine-running.* Crown 8vo, 8s. 6d.
────── *Mechanical Drawing.* Illustrated, small 4to, 16s.
────── *Modern Steam Engines.* Illustrated. 31s. 6d.
────── *Steam Boilers. Boiler Construction and Examination.* Illust., 8vo, 12s. 6d.
Rose Library. Each volume, 1s. Many are illustrated—
  Little Women. By LOUISA M. ALCOTT.
  Little Women Wedded. Forming a Sequel to "Little Women.
  Little Women and Little Women Wedded. 1 vol., cloth gilt, 3s. 6d.
  Little Men. By L. M. ALCOTT. Double vol., 2s.; cloth gilt, 3s. 6d.
  An Old-Fashioned Girl. By LOUISA M. ALCOTT. 2s.; cloth, 3s. 6d.
  Work. A Story of Experience. By L. M. ALCOTT. 3s. 6d.; 2 vols., 1s. each.
  Stowe (Mrs. H. B.) The Pearl of Orr's Island.
  ────── The Minister's Wooing.
  ────── We and our Neighbours. 2s.; cloth gilt, 6s.
  ────── My Wife and I. 2s.
  Hans Brinker; or, the Silver Skates. By Mrs. DODGE. Also 5s.
  My Study Windows. By J. R. LOWELL.
  The Guardian Angel. By OLIVER WENDELL HOLMES.
  My Summer in a Garden. By C. D. WARNER.
  Dred. By Mrs. BEECHER STOWE. 2s.; cloth gilt, 3s. 6d.
  City Ballads. New Ed. 16mo. By WILL CARLETON.

Rose Library (The)—continued.
   Farm Ballads. By WILL CARLETON. ⎫
   Farm Festivals. By WILL CARLETON. ⎬ 1 vol., cl., gilt ed., 3s. 6d.
   Farm Legends. By WILL CARLETON. ⎭
   The Rose in Bloom. By L. M. ALCOTT. 2s.; cloth gilt, 3s. 6d.
   Eight Cousins. By L. M. ALCOTT. 2s.; cloth gilt, 3s. 6d.
   Under the Lilacs. By L. M. ALCOTT. 2s.; also 3s. 6d.
   Undiscovered Country. By W. D. HOWELLS.
   Clients of Dr. Bernagius. By L. BIART. 2 parts.
   Silver Pitchers. By LOUISA M. ALCOTT. Cloth, 3s. 6d.
   Jimmy's Cruise in the "Pinafore," and other Tales. By LOUISA M. ALCOTT. 2s.; cloth gilt, 3s. 6d.
   Jack and Jill. By LOUISA M. ALCOTT. 2s.; Illustrated, 5s.
   Hitherto. By the Author of the "Gayworthys." 2 vols., 1s. each; 1 vol., cloth gilt, 3s. 6d.
   A Gentleman of Leisure. A Novel. By EDGAR FAWCETT. 1s.

Ross (Mars) and Stonehewer Cooper. Highlands of Cantabria; or, Three Days from England. Illustrations and Map, 8vo, 21s.

Rothschilds, the Financial Rulers of Nations. By JOHN REEVES. Crown 8vo, 7s. 6d.

Rousselet (Louis) Son of the Constable of France. Small post 8vo, numerous Illustrations, gilt edges, 3s. 6d.; plainer, 2s. 6d.

—— *King of the Tigers: a Story of Central India.* Illustrated. Small post 8vo, gilt, 3s. 6d.; plainer, 2s. 6d.

—— *Drummer Boy.* Illustrated. Small post 8vo, gilt edges, 3s. 6d.; plainer, 2s. 6d.

Russell (Dora) Strange Message. 3 vols., crown 8vo, 31s. 6d.

Russell (W. Clark) Jack's Courtship. New Ed., small post 8vo, 6s.

—— *English Channel Ports and the Estate of the East and West India Dock Company.* Crown 8vo, 1s.

—— *Frozen Pirate.* New Ed., Illust., small post 8vo, 6s.

—— *Sailor's Language.* Illustrated. Crown 8vo, 3s. 6d.

—— *Sea Queen.* New Ed., small post 8vo, 6s.

—— *Strange Voyage.* New Ed., small post 8vo, 6s.

—— *The Lady Maud.* New Ed., small post 8vo, 6s.

—— *Wreck of the Grosvenor.* Small post 8vo, 6s. 4to, sewed, 6d.

SAINTS *and their Symbols: A Companion in the Churches and Picture Galleries of Europe.* Illustrated. Royal 16mo, 3s. 6d.

Samuels (Capt. J. S.) From Forecastle to Cabin: Autobiography. Illustrated. Crown 8vo, 8s. 6d.; also with fewer Illustrations, cloth, 2s.; paper, 1s.

Sandlands (J. P.) How to Develop Vocal Power. 1s.

Saunders (A.) Our Domestic Birds: Poultry in England and New Zealand. Crown 8vo, 6s.
—— *Our Horses: the Best Muscles controlled by the Best* Brains. 6s.
Scherr (Prof. J.) History of English Literature. Cr. 8vo, 8s. 6d.
Schley. Rescue of Greely. Maps and Illustrations, 8vo, 12s. 6d.
Schuyler (Eugène) American Diplomacy and the Furtherance of Commerce. 12s. 6d.
—— *The Life of Peter the Great.* 2 vols., 8vo, 32s.
Schweinfurth (Georg) Heart of Africa. 2 vols., crown 8vo, 15s.
Scott (Leader) Renaissance of Art in Italy. 4to, 31s. 6d.
—— *Sculpture, Renaissance and Modern.* 5s.
Semmes (Adm. Raphael) Service Afloat: The "Sumter" and the "Alabama." Illustrated. Royal 8vo, 16s.
Senior (W.) Near and Far: an Angler's Sketches of Home Sport and Colonial Life. Crown 8vo, 6s.
—— *Waterside Sketches.* Imp. 32mo, 1s. 6d.; boards, 1s.
Shakespeare. Edited by R. GRANT WHITE. 3 vols., crown 8vo, gilt top, 36s.; *édition de luxe*, 6 vols., 8vo, cloth extra, 63s.
—— See also CUNDALL, DETHRONING, DONNELLY, MACKAY, and WHITE (R. GRANT).
Shakespeare's Heroines: Studies by Living English Painters. 105s.; artists' proofs, 630s.
—— *Songs and Sonnets.* Illust. by Sir JOHN GILBERT, R.A. 4to, boards, 5s.
Sharpe (R. Bowdler) Birds in Nature. 39 coloured plates and text. 4to, 63s.
Sidney (Sir Philip) Arcadia. New Edition, 6s.
Siegfried, The Story of. Illustrated, crown 8vo, cloth, 6s.
Simon. China: its Social Life. Crown 8vo, 6s.
Simson (A.) Wilds of Ecuador and Exploration of the Putumayor River. Crown 8vo, 8s. 6d.
Sinclair (Mrs.) Indigenous Flowers of the Hawaiian Islands. 44 Plates in Colour. Imp. folio, extra binding, gilt edges, 31s. 6d.
Sloane (T. O.) Home Experiments in Science for Old and Young. Crown 8vo, 6s.
Smith (G.) Assyrian Explorations. Illust. New Ed , 8vo, 18s.
—— *The Chaldean Account of Genesis.* With many Illustrations. 16s. New Ed. By PROFESSOR SAYCE. 8vo, 18s.
Smith (G. Barnett) William I. and the German Empire. New Ed., 8vo, 3s. 6d.
Smith (J. Moyr) Wooing of Æthra. Illustrated. 32mo, 1s.

Smith (Sydney) Life and Times. By STUART J. REID. Illustrated. 8vo, 21s.

Smith (W. R.) Laws concerning Public Health. 8vo, 31s. 6d.

Spiers' French Dictionary. 29th Edition, remodelled. 2 vols., 8vo, 18s.; half bound, 21s.

Spry (W. J. J., R.N., F.R.G.S.) Cruise of H.M.S." Challenger." With Illustrations. 8vo, 18s. Cheap Edit., crown 8vo, 7s. 6d.

Spyri (Joh.) Heidi's Early Experiences: a Story for Children and those who love Children. Illustrated, small post 8vo, 4s. 6d.

———— *Heidi's Further Experiences.* Illust., sm. post 8vo, 4s. 6d.

Stanley (H. M.) Congo, and Founding its Free State. Illustrated, 2 vols., 8vo, 42s.; re-issue, 2 vols. 8vo, 21s

———— *How I Found Livingstone.* 8vo, 10s. 6d. ; cr. 8vo, 7s. 6d.

———— *Through the Dark Continent.* Crown 8vo, 12s. 6d.

Start (J. W. K.) Junior Mensuration Exercises. 8d.

Stenhouse (Mrs.) Tyranny of Mormonism. An Englishwoman in Utah. New ed., cr. 8vo, cloth elegant, 3s. 6d.

Sterry (J. Ashby) Cucumber Chronicles. 5s.

Stevens (E. W.) Fly-Fishing in Maine Lakes. 8s. 6d.

Stevens (T.) Around the World on a Bicycle. Vol. II. 8vo. 16s.

Stockton (Frank R.) Rudder Grange. 3s. 6d.

———— *Bee-Man of Orn, and other Fanciful Tales.* Cr. 8vo, 5s.

———— *The Casting Away of Mrs. Lecks and Mrs. Aleshine.* 1s.

———— *The Dusantes.* Sequel to the above. Sewed, 1s.; this and the preceding book in one volume, cloth, 2s. 6d.

———— *The Hundredth Man.* Small post 8vo, 6s.

———— *The Late Mrs. Null.* Small post 8vo, 6s.

———— *The Story of Viteau.* Illust. Cr. 8vo, 5s.

———— See also LOW'S STANDARD NOVELS.

Stoker (Bram) Under the Sunset. Crown 8vo, 6s.

Storer (Professor F. H.) Agriculture in its Relations to Chemistry. 2 vols., 8vo, 25s.

Stowe (Mrs. Beecher) Dred. Cloth, gilt edges, 3s. 6d.; cloth, 2s.

———— *Flowers and Fruit from her Writings.* Sm. post 8vo, 3s. 6d.

———— *Little Foxes.* Cheap Ed., 1s.; Library Edition, 4s. 6d.

———— *My Wife and I.* Cloth, 2s.

Stowe (*Mrs. Beecher*) *Old Town Folk.* 6s.
—— *We and our Neighbours.* 2s.
—— *Poganuc People.* 6s.
—— See also ROSE LIBRARY.
Strachan (J.) Explorations and Adventures in New Guinea.
Illust., crown 8vo, 12s.
Stultfield (Hugh E. M.) El Maghreb: 1200 *Miles' Ride through*
Marocco. 8s. 6d.
Sullivan (A. M.) Nutshell History of Ireland. Paper boards, 6d.

TAINE (H. A.) "Origines." Translated by JOHN DURAND.
  I. The Ancient Regime. Demy 8vo, cloth, 16s.
  II. The French Revolution. Vol. 1. do.
  III. Do. do. Vol. 2. do.
  IV. Do. do. Vol. 3. do.
Tauchnitz's English Editions of German Authors. Each
volume, cloth flexible, 2s.; or sewed, 1s. 6d. (Catalogues post free.)
Tauchnitz (B.) German Dictionary. 2s.; paper, 1s. 6d.; roan,
2s. 6d.
—— *French Dictionary.* 2s.; paper, 1s. 6d.; roan, 2s. 6d.
—— *Italian Dictionary.* 2s.; paper, 1s. 6d.; roan, 2s. 6d.
—— *Latin Dictionary.* 2s.; paper, 1s. 6d.; roan, 2s. 6d.
—— *Spanish and English.* 2s.; paper, 1s. 6d.; roan, 2s. 6d.
—— *Spanish and French.* 2s.; paper, 1s. 6d.; roan, 2s. 6d.
Taylor (R. L.) Chemical Analysis Tables. 1s.
—— *Chemistry for Beginners.* Small 8vo, 1s. 6d.
Techno-Chemical Receipt Book. With additions by BRANNT
and WAHL. 10s. 6d.
Technological Dictionary. See TOLHAUSEN.
Thausing (Prof.) Malt and the Fabrication of Beer. 8vo, 45s.
Theakston (M.) British Angling Flies. Illustrated. Cr. 8vo, 5s.
Thomson (Jos.) Central African Lakes. New edition, 2 vols.
in one, crown 8vo, 7s. 6d.
—— *Through Masai Land.* Illust. 21s.; new edition, 7s. 6d.
—— *and Miss Harris-Smith. Ulu: an African Romance.*
crown 8vo, 6s.

Thomson (W.) Algebra for Colleges and Schools. With Answers,
5*s*. ; without, 4*s*. 6*d*. ; Answers separate, 1*s*. 6*d*
Tolhausen. Technological German, English, and French Dictionary. Vols. I., II., with Supplement, 12*s*. 6*d*. each ; III., 9*s*.; Supplement, cr. 8vo, 3*s*. 6*d*.
Tromholt (S.) Under the Rays of the Aurora Borealis. By C. SIEWERS. Photographs and Portraits. 2 vols., 8vo, 30*s*.
Tucker (W. J.) Life and Society in Eastern Europe. 15*s*.
Tupper (Martin Farquhar) My Life as an Author. 14*s*.
Turner (Edward) Studies in Russian Literature. Cr. 8vo, 8*s*. 6*d*.

UPTON (H.) Manual of Practical Dairy Farming. Cr. 8vo, 2*s*.

VAN DAM. Land of Rubens; a companion for visitors to Belgium. See HUET.
Vane (Denzil) From the Dead. A Romance. 2 vols., cr. 8vo, 12*s*.
Vane (Sir Harry Young). By Prof. JAMES K. HOSMER. 8vo, 18*s*.
Veres. Biography of Sir Francis Vere and Lord Vere, leading Generals in the Netherlands. By CLEMENTS R. MARKHAM. 8vo, 18*s*.
Victoria (Queen) Life of. By GRACE GREENWOOD. Illust. 6*s*.
Vincent (Mrs. Howard) Forty Thousand Miles over Land and Water. With Illustrations. New Edit., 3*s*. 6*d*.
Viollet-le-Duc (E.) Lectures on Architecture. Translated by BENJAMIN BUCKNALL, Architect. 2 vols., super-royal 8vo, £3 3*s*.

WAKEFIELD. Aix-les-Bains: Bathing and Attractions. 6*d*.
Walford (Mrs. L. B.) Her Great Idea, and other Stories. Cr. 8vo, 10*s*. 6*d*.
Wallace (L.) Ben Hur: A Tale of the Christ. New Edition, crown 8vo, 6*s*.; cheaper edition, 2*s*.
Waller (Rev. C. H.) The Names on the Gates of Pearl, and other Studies. New Edition. Crown 8vo, cloth extra, 3*s*. 6*d*.
——— *Words in the Greek Testament.* Part I. Grammar. Small post 8vo, cloth, 2*s*. 6*d*. Part II. Vocabulary, 2*s*. 6*d*.

BOOKS BY JULES VERNE.

WORKS.	Large Crown 8vo. Containing 350 to 600 pp. and from 50 to 100 full-page illustrations.		Containing the whole of the text with some illustrations.	
	In very handsome cloth binding, gilt edges.	In plainer binding, plain edges.	In cloth binding, gilt edges, smaller type.	Coloured boards.
	s. d.	s. d.	s. d.	
20,000 Leagues under the Sea. Parts I. and II.	10 6	5 0	3 6	2 vols., 1s. each.
Hector Servadac	10 6	5 0	3 6	2 vols., 1s. each.
The Fur Country	10 6	5 0	3 6	2 vols., 1s. each.
The Earth to the Moon and a Trip round it	10 6	5 0	2 vols., 2s. ea.	2 vols., 1s. each.
Michael Strogoff	10 6	5 0	3 6	2 vols., 1s. each.
Dick Sands, the Boy Captain	10 6	5 0	3 6	2 vols., 1s. each.
Five Weeks in a Balloon	7 6	3 6	2 0	1s. 0d.
Adventures of Three Englishmen and Three Russians	7 6	3 6	2 0	1 0
Round the World in Eighty Days	7 6	3 6	2 0	1 0
A Floating City	7 6	3 6	2 0	1 0
The Blockade Runners			2 0	1 0
Dr. Ox's Experiment	—	—	2 0	1 0
A Winter amid the Ice	—	—	2 0	1 0
Survivors of the "Chancellor"	7 6	3 6	3 6	2 vols., 1s. each.
Martin Paz			2 0	1s. 0d.
The Mysterious Island, 3 vols.:—	22 6	10 6	6 0	3 0
I. Dropped from the Clouds	7 6	3 6	2 0	1 0
II. Abandoned	7 6	3 6	2 0	1 0
III. Secret of the Island	7 6	3 6	2 0	1 0
The Child of the Cavern	7 6	3 6	2 0	1 0
The Begum's Fortune	7 6	3 6	2 0	1 0
The Tribulations of a Chinaman	7 6	3 6	2 0	1 0
The Steam House, 2 vols.:—				
I. Demon of Cawnpore	7 6	3 6	2 0	1 0
II. Tigers and Traitors	7 6	3 6	2 0	1 0
The Giant Raft, 2 vols.:—				
I. 800 Leagues on the Amazon	7 6	3 6	2 0	1 0
II. The Cryptogram	7 6	3 6	2 0	1 0
The Green Ray	6 0	5 0	—	1 0
Godfrey Morgan	7 6	3 6	2 0	1 0
Kéraban the Inflexible:—				
I. Captain of the "Guidara"	7 6	3 6	2 0	1 0
II. Scarpante the Spy	7 6	3 6	2 0	1 0
The Archipelago on Fire	7 6	3 6	2 0	1 0
The Vanished Diamond	7 6	3 6	2 0	1 0
Mathias Sandorf	10 6	5 0		
The Lottery Ticket	7 6			
Clipper of the Clouds	7 6			
North against South	7 6			
Adrift in the Pacific	7 6			
Flight to France	7 6			

CELEBRATED TRAVELS AND TRAVELLERS. 3 vols., 8vo, 600 pp., 100 full-page illustrations, 12s. 6d.; gilt edges, 14s. each:—(1) THE EXPLORATION OF THE WORLD. (2) THE GREAT NAVIGATORS OF THE EIGHTEENTH CENTURY. (3) THE GREAT EXPLORERS OF THE NINETEENTH CENTURY.

Waller (Rev. C.H.) Adoption and the Covenānt. On Confirmation. 2s. 6d.

—— *Silver Sockets; and other Shadows of Redemption.* Sermons at Christ Church, Hampstead. Small post 8vo, 6s.

Walsh (A.S.) Mary, Queen of the House of David. 8vo, 3s. 6d.

Walton (Iz.) Wallet Book, CIƆIƆLXXXV. Crown 8vo, half vellum, 21s.; large paper, 42s.

—— *Compleat Angler.* Lea and Dove Edition. Ed. by R. B. MARSTON. With full-page Photogravures on India paper, and the Woodcuts on India paper from blocks. 4to, half-morocco, 105s.; large paper, royal 4to, full dark green morocco, gilt top, 210s.

Walton (T. H.) Coal Mining. With Illustrations. 4to, 25s.

Wardrop (O.) Kingdom of Georgia. Illust. and map. 8vo. 14s.

Warner (C. D.) My Summer in a Garden. Boards, 1s.; leatherette, 1s. 6d.; cloth, 2s.

—— *Their Pilgrimage.* Illustrated by C. S. REINHART. 8vo, 7s. 6d.

Warren (W. F.) Paradise Found; the North Pole the Cradle of the Human Race. Illustrated. Crown 8vo, 12s. 6d.

Washington Irving's Little Britain. Square crown 8vo, 6s.

Wells (H. P.) American Salmon Fisherman. 6s.

—— *Fly Rods and Fly Tackle.* Illustrated. 10s. 6d.

Wells (J. W.) Three Thousand Miles through Brazil. Illustrated from Original Sketches. 2 vols. 8vo, 32s.

Wenzel (O.) Directory of Chemical Products of the German Empire. 8vo, 25s.

White (R. Grant) England Without and Within. Crown 8vo, 10s. 6d.

—— *Every-day English.* 10s. 6d.

—— *Fate of Mansfield Humphreys, &c.* Crown 8vo, 6s.

—— *Studies in Shakespeare.* 10s. 6d.

—— *Words and their Uses.* New Edit., crown 8vo, 5s.

Whitney (Mrs.) The Other Girls. A Sequel to "We Girls." New ed. 12mo, 2s.

—— *We Girls.* New Edition. 2s.

Whittier (J. G.) The King's Missive, and later Poems. 18mo, choice parchment cover, 3s. 6d.

—— *St. Gregory's Guest, &c.* Recent Poems. 5s.

Wilcox (Marrion) Real People. Sm. post 8vo, 3s. 6d.

—— *Señora Villena; and Gray, an Oldhaven Romance.* 2 vols. in one, 6s.

William I. and the German Empire. By G. BARNETT SMITH. New Edition, 3s. 6d.
Willis-Bund (J.) Salmon Problems. 3s. 6d.; boards, 2s. 6d.
Wills (Dr. C. J.) Persia as it is. Crown 8vo, 8s. 6d.
Wills, A Few Hints on Proving, without Professional Assistance. By a PROBATE COURT OFFICIAL. 8th Edition, revised, with Forms of Wills, Residuary Accounts, &c. Fcap. 8vo, cloth limp, 1s.
Wilmot (A.) Poetry of South Africa. Collected and arranged. 8vo, 6s.
Wilson (Dr. Andrew) Health for the People. Cr. 8vo, 7s. 6d.
Winsor (Justin) Narrative and Critical History of America. 8 vols., 30s. each; large paper, per vol., 63s.
Woolsey. Introduction to International Law. 5th Ed., 18s.
Woolson (Constance F.) See "Low's Standard Novels."
Wright (H.) Friendship of God. Portrait, &c. Crown 8vo, 6s.
Wright (T.) Town of Cowper, Olney, &c. 6s.
Written to Order; the Journeyings of an Irresponsible Egotist. By the Author of "A Day of my Life at Eton." Crown 8vo, 6s.

*Y*RIARTE *(Charles) Florence: its History.* Translated by C. B. PITMAN. Illustrated with 500 Engravings. Large imperial 4to, extra binding, gilt edges, 63s.; or 12 Parts, 5s. each.
History; the Medici; the Humanists; letters; arts; the Renaissance; illustrious Florentines; Etruscan art; monuments; sculpture; painting.

London:

SAMPSON LOW, MARSTON, SEARLE, & RIVINGTON, LD.,

St. Dunstan's House,

FETTER LANE, FLEET STREET, E.C.

Gilbert and Rivington, Ld., St. John's House, Clerkenwell Road E.C.

www.ingramcontent.com/pod-product-compliance
Lightning Source LLC
Chambersburg PA
CBHW030600300426
44111CB00009B/1052